D0911142

25 METERS TO GOD

TAD M. WEISS

25 METERS TO GOD

REDEMPTION PRESS

© 2022 by Tad M. Weiss. All rights reserved.
Published by Redemption Press, PO Box 427, Enumclaw, WA 98022.
Toll-Free (844) 2REDEEM (273-3336)

Redemption Press is honored to present this title in partnership with the author. The views expressed or implied in this work are those of the author. Redemption Press provides our imprint seal representing design excellence, creative content, and high quality production.

No part of this publication may be reproduced, stored in a retrieval system, or transmitted in any way by any means—electronic, mechanical, photocopy, recording, or otherwise—without the prior permission of the copyright holder, except as provided by USA copyright law.

The author and others have tried to recreate events, locales, and conversations from their memories of them. In order to maintain their anonymity, in some instances he has changed the names of individuals and may have changed some identifying characteristics and details, such as physical properties, occupations, and places of residence.

Scripture is taken from the *Holy Bible, New International Version* (*NIV*). Copyright © 1973, 1978, 1984 by International Bible Society. Used by permission of Zondervan. All rights reserved.

Any other Scriptures included in CaringBridge posts that did not indicate version information were quoted as they were provided.

ISBN 13: 978-1-64645-790-8 (Paperback)
          978-1-64645-532-4 (Hardcover)
          978-1-64645-792-2 (ePub)
          978-1-64645-791-5 (Mobi)
          978-1-64645-530-0 (Audiobook)

LCCN   2022909026

When you pass through the waters,
I will be with you;
and when you pass through the rivers,
they will not sweep over you.
When you walk through the fire,
you will not be burned;
the flames will not set you ablaze.
Isaiah 43:2

ACKNOWLEDGMENTS

There are so many people to thank for helping our story become a book. Many have already been acknowledged in these pages; without them our story wouldn't have played out as it did. Thank you to the people of Seville, the doctors and medical teams in Spain and in the United States, and the body of believers that supported us so beautifully during the aftermath of Maggie's accident. This book wouldn't have been written without you.

Thank you to CaringBridge for their fantastic website and service; this was our main communication tool throughout our journey. The ability to easily keep our friends and loved ones informed and receive words of encouragement in return was an incredible blessing to us.

Thank you to Rosey Brausen, Jim Jackson, and Morgan Wood. Your words of encouragement would always send me back to the computer with a renewed energy to finish the project.

A special thanks to my editor, Lesley Ann McDaniel. I'm amazed at how quickly you took my rough draft and turned it into a book. Thanks also to the team at Redemption Press for your passion and professionalism in working with a first-time author.

My coworkers Kari Haanstad and Diane York were a great sounding board for me. Thanks for your review of the original manuscript and your help in promoting the book. A special thank you to Tom Sadowski for all your work editing and improving our photos.

I'd like to thank our extended family for their support and love for Maggie and us throughout this journey. Peter, you have been a rock supporting your sister, Mom, and me. Paul, thank you for all you do for Maggie and for us, and for your willingness to have this story told.

Maggie, it is impossible to thank you enough. You are the main character in the story, and you suffered the most. I thank God for you every day, and that your bright light continues to shine for all to see.

Words can't express my thankfulness for my wife, Wendy. We walked side by side through this storm and came out the other side stronger. She cowrote this story with me and continues to support me in all areas of my life. She is a true servant of God, and I'm truly honored and blessed to be married to her.

God, this book is about You. Thank You for giving me the inspiration to tell this story and the words to write, both in the CaringBridge posts and in the book. My hope and prayer is that Your name will be lifted high through the telling of our story, and that the reader will come to know Jesus Christ in a new way, for Your glory and honor.

INTRODUCTION

This book tells the story of our daughter Maggie's accident that occurred in Seville, Spain, in June of 2014. It is a story about God and how He performs miracles today, just as He did in Old Testament times and when Jesus walked the earth.

Each chapter consists of three viewpoints, starting with the perspective from my wife, Wendy, and me and based on our memory and on the notes we took at the time, as well as hundreds of emails and other communications.

The second viewpoint comes from our CaringBridge posts that we wrote to update our friends and family about Maggie. The book contains the posts as written at that time, although some have been shortened. Most of the posts were written by me—a few by Wendy. She reviewed every post I typed and provided her input. She corrected all my grammar and sentence structure errors, making me sound smarter than I am. She knew the Bible verse that would apply to each post and is the coauthor of this book.

The third viewpoint is a sampling of responses to our CaringBridge posts—responses that either encouraged us greatly, showed how Maggie's accident was impacting others, or revealed to us how God was moving. We literally received thousands of responses to our posts and they were all meaningful to us, but only a handful are captured in this book.

When writing our CaringBridge posts, we couldn't tell the whole story. There were time constraints, and we didn't have all of the information that we now have. There were details and events that weren't appropriate to share. But as time has passed and the situation has evolved, we can now tell a more complete story. Eight years have passed since the accident, and my memory has its limitations. There are certainly things I've forgotten since the accident, but the ability to see God's plan unfold over time offsets any missed details.

Our hope is that you will find a new or renewed faith in God through our story. We pray that you will see how God works through a tragedy and that you gain a deeper understanding of God and His promises to you. We also hope you will see how you can help and support others during a crisis, as so many of our family and friends did for us.

Finally, we hope that this book will be a help to you should you ever find yourself in a similar situation. God doesn't promise us a life free of worry or hardship, but He does promise He will walk through the fire with us.

God bless,
Tad and Wendy

PART ONE

DAY BY DAY

CHAPTER ONE

Day 1—June 5, 2014

A knock at the door of the conference room interrupted my 8:00 a.m. meeting.

My assistant, Denise, poked her head in and said she needed to talk to me. It was strange that she would interrupt a meeting, and she looked like she had seen a ghost. I excused myself from my clients.

Something was wrong.

As we hustled to my office, Denise told me there was a woman on the phone from Spain who had been trying to track me down for hours. I went into my office and closed the door.

My heart racing, I picked up the phone.

"Mr. Weiss?" The woman on the line quickly introduced herself as Morgan Reiss, the director of student services at the Council on International Educational Exchange (CIEE) Study Center in Seville, Spain. "I'm sorry, but . . . it seems there's been an accident."

The blood drained from my face. My daughter, Maggie, had been in Spain for ten days, just starting a summer study program in Seville. Morgan told me that at 7:35 that morning in Seville—12:35 a.m. in Minnesota—Maggie had been out for a run and was hit by a bus. She was at a hospital in Seville in serious condition.

Morgan gave me what details she knew. I took notes furiously, which in hindsight looked like the scribbles of a first grader. Maggie had been hit by a city bus. They believed her spleen had ruptured. She had a head injury, a broken pelvis, and broken ribs. She was unconscious and in the ICU.

I'm a planner by nature. I like to map out strategies and work toward logical conclusions. This phone call wasn't part of the plan. I was shaken to the core, and my mind reeled with questions. What do I do? Is Maggie getting the care she needs? Is she going to live? Someone needs to go to Spain right away. Do I go or does Wendy? Do we both go? What about my clients and my business? Who is going to take care of our seventeen-year-old son, Peter? And how is Wendy going to react when I call her?

I told Morgan that one of us would be going to Spain as soon as possible. We exchanged phone numbers and hung up.

I went back into the conference room and told my clients that my daughter had been in an accident in Spain. They sensed the urgency of the situation, and I told them I would give them an update when I knew more. Our five-minute meeting ended, and I went back into my office to call Wendy . . . the hardest phone call I'd ever made.

When I told her the news, Wendy, of course, freaked out.

She cried, "No, no, no!" for about ten seconds. Then her motherly instincts kicked in, and she pulled herself together. "What do we need to do?"

We talked through which of us would go to Spain and quickly decided that we both needed to go. I told her to pack us each a small suitcase and grab our passports and to meet me at my office as soon as possible. I would call the airline to get us on the earliest flight from Minneapolis to Seville. We said a quick prayer and hung up.

There was so much to figure out, and my decision-making was clouded by the magnitude of the news that had just hit me out of the blue. Part of me thought this couldn't be happening, and that it was all some sort of sick joke. But I knew the news was true, and it was paralyzing. My daughter was in an ICU 4,300 miles away with people she didn't know watching over her and keeping her alive. It would be a full day before we could get to her.

We didn't know anyone in Seville. There was no one to call who could be by her side. There were a hundred things we needed to do, but the first was get to Maggie. I called American Airlines to start that process.

Maggie had flown to Spain just ten days earlier on American, and we had planned for Wendy to fly over at the end of the summer session in late July. I needed to book a flight for myself and change Wendy's existing ticket. I called the airline and eventually connected with a customer service agent at 8:15 a.m.—ten minutes after receiving that awful phone call. I explained the situation to her, and she jumped into action.

She found a flight to Chicago, then Madrid, then on to Seville. The flight to Chicago would leave at 10:40 a.m., and we would arrive in Seville the next morning at 9:00. There were two seats on that flight and several seats on the connecting flights. She said the airfare would be $3,600. This wasn't a time to scour the internet for a cheaper fare.

She moved on to change Wendy's ticket, once again giving me the play-by-play as she did so. Her next words were "Oh no." The seat that had shown when she was booking my flight was no longer available.

My heart sank. She worked furiously, checking every available option for getting the seat for Wendy. Finally, she changed Wendy's ticket to leave that day, on the same flight as me, with the return date left open to be decided later. The change fee was $1,800, but cost was completely irrelevant.

She told me she couldn't email me our itinerary and that we would just have to go to the airport and check in. We didn't have assigned seats, but we were on the flights. I thanked her from the bottom of my heart and called Wendy back with the news that we were booked to Seville and would be leaving in less than two hours.

Wendy had us ready to go in thirty minutes. Packing for a long trip is often a multiday process, with checklists and a constant review of what needs to be packed. This wasn't one of those trips. She had thrown together a few changes of clothes and grabbed our toiletries and passports. She was ready to leave our house in Victoria for the twenty-minute drive to my office in Eden Prairie. I told her I would call Peter, who was finishing his junior year of high school, and that she should call her parents to see if they could come to our house and stay with him.

I left a message on Peter's cell phone, and he called me in between classes. I told him what I knew about the accident and that his mom and I would be leaving in a couple of hours to go be with Maggie in Spain. We wouldn't have time to say good-bye, and his grandparents would be coming to the house to stay with him.

"How long will you be gone?" His voice sounded weak with concern that I could do nothing to assuage.

"No idea." I sighed. "But we'll call as soon as we can."

Wendy arrived at my office at 9:15. I asked Denise to cancel my meetings for the next week and promised I'd be in contact as soon as we knew more.

The airport was fifteen minutes away, but we needed to go through security, check in, and get our seats. It would be tight but doable. As we drove, we talked about what little we knew, and we prayed.

"Dear God," I said as I navigated traffic, "be with Maggie. Keep her alive, Lord, and help us to get to her side as soon as we possibly can. Be with her doctors and nurses to give her the best care that is humanly possible."

"We're scared, Lord," Wendy added. "We don't know what to do. All we can do is trust in You. Amen."

We arrived at the airport, sped through security, and hurried to the gate. The waiting area brimmed with people waiting to board the plane to Chicago. At the check-in counter, I explained the situation and asked if there was any way she could seat us together.

After several seconds of tapping on her computer, she looked up with a small smile. "I have two adjoining seats." Still typing, she creased her brow. "I have no idea how you got on this flight. It's been oversold for two weeks."

We didn't know it at the time, but this was our first God sighting. God was at work for us, freeing up two seats on an oversold flight so we could get to our daughter's side as soon as possible. He was taking care of the details that we couldn't manage on our own.

The flight from Minneapolis to Chicago was less than an hour. We had a two-hour layover before we would board our flight to Madrid. We called Morgan in Spain, but there was no updated news on Maggie's condition. I called AT&T because we were going to need the biggest international phone package they had.

We called Wendy's parents and my parents in Florida. I told my mom and dad we might need them to travel to Minnesota to stay with Peter if we found out we needed to be in Spain for an extended time. We called our friends Vibhu and Julia Sharma, who lived and worked in Zurich, to see if maybe they could get to Maggie's side faster than we could. It helped a little to be able to do things—to try to gain control of an uncontrollable situation.

During the flight to Madrid, we talked, but we knew so little of the situation. We held out hope that we'd get to Spain and find Maggie in better shape than expected.

Iberia Airlines, a partner of American, has a great entertainment system on their overseas flight, but neither of us could watch a movie or TV show or play the games that were offered. We tried to think through all the details we would need to take care of, but we were headed to a foreign country . . . a place where we knew no one and didn't speak the language. We knew we were going into battle and had no idea what would be required of us. All we could do was pray—for Maggie, for us, and for the time to pass quickly.

It didn't. Nine hours of fear wondering about what we would find in Spain felt like nine days.

Midway through the flight, a young man across the aisle asked me where I was going on vacation. I told him about our nineteen-year-old daughter's accident.

As I talked, the tears started to flow—the first of many over the coming weeks. The poor man was probably kicking himself for his innocent question. He told me he was eighteen years old, just finished with high school, and heading to Spain to travel for a few weeks before starting college at Indiana University. From what little he shared, I could tell he was a sharp young man—an entrepreneur at heart—with his whole life ahead of him.

Our daughter was a sharp young lady—a great student with many talents and the kindest heart. Earlier that morning, before she left her house for a run, she had her whole life ahead of her. Now we weren't so sure.

Maggie was born in July 1994, our first child. She was a cute kid, a typical firstborn in many ways—smart and determined with quite a bit of spunk. When she was about to enter kindergarten, Wendy did a search of the school options in the area, and we ended up enrolling her at Chapel Hill Academy, a Christian K–8 school in Chanhassen, Minnesota. Along with her academic education, Maggie learned the Bible, and she committed her life to Christ in the first grade. She was compassionate toward others and loved to give her teachers hugs. She excelled at sports, drama, and singing, as well as in academics.

Wendy did a lot of legwork to determine where Maggie should go to high school. We decided to enroll her at Minnetonka High School, a public school with a great reputation, about ten miles from our home. Her class of fifty kids at Chapel Hill was tiny compared to the seven hundred and fifty freshmen at Minnetonka!

Maggie had grown up swimming for a local swim club, and she joined the high school team as a freshman. While she enjoyed swimming, what she really wanted to participate in was theatre, and she couldn't do both. She was cast in her first musical in the spring of that year and loved becoming a part of the theatre community at Minnetonka.

Minnetonka High School has one of the best theatre programs in the state, if not the country. The school attracted talent from the entire region, and Maggie had a tough time breaking through to get a lead role. She experienced more success in the choir program.

As Maggie transitioned from swimming to these other activities, she wanted to maintain the physical condition she'd achieved through swimming every day. We encouraged her to cross-country ski in the winter and then start running in the spring. It took about a month of running for her to get over the hump, but once she did, she fell in love with it and ran almost every day.

In her junior year, I planted a seed that it would be really cool if we ran a marathon together before she left for college. She thought about it for a while, and we signed up to run the Twin Cities Marathon in October 2011, the fall of her senior year. I encouraged her through countless hours of training as we prepared for the marathon, and then she inspired me through the last few miles of the race. It was a grueling but beautiful experience that we shared, crossing the finish line together in our matching father-daughter shirts.

Maggie continued to have success with singing and was admitted as a vocal performance major to St. Olaf College, a small liberal arts school forty miles south of the Twin Cities in Northfield, Minnesota. It didn't take her long to realize she wasn't cut out to be a music major, and she switched to a double major of Spanish and Latin American studies. She sang with the freshman choir at St. Olaf and continued running on her own as she had for the past four years.

Maggie enjoyed being in the choir, but her heart was in running.

Toward the end of her freshman year, she asked the cross-country coach, Chris Daymont, if she could join the team. She said yes, and Maggie joined in the fall of her sophomore year. She had other young women to run with and loved the competitive aspect and continual challenge to improve her times. Cross-country rolled into track in the spring. Maggie had become a collegiate runner, and she loved it!

As she continued working toward her double major, she got the idea to study abroad to become fluent in Spanish. Since she didn't want to miss the cross-country or track season, we found a summer program for her through CIEE.

So in the summer of 2014, just after completing her sophomore year at St. Olaf, Maggie traveled to Seville, Spain. The plan was to spend two months studying in Seville, running in the mornings before class to get ready for the upcoming cross-country season.

Life has many twists and turns, and that is the crooked line that took Maggie from Victoria, Minnesota, to Seville, Spain, and had her out for a training run on the morning of June 5, 2014.

CHAPTER TWO

Day 2—June 6, 2014

Wendy and I landed in Madrid at 6:00 a.m., which was 11:00 p.m. back home. The lines in customs were long but moved quickly. We made it to our gate an hour before the 8:00 a.m. flight to Seville.

As we flew into Seville, the landscape reminded us of Arizona with arid land and houses with swimming pools to escape the heat. We were going to the desert at the beginning of summer.

The airport there is older and smaller than what we're used to. My initial thoughts were that we were entering a city that wasn't up to modern standards.

We found Morgan Reiss waiting for us and made the short walk to the taxi. She told us it would be a twenty-minute drive to the hospital where we could finally get in to see Maggie. It was 9:30 in the morning in Spain, eighteen-and-a-half hours since I had received the call from Morgan in my office back home. We had made it there as quickly as we could.

Twenty-six hours had passed since Maggie's accident. She had gotten through the night.

We talked as we drove to the hospital. Morgan told us what she had learned since we had talked the day before. Maggie's spleen had not ruptured. She had an enlarged spleen, and the X-rays made it look as if it had ruptured. The ER doctors cut her open, but they found no internal organ damage. She had seven broken ribs and a badly shattered pelvis on both sides. She had traumatic brain injuries in two places, which was the biggest concern. Beyond that, Morgan didn't have much new information.

As we pulled up to Hospital Universitario Virgen Del Rocio, a feeling of dread came over me. The hospital looked old and rundown. We couldn't wait to get in and see Maggie, but in my heart, I felt there was no way she could get the care she needed in this facility. My fatherly instincts took over, and I was determined to get my daughter out of this hospital, out of this city and country, and back to the United States as soon as humanly possible!

Morgan, Wendy, and I entered the hospital, dragging our luggage behind us. The inside looked better than the outside, and we were quickly escorted to an office where we would wait until we could get in to see Maggie. The intensive care unit in Spain is called the UCI and is pronounced "ooh-see." Our daughter was in the UCI, and they needed to make sure all the patients were stable before we could enter.

After a twenty-minute wait, we were escorted in.

Our prayers and hopes that Maggie would somehow be in better shape were not realized. The young lady lying in the hospital bed was hooked up to every machine and monitor imaginable. She had tubes running in and out of her mouth, nose, and body. The hardest part was that the swelling on her face from the trauma made her almost unrecognizable. Her head was partially shaved, with a cranial pressure monitor attached to the bare skin.

Wendy and I were undone. The shock of seeing our daughter in this condition, combined with the adrenaline of the past nineteen hours, was all we could take. We prayed over Maggie and cried. We talked to her and told her that everything would be okay, believing she could hear us through her coma. We told her that we were there, that we wouldn't leave her, and that she would be healed. We had no way of knowing this, but at least there was a chance. God and the doctors had kept her alive, and we had made it to her side. That prayer had been answered with a yes.

We could stay with Maggie for only a few minutes, as it was outside of regular visiting hours for the UCI. The doctors and nurses spoke only Spanish, so Morgan translated for us.

As our visit neared its end, a male nurse came up to Wendy and said in English, "She is going to be okay. She is going to be okay."

He told Wendy he had seen many accidents like this, and although everything looked grim to us, he provided some hope and assurance that Maggie was going to make it. He was the only nurse who spoke English to us, and we never saw him again after that first visit.

Looking back, we believe he was an angel sent by God to calm two parents who feared the worst for their precious daughter.

We left the hospital with Morgan, our luggage in tow. The hospital is on a large campus—six square blocks. We walked between the buildings on our way to the closest hotel where arrangements had been made for us. The temperature was rising; it was going to be a sweltering day in Seville.

After a short walk, we entered the hotel, but they had received the wrong information. They thought we would be arriving tomorrow, and there was no room available. Morgan knew of another hotel a few blocks away. As we walked, Wendy talked to Morgan, with me a few steps behind. Dragging our roller bags over cobblestone, I felt helplessness start to sink in.

We made it to the AC Marriott, five blocks and a ten-minute walk from the hospital. This looked like a nicer hotel to me, and I asked Morgan if we could just stay there the entire time. She made the arrangements for us, and we moved into room 127—basecamp for our entire time in Spain.

We fell onto the bed, exhausted. It was noon in Spain, and 5:00 a.m. back home in Minnesota. Twenty-one hours had passed since I'd received the phone call. It seemed like an eternity.

Wendy said the first thing we should do was set up a CaringBridge site.[1] She explained that instead of making hundreds of phone calls or sending out mass emails, we could update everyone with regular posts. Our family and friends would be able to log on to CaringBridge, go to Maggie's page, and get the latest updates on her situation.

Wendy had been on the site several times throughout the years, following and supporting others who had used it to send out updates about their loved ones.

She burst into tears. "I can't believe it's our turn to host a CaringBridge site."

I went to the front desk and bought an access card to have Wi-Fi in our room. We quickly established Maggie's CaringBridge site on my laptop and sent the link to our friends and family back home.

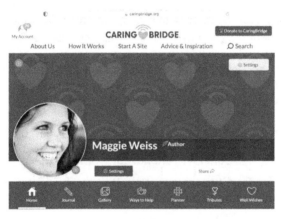

Maggie's Story

Site created on June 6, 2014

Then I wrote the first post:

Trusting God

By Tad Weiss, June 6, 2014

Our daughter, Maggie, has been in Seville, Spain, for two weeks as part of a summer study program, after finishing her sophomore year at St. Olaf. She was out running in the morning on Thursday, June 5, and was literally hit by a bus.

We received the phone call at 8:00 a.m. in Minnesota.

Wendy and I left for Seville to be with her. We arrived at 9:00 a.m. on Friday (Spain is seven hours ahead of Minnesota) and were at the University Hospital by 10:00.

Maggie is in intensive care. The doctors had performed exploratory surgery, as they were concerned with internal bleeding, but they didn't find any.

Maggie has broken ribs, a broken pelvis, and possibly other broken bones. Our main concern right now is head trauma. She is in a medically induced coma, and the doctors are watching for swelling or fluid on the brain. We hope to know more about this in the next day or two. We will talk with the doctors in a couple of hours for the first time and will provide any updates.

We believe this is going to be a long journey. We can feel your prayers of support and love. We know that God preserved Maggie's life. We have a lot to deal with, being in a foreign country and figuring this all out. Wendy and I have been fairly calm as we know that all we can do is trust God on this one. But we certainly have our moments. It was hard seeing our beautiful Maggie broken, but she's not beaten. If anyone can overcome this, it is Maggie, and she will, with God's help!

Thank you for your prayers and words of encouragement! We can definitely feel them. We'll keep you posted as we learn more.

"For the Lord God is a sun and shield; the Lord bestows favor and honor; no good thing does he withhold from those whose walk is blameless" (Psalm 84:11).

To our delight, we soon noticed that my post had received a few comments:

Janet McFarland, June 6, 2014

Praying for God's peace over you, Wendy, Tad, Peter, and the entire family. Know that you have an army of people praying for Maggie's recovery.

Carey and Sharon Owen, June 6, 2014

You don't know us and we don't know you yet. But perhaps God is connecting us.

We have lived here in Seville for the last eighteen years and in Spain for twenty-four years. We are TEAM Missionaries.[2] We are fluent in Spanish and live just fifteen minutes from downtown Seville. Through a chain of connections, we heard about your daughter. We would like to help however we can.

That second comment stopped us in our tracks. God was already at work, orchestrating the support team we would need on the ground in Spain. We continued to be astonished by the outpouring of calls, emails, and comments to our site.

At 1:45 p.m. we made our first walk from the AC Marriott to the hospital. It was Friday afternoon, and the traffic was heavy. Seville has a metropolitan population of one and a half million people, and it is the fourth largest city in Spain. The sidewalks are tight and right next to the street. Cars and buses flew by a few feet from where we were walking. The five-block walk took about ten minutes. We would get very used to making this trek.

We met Morgan in the waiting room of the hospital on the bottom floor. The room was filled with anxious people waiting to get an update on their loved ones from the ER doctors. At 2:37, our name was called. Morgan, Wendy, and I were led into a small room for our first official medical update.

Dr. Marin came into the room. He understood English but preferred to speak Spanish. He relayed what he could tell us to Morgan who then translated for us.

Maggie had head trauma that didn't need surgery at this time. The inflammation inside her head was under control. She had a sensor on her cranium to monitor any brain swelling. She was in a coma from the head injury, and they would keep her under sedation to control the brain pressure. She had broken ribs, and they were using mechanical ventilation. Her spleen was okay. Her pelvic injury would need surgery to reset the bone, and they hoped to do that sometime in the next week.

Dr. Marin was very straightforward but had a calming influence. Morgan assured us that we were at a great hospital, one of the three best trauma centers in Spain.

We made the five-block walk back to our hotel. The new day had started back home, and now we could make phone calls and start to figure out a plan amid the chaos. We felt completely out of control and started contacting people who could help us make sense of the situation.

Earlier in the day, we had left a message for Dr. Mark Solfelt, a family friend from our Chapel Hill days and a thoracic and cardiac surgeon. He was on a medical mission trip to South America but had received our message and called us back.

We explained what we knew about the accident and the care Maggie was receiving. He offered to coordinate Maggie's care, offering to consult with the doctors in Spain if that would be helpful. He would be flying to Minneapolis in a couple of days but said to call at any time with questions. It was nice to have some of our medical questions answered in English and to have an expert in the field available to us around the clock. Time zones, the time of day, and sleep mean nothing to these medical professionals, and Dr. Solfelt was a huge source of encouragement and comfort.

While on our layover in Chicago, we had left a message for Vibhu Sharma in Zurich, Switzerland. We connected with him that afternoon. Vibhu is also a family friend from our days at Chapel Hill. At the time, he was the acting CFO for Zurich Insurance, the global financial services firm headquartered in Zurich. He offered to contact his business associates in Spain to provide us with any support they could.

Wendy and I also called Maggie's boyfriend, Matthew, back home in Minnesota. They had met at school and had been dating for six months. Matthew was interning at my company that summer, so he had heard about Maggie's accident when I did. He'd had a sleepless night waiting for an update.

Maggie's family, friends, and loved ones back home were dependent on us for updates, and the waiting was the hardest part. They were already hanging on our CaringBridge updates and calls, filling the time back home with prayer and attempting to go on with their normal lives. We vowed to do our best to provide regular updates as much as possible.

Wendy and I tried to eat, but neither of us could. We tried to figure out what to do next, but these attempts were mostly futile. This was not a situation that could be controlled. No amount of intelligence or effort on our part was going to make things better for Maggie. We weren't in control, and that realization hit us hard. If Maggie was going to make it, if our family was going to emerge from this trial intact, it would only be by trusting God and His healing powers.

We went back to the hospital to see Maggie for the evening visit, and Morgan met us there. The UCI waiting area was again filled with people waiting to be let in to see their loved ones. Although the visiting time was scheduled for 6:30, all the patients needed to be stable before we could be let in.

After waiting for over an hour, we were escorted into the UCI with twenty other people. We put on gowns, gloves, and masks and were led into Maggie's cubicle by a nurse.

At first it seemed as if nothing had changed in the nine-plus hours since we had seen her that morning. In examining her face, though, it seemed to me like her swelling had gone down just a little. There were glimpses of Maggie behind the bruising, tubes, and monitors. Could it be that she was already healing in such a short period of time? Or was God giving us a little glimpse of hope to carry us through the night?

The visit lasted about thirty minutes. We said goodbye to Morgan and made the lonely walk back to our hotel. We found a little something to eat, then called our family back home. It was midnight and we were exhausted, but I typed our second CaringBridge post.

A Long Day

By Tad Weiss, June 6, 2014

It has been a long day.

We were able to talk with Maggie's doctor at around 3:00 p.m. Seville time. He said she has broken ribs that will heal on their own. They did their job and protected her internal organs. She has a broken pelvis that will need to be operated on in a week or so. The main concern is the head trauma and we won't know any more on that for a few days. They plan to keep Maggie sedated and let her brain rest and heal. In a few days, they plan to take her off the sedation and then we'll have a better idea of her situation. It will be a trying few days as we are forced to wait patiently.

We had a great thirty minutes with Maggie tonight. We thought she looked better already, but we're not kidding ourselves about this being a long process.

We laid hands on her and prayed. We told her about all the emails, texts, calls, and responses coming in from around the world, and we know she heard us. We are blown away by your care for Maggie and us. We cannot do this without you.

We read from the Bible, Psalms 23, 100, and the beginning of 119. We read to her about Jesus's healing the sick and the crippled, and we know that He can heal Maggie too.

We've been up for thirty-six hours and we're running on fumes. It has been one of the longest, hardest, most incredible days you can imagine. We have so many people to thank. From the airlines getting us here so quickly, to Dr. Mark giving us guidance and encouragement, to Vibhu in Zurich helping us negotiate Spain, to our CIEE contact, Morgan, who has been translating for us all day, to Matthew and his solid support, and our family. Maggie is at one of the three best hospitals in Spain and we believe she is getting great care from her doctors.

And to everyone who is praying for Maggie and sending words of encouragement and hope, we can't tell you how much that has strengthened us through this day.

We're going to get some sleep and see Maggie in the morning. We will continue to update the site, even if there is no news.

Please pray specifically that Maggie remains stable and that her brain continues to rest and heal. God bless you!

"So do not fear for I am with you; do not be dismayed for I am your God. I will strengthen you and help you; I will uphold you with my righteous right hand" (Isaiah 41:10).

Before we could log off for the night, we started receiving replies, which once again lifted us up and blew us away.

Joelle Syverson, June 6, 2014

Thanks for the update, especially at the end of a long and trying day for you and Wendy. It helps to know how to pray specifically. "Fear not, for I have redeemed you; I have summoned you by name, you are mine. When you pass through the waters, I will be with you: and when you pass through the rivers, they will not sweep over you. When you walk through the fire, you will not be burned; the flames will not set you ablaze. For I am the Lord your God, the Holy One of Israel, your Savior" (Isaiah 43:1–3).

Sarie Anderson, June 6, 2014

I don't believe we have met personally, but my husband and I are global partners with TEAM from Wooddale, living in Madrid. We wish we could be of more help to you at this time, but we are on our way back to Minnesota in just a couple of days. We contacted colleagues and good friends in Seville, and they will be of great help and support for you. Their names are Carey and Sharon Owen and Juan Carlos and Ana. We have rallied many prayer partners in Spain who are lifting all of you up to the Father. *Un abrazo fuerte*, as they say here in Spain.

Wendy and I fell asleep at around 2:00 a.m., after being up for thirty-seven hours straight. It had indeed been a long day.

CHAPTER THREE

Day 3—June 7, 2014

W e slept solidly until the alarm went off at 7:00 a.m. to start the second day of our journey, which was really day three, since the first day essentially covered two days. It had been forty-eight hours since the accident.

Both of us were hungry, as we hadn't eaten much of anything for two days, so we went downstairs for the hotel breakfast. The café con leche (strong coffee mixed with scalded milk) was delicious and much needed. Then it was off to the hospital for our 8:30 a.m. visit. We didn't know it at the time, but we were starting a routine that would become very familiar.

After our visit with Maggie, it was time to update CaringBridge.

A New Day

By Tad Weiss, June 7, 2014

We just returned from the hospital and our thirty-minute morning visit with Maggie. Here is a picture of Wendy reading to Maggie from the Bible.

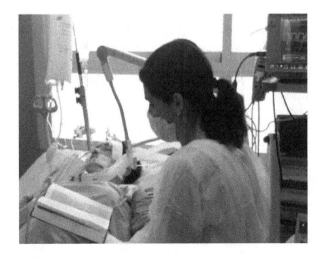

I'm reminded of when she was an infant, and we would read to her. She couldn't say anything then either, but we knew the importance of grounding her in God's Word at a young age.

Now we spend our time with her reading from the Bible and praying. We also tell her of the astounding support from all of you. We are absolutely blown away that Maggie has had 2,171 visits to this site in the twenty hours it has been up! God's army is mobilized for our precious daughter!

We finally fell asleep at 2:00 this morning, local time, and had five hours of solid sleep and a good breakfast. We have only been in Seville for twenty-four hours, yet so much has happened. The first day felt like five days! Hopefully, today will only feel like three.

Maggie rested peacefully last night and let her brain heal. That is what we continue to request prayer for. We are confident that her body can be put back together, and we pray for total and fast healing for her brain.

There is no new medical news to report. We will meet with her lead doctor at 2:00 p.m. and hope to give you a positive update. They did a brain scan that we hope to receive a report on.

Having patience is hard. We have no idea how long we will be here and we're trying not to even think about it. We will be here until we can triumphantly bring our daughter home.

Continue to pray that Maggie's brain will rest and heal and that when they take her off the sedation, she will regain consciousness soon. Pray for total healing for her. Pray for Wendy and me that we will have patience throughout this process. We can feel your prayers and support!! God's sovereign strength and the prayers of our family and friends are sustaining us at this time. To Him be the glory!

We're on day three of the most difficult journey either of us has been on. We will continue to share with you; it is therapeutic for us to write about it.

"We ourselves, who have the first fruits of the Spirit, groan inwardly as we wait eagerly for our adoption as sons, the redemption of our bodies. For in this hope, we were saved. But hope that is seen is no hope at all. Who hopes for what he already has? But if we hope for what we do not yet have, we wait for it patiently . . . And we know that in all things God works for the good of those who love Him, who have been called according to His purpose" (Romans 8:23–25 and 28).

As we had come to expect, replies to my post began arriving quickly.

Bonnie Gasper, June 7, 2014

Each morning as I open my eyes, the first thing I do is pray for Maggie and all of you, and continue to pray throughout the day. Thank you for these updates as they are probably as therapeutic to us as they are to you. It is hard to be so far away from your family in your time of great need. This picture both breaks and warms my heart at the same time.

After seeing Maggie on our morning visit and writing the update, we went back to our hotel room and crashed. But we had only rested for what seemed like a minute when the phone rang. A couple from Seville, who had replied on our site, wanted to see us and bring some food. I was a little irritated and just wanted to rest. I didn't want to see anybody, particularly someone we didn't know or need to see. Not wanting to be rude, I said they could come by our hotel in an hour.

At around noon, Carey and Sharon Owen showed up. We already knew from the CaringBridge comments that they were a missionary couple living in Seville and that they had heard of our situation from a missionary couple in Madrid who were connected to Wooddale Church in Minneapolis. They brought some meat, cheese, and crackers that we put in the refrigerator in our room. They drove us to the hospital, then took us to lunch in the hospital cafeteria, where we talked until our two o'clock doctor visit.

My initial reaction when they called could not have been more misguided. Carey and Sharon would turn out to be the rock of stability that we would need to navigate our time in Spain.

We met with Dr. Flores for our afternoon medical update. The doctors who handled these consultations were a team of five that rotated.

Dr. Flores told Morgan, who translated for us, "Maggie is clinically stable."

Wendy and I clutched each other's hands as Morgan relayed the doctor's description of Maggie's current condition.

After our doctor's visit, Morgan drove us to Maggie's host family in the city. Maggie was staying with a couple named M'awy and Antonio. They lived in the *Casco Antiguo* (the historic center of Seville), a fifteen-minute drive from the hospital. They didn't speak English, so Morgan translated for us again.

We had a nice visit with them. It was hard to see Maggie's room and all her belongings and the routines she was settling into in Spain—a book she was reading by her bedside, her journal, clothes laid out for last Thursday that weren't needed. She had packed enough to live for two months in Spain.

An intense sadness came over us as we realized that this plan, this dream, wasn't going to be fulfilled. The enormity of the situation was almost unbearable. All the planning, preparation, travel, and expense wiped away in the blink of an eye—a step off the curb.

M'awy, Maggie's "host mom," was the one who helped the police identify Maggie after the accident. Maggie was unrecognizable after being hit by the bus and had no identification on her. The paramedics rushed her to the hospital a few miles from the accident scene. There was a closer hospital, but the one they took her to was one of the best trauma centers in all of Europe. The first responders didn't think she would make it, but if she were to have any chance, she needed the best care Seville could offer.

M'awy had been at work that morning and heard on the radio that a young female had been hit by a bus on the Torneo (a main thoroughfare in Seville), which is close to their house. She went home to check on Maggie and saw that the breakfast she had set out for her hadn't been touched. She called the school, who then called the police. Three hours passed before anyone knew who the victim was.

M'awy and Antonio took us to their rooftop garden, and it was nice to see Wendy looking at their plants and talking about the varied species that grow well in Seville. Wendy loves to garden and loves flowers. It was heartening to see her enjoying those things in the midst of the trial we had been thrown into.

Morgan drove us back to our hotel, and we made a call to Dr. Solfelt, still on his mission trip in South America. We told him what we had heard from the doctors, and he said we were at least a week out from deciding to fly Maggie home. The next hurdle to get over was her pelvic surgery. He encouraged us to look for the little things—the small changes—and not to consider moving Maggie until she was off the ventilator.

From what we'd told him, he felt the doctors in Spain were doing all of the right things. He said as soon as he was back in Minneapolis, he would start pulling together the medical experts to support us in Spain and, ultimately, when Maggie made it back to Minnesota.

Later that afternoon, we had a visit to our hotel from Carlos Lopez, an attorney with Garrigues, the oldest law firm in Seville. Our friend Vibhu Sharma had put in motion the resources of his employer, Zurich Insurance Group—Switzerland's largest insurance company and the seventy-fifth largest company in the world.

We had been contacted by Giuseppe Gamucci, general counsel for Zurich Insurance Group in Spain, who had told us we would be contacted by Carlos. Garrigues did legal work for Zurich. The law offices of Garrigues were right across the street from our hotel, another coincidence that worked in our favor.

Carlos was very compassionate and comforting. In addition to being a partner at one of the best law firms in Spain, he had his own children and could understand the position we were in. Carlos was fluent in English, allowing us the ability to speak directly with him. He didn't have much information on the accident at this point, but he walked us through the legal process in Spain. Their law firm didn't handle traffic accidents like this one, but he would hire another firm for us, and he would stay involved in the investigation.

"Our law firm has worked with Zurich for many years," Carlos said. "We received word from the top of the organization to leave no stone unturned in helping Maggie in her recovery and helping you navigate the situation."

Carlos said that he would have more information on Monday, and we agreed to meet again Monday afternoon after our visit with the doctors.

We went back to the hospital for our 6:30 p.m. visit with Maggie. Carey and Sharon were waiting there for us, as was Madeline Marfe from CIEE. The school sent someone to be with us at each visit to translate, and Madeline would end up being with us many times.

We were able to get in to see Maggie after just a short wait. Afterward we walked back to our hotel and wrapped up the day with another CaringBridge post.

Praise God!

By Tad Weiss, June 7, 2014

I guess we didn't need to worry about today going by slowly; it has been a whirlwind! The good news is that we talked with one of Maggie's lead physicians this afternoon who told us that Maggie is stable, and they are confident she will recover . . . praise God!!

The doctor was very open and honest with us, and here is what we know: Maggie is clinically stable. They were concerned yesterday with some mucus around her lung but the doctors removed it. She will need pelvic surgery, probably early next week. She has been sedated and will continue to be for at least three to four more days. We are encouraged that the doctors believe Maggie will soon be strong enough to have the surgery.

Her brain injury does not require surgery. Praise God! All of the monitoring of her brain is normal and we simply need to continue to pray that it will heal and be patient with the process.

For the next few days, no news is good news. Maggie simply needs to rest and give her brain time to heal. We can go into ICU two times per day for roughly thirty minutes to be with her. These are awesome times of praise and prayer.

Our first visit yesterday morning was the hardest. On the flight over, we didn't know what to think and just tried not to let our imaginations run wild. But walking into the room and seeing our beautiful daughter hooked up to every machine, bruised and broken, was all we could take at the time. She just didn't look like Maggie.

Last night was better. We could see the swelling coming down and she started to look like Maggie again. Maybe it was wishful thinking that she was improving, but we don't think so. God needed to show us what we were in for and give us hope.

This morning Maggie looked better again, and at tonight's visit she showed continued improvement. It has only been sixty hours since the accident, but God is healing Maggie before our eyes! Praise God!!

Wendy and I are starting to write down everything that is happening on this journey. If you know God, you aren't surprised by what He does, but it is truly amazing to witness it firsthand! Our society calls these events "coincidences" but we know it is simply God in action.

There is no earthly explanation for the outpouring of love and support we are receiving. We have an unbelievable support team in Seville and people to contact for help that we haven't even gotten to. This site has over 2,700 visits in the thirty hours it has been up! Can you even imagine how much that encourages us? We have doctors in the US that are on call and willing to work with the doctors in Seville as needed.

We met with an attorney today who provided us with great comfort so we can concentrate on Maggie's health.

We met Maggie's host family and had a wonderful visit. Two missionaries brought us groceries and took us to lunch. We can't wait to share the numerous "coincidences" that God has orchestrated for us. You all are the hands and feet of God!!

My wife is a warrior. God is strengthening her, and she is there for me every time I start to crash. Please keep Wendy, Peter, and me in your prayers. Today, pray specifically that Maggie will remain stable with no setbacks, that her brain and body will continue to mend and heal, and that we all will get much-needed rest.

Maggie has endured a terrible accident and our hearts are broken. We have our moments when we ask God why this happened. But we know that God can do good through all things, and we already see this happening. One of the most marvelous things is the outpouring of love, support, prayers, and resources from all of you. We received this verse from Joann Hall Swenson today from *The Message,* Maggie's favorite Bible paraphrase/translation:

"When two of you get together on anything at all on earth and make a prayer of it, my Father in heaven goes into action. And when two or three of you are together because of me, you can be sure that I'll be there" (Matthew 18:19–20).

Jesus didn't say what happens when hundreds and hundreds of you get together, and Wendy and I look forward to telling you about it! Praise God!!

I had scarcely hit "post" when the replies started showing up.

Donna Even, June 7, 2014

Praise God for the good news! Tad, I agree with you that Wendy is a warrior. I have had the privilege of serving with her in the trenches of the Bible Study Fellowship children's program for five years. She inspires me every week. I'm blown away by the wondrous way that God is working through this trial.

Dawn Eber, June 7, 2014

Reading this through tears! Although I don't know Maggie, I know the wonderful family she has, and as a mother of a daughter close to Maggie's age, I can only imagine the fear and pain this event has brought on your hearts. Praise for the faith you have to carry you through and for the miracles He is doing. On top of the 2,700 visits to your site, I've had over 100 people praying through a request on Facebook. God's army is at work!!

The third day had been a busy day but a good one. We could see Maggie healing before our eyes, and the doctor felt confident that she would recover from the accident.

It was late in the evening in Spain but the middle of the day back home. We made a few phone calls to our family and were able to climb into bed around midnight. I was hoping for seven hours of solid sleep, but as I would soon find out, God had something else in mind.

At 2:00 a.m., I woke up. The room was dark, and I felt disoriented. Where was I? Was this all a dream?

As my head cleared and I realized I was in Spain with Wendy sleeping beside me, I felt the presence of God in the room. My mind went to an email I'd received from one of my best friends, Bill Sternard.

Billy and I go way back. We met our freshman year at Gustavus Adolphus College in St. Peter, Minnesota, at the first fall practice of the tennis team. We've been the best of friends ever since, always living near each other, raising our families together, taking trips together, and going to the same church. In the email, Bill said he'd seen me do a lot of things over the years, but this "writing thing" I was doing on CaringBridge was unexpected and was throwing him for a loop. He could see and understand God in a completely new way.

I didn't start writing on CaringBridge to be an author and certainly not a theologian. We simply needed to get the word about Maggie out to our friends and family. Writing the CaringBridge posts was an outlet and a release for me, and it felt good to type everything I was feeling. But lying there, staring at the ceiling, God told me to keep writing and to be bold.

And then a thought entered my mind. *What happens if you get hit by a bus?* Where had I heard that, recently in fact? A client had asked me that just a couple of weeks ago. Now I was in Spain because my daughter had been hit by a bus.

Lying in bed, I thought through my morning post. Every sentence and paragraph flowed through my mind in a matter of minutes, as if God was telling me what to write. I'm a note taker, and normally I would get up and write these thoughts down so I wouldn't lose them. But God told me not to worry, to go back to sleep, and to write in the morning.

CHAPTER FOUR

Day 4—June 8, 2014

After my middle-of-the-night download from God, I slept for a few more hours, then snuck out of the room and to the lobby to scare up some coffee and started typing.

What Happens If You Get Hit by a Bus?

By Tad Weiss, June 8, 2014

"What happens to us and to our accounts if something happens to you? What happens if you get hit by a bus?"

Believe it or not, I get asked that question quite frequently. In my business (financial planning) I have a great team that works with me, but I'm the front man and I meet with all of our clients.

It is a perfectly fair and reasonable question to ask.

The phrase "hit by a bus" is a socially acceptable way of asking what happens if you die. If you get hit by a bus, you usually die. The bus that hit Maggie weighs twenty-two tons. It was probably going 30 miles per hour when it hit her. She was wearing nothing but running shoes, shorts, and a shirt. She had absolutely no protection except for a strong body and the armor of God. Without that, she would be dead. It is only by God's grace and protection that she is still with us and that we have hope for her recovery.

What would we be going through right now if Maggie weren't alive? Her mother and best friend, who brought her into this world, would be totally devastated. Her father and protector would have lost his favorite skiing buddy. Her big "little brother" would have lost his very first friend who held him on her lap when he was a baby. Her boyfriend would have lost the girl he wants to spend the rest of his life with. Her grandparents, aunts, uncles, and cousins would miss her dearly, and family gatherings would be less joyful. The St. Olaf octet would only have seven. The cross-country and track teams would not be as deep or as strong.

All of you would miss Maggie and the way she has brightened your life and touched you. The world would be a darker place without the bright light of Maggie. That would be the sad news for those of us left here on earth.

But the great news is that Maggie accepted Jesus as her Savior as a little girl, and heaven would rejoice with her as she triumphantly entered heaven! Jesus would greet her and say, "Well done, my good and faithful servant." There would be great reward for her as the angels celebrate the life Maggie lived on earth. Her body would be made perfect again, better than before the accident. She would be in heaven, where there is no sin, death, or hardship. She would be there for eternity.

So I ask the question: What happens if *you* get hit by a bus? What happens when your time here on earth is up? Maggie didn't wake up on Thursday morning thinking she would get hit by a bus, but that is what happened. We don't know the future or how long each of us has on this earth. Only God knows.

For anyone reading this who does not know Jesus as their personal Lord and Savior, I pray that you will think and meditate on these words today. If you do not know Jesus, there is a hole in your heart that only He can fill. He is waiting for you to come to Him. It is as easy as ABC:

A—Admit that you are a sinner in need of a Savior.

B—Believe that God sent His one and only Son to earth to die on the cross for the forgiveness of your sin.

C—Choose to follow Jesus all the days of your life.
It is the best decision you will ever make.

By the time you read this, it will be Sunday morning in the US. The churches are opening their doors. There will be great prayer and praise for Maggie in God's house! You can bring no greater purpose to this accident, no greater honor to God by what Maggie and we are going through, than by committing your life to Jesus Christ today. Ask a pastor or a Christian friend to help you. If the Holy Spirit is prompting you, it only takes a minute, but the rewards last forever.

"For God so loved the world that He gave his one and only Son, that whoever believes in Him shall not perish but have eternal life" (John 3:16).

Amy Fisher, June 8, 2014

Such wonderful words! So thankful that God has spared Maggie's life and that you are using this experience to save the lives of others for eternity!

Over breakfast that morning, I joyfully recounted to Wendy my experience with God the night before. She could see how much the writing was helping me, as well as our friends and family, and she wrote her first of many updates to our CaringBridge site.

God is So Good!

By Wendy Weiss, June 8, 2014

Everyone from Bible Study Fellowship (BSF) who knows the children's program will recognize the title of this entry as the title of a hymn we sing with the children nearly every week in BSF . . . and you will also then know that this is not Tad, but Wendy, who is writing this journal entry!

God is so good! God is so good! God is so good; He's so good to me!

Glory Hallelujah! Glory Hallelujah! Glory Hallelujah; He's so good to me!

God is so good to me! True! We see Him and His hand everywhere, while we are here. Tad has done a great job with this journal, and I would like to add my heartfelt thanks to all of you. There have been so many comments, posts, personal texts, and emails, we can hardly get through them all. But it really has helped us so much to know how very many people love Maggie and us and are praying on our behalf. The body of believers is a gift on earth; thanks be to God! Please do not stop praying. Please do not stop trusting that God will heal Maggie. Please do not stop writing to us; we treasure every word in our hearts, and I know Maggie will be blessed to be able to hear all you have to say to her when she wakes up.

When we are with her for the short visits twice a day, we talk to her, tell her about all your love and prayers, lay hands on her and pray over and for her, kiss her shoulders and arms, and play the *Choral Benediction* that the Minnetonka choir kids sang for her. Thank you, dear choir friends and thank you, Barb, for sending the video!

We were told that though she is currently unresponsive due to the heavy sedation, she can hear us. I personally believe, because music has been such an integral part of Maggie's life, that she will be blessed by this music in her unconscious state of mind. For those of you who do not know the words of this blessing, here they are:

"The Lord bless you and keep you; the Lord make His face

shine upon you and be gracious to you; the Lord turn His face toward you and give you peace" (Numbers 6:24–26).

I pray this for each one of you who are following Maggie! Thanks for all you are doing for us!

The outpouring of love, support, and responses ushered us forward with our day.

Nancy Wagner, June 8, 2014

Maggie is everyone's child right now. She is loved and treasured by God and all of us who are touched by her story.

Lindsey Finch, June 8, 2014

Wendy, I remember years ago while going through a trial reading the words, "Tear-filled eyes can still focus on Jesus." I see this happening now as you and Tad share how God is with you and for you and evident even in this trial. God is ministering to others through you and your faith in Him!

Matt, Jana, Andy, and Ellie, June 8, 2014

Praying for Maggie constantly. There are so many congregations this morning, here in Iowa and Minnesota, at this very moment, praying together for our sweet Maggie. I know she will feel God's power. You are in our every thought and prayer. God is good!

The "business" end of our journey had already begun, which was inevitable. Maggie's college, St. Olaf, had been in contact with Morgan at CIEE from the date of the accident, since they coordinate student exchange programs together. FrontierMEDEX provided travel insurance for St. Olaf. Maggie had emergency medical coverage of $100,000 and medical repatriation coverage up to $1,000,000 through EIAA/Navigators, if deemed necessary by FrontierMEDEX.

When Maggie signed up for the program, I had wanted to decline this coverage as I don't usually buy travel insurance, but fortunately, that wasn't an option. Our health insurance was with PreferredOne, and they were brought onto the case, and the bus company had their insurance coverage too.

We were working behind the scenes to get Maggie's medical updates to the doctors in the US. Through friends, we had access to the best specialists in the Twin Cities, but getting the information released was going to be tricky. The language barrier added another level of complexity.

We received an email from a friend with a link to an article about the accident. The bus driver had tested positive for cocaine in a drug test taken immediately after the accident. We had a meeting already scheduled with our attorney, Carlos, for Monday. Our world was moving fast!

Riding the Rollercoaster

by Tad Weiss, June 8, 2014

It is after 11:00 p.m. here in Seville and it has been another busy day. We are grateful that the days are full, as it helps them go by quickly. Wendy and I need to try and get some sleep, so this will be short.

We followed our new routine of visiting Maggie in the morning for thirty minutes in the ICU, met with the doctor at around 2:00, then saw Maggie again at 7:00 this evening. She continues to look better to us. The swelling is going down at each visit. We will reach the ninety-six-hour mark since the accident tomorrow morning at seven. The first three to four days are the most critical after such a serious trauma, and Maggie remains stable and is resting. We are so thankful for your prayers and God's protective hand that has gotten Maggie to this point.

The doctors plan to operate to fix Maggie's broken pelvis this Wednesday. They will evaluate her tomorrow to make sure she is ready for the surgery. Her ribs are broken but they will heal on their own.

The main concern continues to be Maggie's head trauma. Once again, the good news is that she is stable and there have been no setbacks. She simply needs to rest and let her brain heal, and she is doing a great job!

After the pelvic surgery, the plan is to take her off sedation and remove the mechanical breathing. Then we see how she responds. There are no guarantees, and it may take time. We are praying that this process can start later in the week.

We met with the doctor at 2:00 today, and all the progress reports were on track. He was the first doctor who spoke directly to us in English, so we were hearing a lot more of the information.

The walk back to the hotel and the ensuing hour was the low point of the day. Our minds ran wild with questions that can't be answered: Will Maggie fully recover? If so, when? How long will we be here?

I wish I could tell you that we are rock solid all the time and that our faith is so great that we have no fears or doubts. But it simply isn't true, and fear had a hold of us this afternoon.

The turning point in the day was watching the 9:45 a.m. online service at Westwood Community Church. Joelle had sent us a Bible verse earlier from Isaiah 43:2 that we loved: "When you pass through the waters, I will be with you; when you pass through the rivers, they will not sweep over you. When you walk through the fire, you will not be burned; the flames will not set you ablaze." The first song of the day, "For I

Am the Lord Your God," was written from this Scripture!

God reminded us, once again, that He is at work in *all* the details. He inspired Joelle to send us that verse, and He inspired the worship leader to choose that song even before Maggie's accident had occurred. God is sovereign, and He is in control.

We were incredibly lifted by the prayer group that met at Westwood to pray for Maggie . . . thank you! We have heard from so many of you that Maggie is being lifted up in churches throughout the country. What a blessing to us in our time of need!

Right before we left to go see Maggie for our 6:30 visit, we received a call from Maritheresa Fraine, consular agent at the US Department of State. Could we meet with her?

She and her husband, Juan, as well as Jaime from CIEE, met us at the hospital and we talked before seeing Maggie. She told us of all the calls the consulate has received about Maggie. We were so inspired and encouraged that no stone was being left unturned in the care of our daughter and in getting her back to the US as soon as we possibly could.

On our walk back to the hotel that night, we marveled at how different we felt. The same walk between the hospital and the hotel, the same route, four hours apart. The first filled with doubt and fear. The second filled with hope, encouragement, and renewed and strengthened faith! God continued to put the right people in our path at exactly the right time. He is in charge of all the details. We need not fear!!

Please continue to pray for Maggie to remain stable, to be strong enough for the upcoming pelvic repair, and that she will receive the best possible care for all her injuries and complete healing of her brain. We also covet your prayers for continued strength and peace for us, that the God of all comfort would be very near to all of Maggie's family and closest friends in this time.

I know that many of you have dealt with extreme grief and suffering in your life. We are so grateful for all your prayers. We know that God is holding Maggie in His hand, and as one of you wrote today, Maggie is everyone's daughter in this journey. God bless and good night.

The road felt long and mostly uphill, but the continued reminders that we were never alone went a long way to ease the burden of the journey.

CHAPTER FIVE

Day 5—June 9, 2014

O n day five we started to put the pieces of the accident together.

In the afternoon we met with Felix and Rafa, the two police officers who were first on the accident scene. They were young family men, and we could see the compassion and concern for Maggie in their eyes.

Felix explained how the paramedics made a wise decision in taking Maggie to Hospital Universitario Virgen Del Rocio, as it has greater emergency room and intensive care capabilities versus the hospital that was closer to the accident. He said that decision alone may have saved Maggie's life.

Then we met with our attorney, Carlos, who said that Maggie was at the best hospital in the south of Spain. Her case was high profile due to her being a young exchange student, the bus company being owned by the city, and the nature of the accident.

Carlos explained that the police report—the *atestado*—would be the key element in the legal process, and it would be considered the truth in the Spanish legal system. The *atestado* would be sent to the judge, who would decide on the criminal case. Carlos said that damages, if any, would be a part of the criminal case. There would be no settlement until Maggie had recovered fully, and it would be a long process.

Carlos said, "Settlements in Spain are nowhere near the amounts awarded in the United States. If her legal case is successful, expect a moderate amount, maybe enough for Maggie to make a down payment on a house at some point in the future."

The case would likely boil down to the speed of the bus and if it was determined that Maggie crossed the intersection against a red light.

Carlos told us that Maggie had been knocked in the air by the bus and had traveled four to five meters. We learned later that this wasn't true—it had been considerably more—but Carlos had a sense for how much we could handle at that time.

We had one of the finest attorneys at our disposal at no charge. His firm,

Garrigues, did not specialize in personal injury traffic accidents, and they brought another local law firm, RZS, on the case. They had already sent an expert to the scene of the accident to gather information.

As we were wrapping up our time with Carlos, Wendy asked him about his family. He told us he had a young daughter who was dealing with some issues. It was awe-inspiring for me to see the compassion Wendy had for him and to see the roles reversed, as if they both stood up and literally changed chairs. Wendy went from the one being comforted to being the comforter, and Carlos from the legal counselor to the one receiving needed encouragement.

As Wendy shared some of the struggles Maggie had gone through at his daughter's age, she assured Carlos that his daughter would survive that challenging period, just as Maggie had. I was in awe of my wife's capacity to listen and care and comfort someone else at that moment. It also was the first time I realized that maybe we weren't there just for Maggie but for another purpose.

God Sightings
by Tad Weiss, June 9, 2014

It is 5:30 p.m. in Seville and the day is literally flying by. My concern that the days would drag on was totally unfounded. We are busy from morning to night, just the right amount. We were in the hotel room at what we thought was noon, but when we looked at the clock, it was 1:45 and time to go to our 2:00 visit with Maggie's doctor.

Seven thirty-five this morning marked the ninety-six-hour point in Maggie's journey. We've been told the first three to four days are crucial, and she passed the four-day mark like a champion!

This morning at 8:30, we had our time with Maggie in ICU.

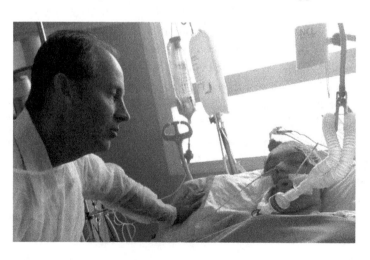

This was the first time we could see Maggie without surgical masks and gloves!! We also were told that they have reduced the amount of sedation medication!!! Three big victories this morning, and we are very encouraged. God is in charge!!!!

The meeting with Maggie's doctor was good also. I think we're getting better at this. We're learning what to ask and what not to ask. Here are some of my notes:

Maggie is quite stable; pressure is under control in her brain. No problem with her respiratory system. Her pelvic bone surgery is likely on Wednesday or Thursday. She'll need a blood transfusion before the surgery to strengthen her, but the doctors are confident she'll be ready to go. The surgery will be more detailed and invasive; her pelvic bone is pretty messed up.

If all goes well with the surgery, they plan to take off the brain sensors and remove the sedation. That may be later in the week. Then we can start to get a handle on the extent of the brain injury, but all indications are positive.

Wendy and I are feeling more peace as we start to grasp the bigger picture. God is meeting us in so many profound ways that it is hard to put into words. We're trying to capture all of these God moments, but there are so many, it's hard to keep up. Some are small, some are *huge!* They constantly remind us that God is in charge, and we don't need to worry. He has our precious Maggie in His hand and He will not let her go.

Here is what we believe: God aches as much as we do at what happened to Maggie. He didn't make the accident happen. It happened because we live in a sinful world. But God can take terrible things and bring amazing good from them. Here are a few God moments from today:

When we were waiting to see the doctor, a man came in from the street and asked for us. We didn't know him. He lives two blocks from the accident scene. He and his girlfriend are runners and they run the same route as Maggie did.

Two weeks ago, they almost got hit by a bus. They filed a complaint that the buses are driving too fast. They were devastated to hear about Maggie, but they knew this was going to happen.

Now, because of the accident, things will change. There are laws but they aren't followed. The buses go over 50 miles per hour in a very busy city area. There is a school in the same block where Maggie got hit.

Maggie's accident and the changes that will happen will save someone's life in this city.

This morning, Wendy and Jorge from CIEE were working on getting Maggie's medical records released to a team of doctors in the US so they can review and consult with our doctors in Spain. Our team on the ground here was able to get Maggie's records released to our team in the US in about three hours. The process usually takes eight days!!

Meanwhile, I was back at the hotel working on getting our car keys FedEx'ed to the US for my mom and dad. Piece of cake, right?

I called FedEx. They wouldn't release my account number over the phone. I would have to talk to the invoice department, and they were closed. Are you kidding me?!?

I explained the whole situation. They had my account number right in front of them, and they wouldn't release it because of some policy?!

Just when I was about ready to lose it, John Hiatt started singing over the hotel radio, "Have a Little Faith in Me." I started laughing.

Now, I don't think this song is about God, and it doesn't even matter. It was just the reminder that I needed to not sweat the small stuff. I thanked the supervisor for his time and hung up. The keys will get there a day later.

When we are with Maggie, we pray and read from Scripture. I always flip through the Gospels and read one to Maggie about Jesus's healing powers. Not planned out, totally random as to where I land.

Today His hand took my finger to John 9:1. "As he went along, he saw a man blind from birth. His disciples asked him, 'Rabbi, who sinned, this man or his parents, that he was born blind?' 'Neither this man nor his parents sinned,' said Jesus, 'but this happened so that the work of God might be displayed in his life.'"

Boom! That is what Wendy and I have been trying to find through the accident, and there it is in God's Word. God didn't want this accident to happen any more than we did, but since it happened, He is going to use it in every possible way for His glory! We feel called to keep our eyes and ears open to the best of our ability to help Him in the process.

We had another great visit with Maggie. Six people from CIEE and a missionary couple were with us. Our support on the ground has been phenomenal. We met with the police and with an attorney and are taking care of business in between our visits with Maggie and the doctors.

Specifically, please pray the following tonight:

- That Maggie will remain stable and continue to heal.
- That the Spanish doctors and US doctors will have wisdom and will effectively share information and agree on Maggie's treatment plan.

Thank you all, God bless, and good night!

After getting ready for bed, we checked for replies.

Candace Wisely, June 9, 2014

Jayme and I continue to pray through the day for the Lord's care of each of you. He has entrusted you with this story because He knew He could trust you to make His name great in the midst of all you are encountering.

Madeline Marfe, June 9, 2014

That ICU unit was filled with God's love . . . Looking through the glass at both of you praying, talking, and even laughing with her multiplied my faith.

Wayne and Pat Schultz (Maggie's Grandparents), June 9, 2014

To all of you out there . . . we are totally overwhelmed by your faith in God. Take heart that God is using Maggie as our inspiration to stand up and be counted. We will never deny God nor our faith in God and know that He will completely heal her for all of us.

We needed to get a good night's sleep. Maggie's pelvic surgery would happen either the following day or the next. We'd been talking with Dr. Mark Solfelt. We trusted the doctors in Spain, but the language barrier made it difficult to have total confidence. Mark told us that from the pictures he could tell they were using intracranial pressure monitoring, just like they would in the US. He assured us that she was in a state-of-the-art location.

All of Maggie's medical records were being downloaded into Dropbox, and Mark planned to review them with the specialists. He had a Spanish-speaking doctor in Minneapolis—Dr. Esguerra—who would talk with Dr. Marin in Seville. Wendy and I bounced back and forth between faith and trust and wanting to make sure we took every step and precaution possible in the care of Maggie.

Wendy had a saying: "Just because you have faith in God doesn't mean you check your brain at the door." God is in control, and we have a part to play too.

CaringBridge was our public communication tool, and we received so many messages through it. We also received lots of emails from friends who didn't feel comfortable posting to CaringBridge. Publicly or privately, the support we received was overwhelming. It was all a part of God's plan to get us through this.

CHAPTER SIX

Day 6—June 10, 2014

Wendy and I had gotten into the habit of checking the number of visits to the site before bed and when we awoke in the morning. We signed off late on day five at 12:15 a.m. and logged back in at 7:25 the next morning. While we slept, there were 1,030 visits to Maggie's CaringBridge site!

The time difference was a comfort in this way. When we went to sleep to get the rest we needed, we did so in peace, knowing that our followers were taking over for us. Maggie was never alone. She was covered in prayer twenty-four hours a day every day.

We told her about this . . . that there was someone somewhere praying for her every second of every day. And we knew that most of the day, there were hundreds of people around the world praying and thinking of Maggie every single second.

How Lovely Is God's Dwelling Place
by Tad Weiss, June 10, 2014

We're going to try and do shorter posts more frequently, especially when we have great news to share. And this morning, there's great news!

At our morning visit with Maggie, we played a video from her boyfriend, Matthew. When we played it, Maggie moved for the first time! Her shoulders moved up and down!! Then as we read to her from Scripture, her hand and arm moved, and then her mouth. We went to get the nurse to make sure it was okay, that she wasn't getting too excited, and it was good! What a beautiful sign of progress.

The first four days we were told that we just wanted Maggie to rest and not go backward. Yesterday was the first day we saw signs of actual forward progress—from stability to improvement. *Praise God!!!!* This morning was an even greater sign. Maggie looked beautiful, more and more like the Maggie we all know.

The title of this post is "How Lovely is God's Dwelling Place."

In the Old Testament, the dwelling place of God was the temple. Because of Jesus's sacrifice on the cross, God's dwelling place is now in those who trust in Jesus as their Lord and Savior. Our lovely daughter is God's dwelling place! The spirit of God, which in Hebrew is the same word as breath, is flowing in and through Maggie to bring her back to a place of wholeness. *Praise God!!*

"How lovely is your dwelling place, O Lord Almighty! Better is one day in your courts than a thousand elsewhere; I would rather be a doorkeeper in the house of my God than dwell in the tents of the wicked. For the Lord God is a sun and shield; the Lord bestows favor and honor; no good thing does he withhold from those whose walk is blameless. O Lord Almighty, blessed is the man who trusts in you" (Psalm 84).

It filled us with joy to share good news with those we knew had been praying so fervently. And we were soon rewarded with their heartfelt responses.

De, Pete, Dan Brandt, June 10, 2014

Our family is praying for God's peace, healing, and wisdom for you. Our son, Dan, is particularly disturbed and was going on about how Maggie is the nicest, most genuine, *good* girl he knows and why would this happen to *her?*

Brittney Johnson, June 10, 2014

Wendy, you are so strong, and the Holy Spirit is flowing from you. I'm crying tears of joy because God's healing your sweet Maggie and you're blessing us by literally letting us watch alongside you.

Niki Klein, June 10, 2014

Your witness and faith are spreading across the world. Who knew you would be on a mission trip this summer!

Wendy and I were called to the hospital early for our evening visit. We were asked to authorize a blood transfusion for surgery.

Have you ever signed a waiver without reading all the terms? How about one written in a foreign language? There was no option but to sign away. Maggie's blood cells were at the lower limit of where they needed to be for surgery.

This same day, we heard from our attorney, who said, "The bus that hit Maggie was going thirty-eight miles per hour."

"What?" I literally questioned what I had heard. "That doesn't add up with what we've been told."

We knew that the accident was severe, but we'd been told that Maggie had only been thrown four or five meters from the impact with the bus. If Maggie was hit head-on by a bus going thirty-eight miles per hour, she would have been thrown much farther than five meters.

I had been so consumed with Maggie and with all the doctor and attorney meetings, I hadn't thought about work at all, but I realized I needed to get some word out to our clients. For the first time since the accident, I checked in with Julie Kaufmann, an associate at the office. I wrote an email update for my clients, steered them to the CaringBridge site, and relayed that I didn't know how long we would be in Spain.

I mentioned our faith and trust in God. Talking about faith with clients is generally considered off-limits, but this was my reality, and I couldn't separate the two. It felt good. Clinging to the edge of a cliff has a way of breaking down barriers and stripping away facades.

Morgan was hard at work behind the scenes getting the Spanish doctors to download Maggie's medical records into Dropbox, which would allow the doctors in the US to see them. Dropbox was a relatively new technology at the time, and this wasn't going to be easy or smooth!

I received an email from Todd Rooke, the first of many over the next couple of months. Todd's wife, Donna, is a friend of Wendy's. He and I met once, briefly. Todd had tracked down my email address and shared that he'd been prompted by the Holy Spirit to encourage me to advocate and communicate effectively with the doctors. He had been through a similar medical emergency with a child and understood the challenge of getting doctors to communicate across the world.

We were advocating for Maggie to the best of our ability, but I felt a renewed strength to do an even better job. This wouldn't be the only time Todd saw into the future and, with God's help, provided guidance for me.

Passing the Baton
by Tad Weiss, June 10, 2014

We have met with four different doctors, and today we met with Dr. Flores again. He said the situation is good based on the severity of the accident. We were told that Maggie's pelvic surgery will likely be on Thursday. Her CT scan was great; they planned to reduce her sedation again and remove the ICP monitors from her brain this afternoon. We had thought they would not reduce the sedation until after the pelvic surgery, but they are separate issues, and this was moved up. Praise God!!

Back to the hotel, and then again to the hospital at 6:30 to see Maggie. Our visit this evening was like the one this morning. At first she just listened to us as we talked to her. We played a voice message for her and read a letter, then we played the voice message from Matthew again—the one that inspired the first movement this morning. And she started moving again!

49

The doctors had removed the ICP monitor. Maggie's dressings for the cuts on her head were removed too. She looks absolutely beautiful! We have witnessed an unbelievable transformation in her face over the five days we've been here. More importantly, we know that God is transforming and healing her whole body, inside and out. We also were told that her pelvic surgery may be Wednesday, tomorrow. We view this as a good sign that she is strong enough and ready for the surgery. We are not anxious or worried about the date. We trust that God will take care of that detail. We will let you know as soon as possible if the surgery is tomorrow so Maggie's prayer warriors can do their thing!

The Scripture verses and words you share touch us deeply. These verses are jumping off the pages as they so beautifully detail what we are going through and how we are to respond and be faithful to God. His Word is so true and good.

We love the idea of "passing the baton" to you when we go to bed. We know that God is watching over Maggie all day every day. But it is comforting to know that you are praying for and thinking of Maggie while we're asleep. We look forward to waking up refreshed, ready to receive the baton back, to be with Maggie, and to see what miracles God has in store for her and for all of us. May God bless you all.

"Therefore, since we are surrounded by such a great cloud of witnesses, let us throw off everything that hinders and the sin that so easily entangles, and let us run with perseverance the race marked out for us" (Hebrews 12:1).

Gary Kriegel, June 10, 2014

Keep passing the baton our way. We got you covered at night so you can rest. "Come to me, all you who are weary and burdened, and I will give you rest" (Matthew 11:28 NIV).

Maritheresa Frain, Carmen Rivera Frain, Juan Rivera,
June 10, 2014

You and Maggie came into our lives when all we thought about were ourselves and our move to the US. I thank you and God for helping us gain perspective. I can only say that *there are no mistakes.* There is a larger plan of what is to happen and whom we are to meet to help in that process. As a family, we would like to thank you for coming into our lives.

I received an email from my friend Brace Helgeson, with a photo of himself and three friends of mine taking a knee on the fourth tee box at a golf course, praying for Maggie and dedicating the day to her.

When guys play golf, they usually spend four or more hours walking and talking about nothing of significance. It's fun, and it's the nature of the game, but our wives are amazed that we can spend that much time together and not even ask the most basic of questions about someone's life and the things that truly matter. Here were four guys stopping, taking a posture of reverence, and praising God on behalf of Maggie. Guys just don't do that, and it meant the world to me.

At our doctor visit, I made a comment about all of the astounding, good things that were happening because of Maggie's accident.

The doctor replied, "The best thing would be if this had not happened to her."

There were a couple of things at play. One was that the Spanish people don't handle tragedy or hardship well. I guess most people don't, and it's perfectly normal to want life to be easy, smooth, and pain free. To them, there was no way this could be seen as a "good" event.

Believe me, I don't view Maggie's accident as good. The bigger issue, though, is how you view God. If you believe God is all knowing and all powerful and a loving God, then you must believe that He allowed Maggie's accident to happen. He must have His reasons.

Our challenge was to find out what those reasons were.

CHAPTER SEVEN

Day 7—June 11, 2014

Wendy and I had a good night's rest and woke up ready to take the baton back!

After our morning visit with Maggie, we went back to the room and had an anxious moment when our Spanish cell phone rang. We had been given a preloaded phone to send and receive calls in Spain. We called it the "bat phone," as it was only used for emergencies. I could barely operate it and couldn't turn down the volume, so it scared me every time it rang.

This particular call was from a lady at the hospital speaking Spanish. *No comprendo.* She put the doctor on the line, and he said, in broken English, that he needed to see us right away.

I panicked. "Is Maggie okay?"

"Yes," the doctor assured us. "She is fine. But we need to speak with you about the surgery."

Respecting that surgeons are busy people, we rushed back to the hospital.

The surgeon's English was quite good in person. Dr. Moreno said that Maggie would go into surgery at approximately 9:00 a.m. the next day. It would be a complicated surgery, lasting a minimum of two hours. They would surgically repair the pelvic fracture on Maggie's left side. She also had a fracture on the right side, but it was not as severe.

I found comfort in our daily routine and in updating everyone on Maggie's progress.

Trying to See

by Tad Weiss, June 11, 2014

Good morning to you all from Seville. Thank you once again for caring for our daughter through the night.

This morning at 7:55 in Seville, we hit the 10,000-visit mark on CaringBridge! Six days and twenty minutes from the time of Maggie's accident. We love seeing that number climb because we need *all* of your prayers. God's Word is being spread and He is being glorified through Maggie. That brings great joy and comfort to Wendy and me. God bless you all!

We saw Maggie this morning, and her improvement continues! Today was the first time we could hold her hand. As they reduce her sedation, she moves around more. They have her hands restrained as she keeps trying to lift them! When we walked in today and spoke our first words, she started raising her hands, we think to praise God!! Maggie's eyes were slightly opened, tiny slits, but they were open!!!

In the area that they shaved her head for the brain monitor (which was removed yesterday) her hair is already starting to grow back. This was a great sign to us that she will be made whole again, both inside and out.

Wendy is amazing. The words she speaks come from a deep knowledge of Scripture. All that time studying the Bible is being put to use so powerfully! I am humbled to witness it.

God pointed my finger this morning to Mark 9:22–26 to read to Maggie. Jesus touched the blind man at Bethsaida and he started to see, though not clearly. Maggie is starting to see again by opening her eyes a little. Jesus touched the man again, his sight was restored, and he saw everything clearly! Once again this encourages us to have faith that Maggie will regain all of her bodily functions according to His timing and His will.

The verse also shouts to me. I was blind to so many things before Maggie's accident. Jesus has touched me (hit me between the eyes with a sledgehammer is more accurate), and I can see many things *so clearly* that I could not see one week ago.

This afternoon, we learned that Maggie will be having her surgery tomorrow! We go back to the hospital to meet with the doctors for our general update, then will visit with Maggie again tonight. That will likely be the last time we see her until after her surgery.

Here are our specific prayer requests for today:

- That the doctors will be able to continue to reduce Maggie's sedation and that her brain will continue to heal.
- That she will remain stable and that all her body continues to function and improve.
- For wisdom and skill for the surgeons, doctors, and nurses as they operate on Maggie. That God will guide their decisions and hands regarding every aspect of the procedure and that the operation will be a complete success.
- That we continue to see signs of Maggie's improvement and healing, yet at the same time remain patient and trust in God for His will and His perfect timing.

"Therefore, I urge you, brothers and sisters, in view of God's mercy, to offer your bodies as living sacrifices, holy and pleasing to God. This is your spiritual act of worship. Do not conform any longer to the pattern of this world, but be transformed by the renewing of your mind. Then you will be able to test and approve what God's will is; his good, pleasing and perfect will" (Romans 12:1–2).

Julia Sharma, June 11, 2014

I can't help but be in awe of all God is doing through this situation and your faithfulness to proclaim His name through it all. You are getting the opportunity to be His servants publicly and strategically and, as we can see from your posts, you know that you serve an incredible Master. We'll be praying tonight and wondering how many North Americans will be awoken at 2:00 a.m. to pray.

Lynne Miller, June 11, 2014

Your family is truly impacting the world for God's glory! I have asked everyone I know to pray for Maggie and her family as God heals her. Every minute of every day, you are all being prayed for.

Yes, another post . . . this time from Wendy. She gave me a little break. I had been posting as often as possible, but I was tired.

Mucho Ánimo!
by Wendy Weiss, June 11, 2014

We are praying for a good night's rest; we have a big day tomorrow! (Those of you who know me well are probably wondering how in the world I have managed to stay so quiet for this long.)

We visited with Dr. Flores this afternoon. The conversation was pretty much what we expected. Maggie is still stable (Praise the Lord!). They continue to reduce the sedation meds, and her responses (shrugging shoulders, moving arms and feet, yawning) are normal. She will receive a transfusion before surgery tomorrow at 9:00 a.m. We do get to see her in the morning, then we will follow her to wherever they will perform surgery (it is a *big* hospital!). We will wait with Morgan (and new friends Carey and Sharon) during the surgery. It could be two hours or a lot more. God is teaching us *paciencia!*

The only new piece of information we got was this. Because of the sedation, they have not been able to tell whether Maggie suffered any nerve damage. So a new prayer request would be for no nerve damage.

I loved what Niki posted about Tad and me being on an

unplanned mission trip! So true! And . . . we unwittingly en-rolled in a crash course for Spanish. God is healing our beauti-ful daughter before our eyes, but the fact that she has *mucho ánimo* (a lot of spirit and a lot of Spirit!) is also helping!

We continue to stand in awe of our God and His ability to hold us together. He has also given us *mucho ánimo,* and we are so grateful; we pray for that to continue tomorrow during the surgery!

"In the same way, the Spirit helps us in our weakness. We do not know what we ought to pray for, but the Spirit inter-cedes for us with groans that words cannot express. And He who searches our hearts knows the mind of the Spirit, because the Spirit intercedes for the saints in accordance with God's will" (Romans 8:26–27).

Roxanne Martin, June 11, 2014

Join us in a prayer vigil from 1:30 a.m. Minnesota time, until we hear God has allowed Maggie to stay with us.

Sarie Anderson, June 11, 2014

We made it from Madrid to Philadelphia and are waiting for our connecting flight to MSP. We have been following Mag-gie's progress and are in awe of all God is doing through you. God is using this very tragic accident to make Himself known in a much bigger way than you could have ever imagined. We will be in prayer for Maggie's surgery tomorrow.

Madeline Marfe, June 11, 2014

"Love is always patient and kind" (1 Corinthians 13:4). Wen-dy, thank you for being so kind to my sixteen-year-old, Sara. She was impressed by your kind smile, serenity, and calm *pa-ciencia.* You and Tad are giving everyone that meets you the incredible gift of your faith and hope, but above all your love. Maggie will be healed, and you are healing us. See you tomor-row at the hospital . . . *Mucho ánimo.*

John Podergois, June 11, 2014

I haven't prayed this much in a long time.

CHAPTER EIGHT

Day 8—June 12, 2014

Wendy and I awoke refreshed on day eight, a Thursday, in Seville. One (or more!) of our prayer warriors had prayed that we would get eight hours of sleep, and that was exactly what we got. We had been very tired the night before, but we woke up feeling rested, renewed, and strengthened for the day.

Do Not Be Afraid
by Tad Weiss, June 12, 2014

"So do not fear, for I am with you, do not be dismayed, for I am your God. I will strengthen you and help you; I will uphold you with my righteous right hand" (Isaiah 41:10).

Thank You, God!! You know exactly what we need and when we need it. You send your servants to us through prayer, Scripture, loving words, and acts of service at exactly the right moment. We see these small moments *all day long* and even when we rest, and they are a comfort to us and proof that You are holding Maggie and all of us in Your righteous right hand.

Today is a big day in Maggie's journey. At 7:35 a.m., just a few minutes from now, it will be exactly one week from the time Maggie was hit. Thank You, God, that she has rested and recovered so miraculously during this week. We could not be more thrilled with her progress. We are not anxious or worried about the surgery. We know that God has put the right doctors, surgeons, and nurses in place. They are confident her surgery will be successful and so are we. Wendy and I will be accompanied by faithful people here, and we know she is covered in prayer by all of you around the world. We will share the news of the completion of her surgery as soon as we can.

Wendy received an email from Cassie yesterday with the prayers of her three-year-old daughter, Penny, that we would like to add to the prayer requests, so here they are:

"Jesus, make Maggie feel better. Help her breathe through her mouth. Help her really big ouchie, God. She wants to do it herself but she can't. Help her, Jesus. Don't let her head be sad. Let her stand up. She loves You."

Amen and *Amen!*

Cindy, June 12, 2014

I learned of you through a fellow missionary with SEND International.[3] We are living and serving outside of Madrid, and I have read each of your posts. I know you would not choose to go through this valley if you had an option, but God is using every step.

We are here to partner with the evangelical church, and we have learned much about the Spanish culture. The people are beautiful with wonderful hearts, but they are slow to let you into their lives. Friendship is a treasured thing and Spaniards do not take it lightly. If they become your friend, they expect it to be for a lifetime. We have been well accepted and loved, but there have been some very lonely days along the nearly three years we have been here.

The Spaniards who are helping you have stepped outside their normal cultural norms to touch your lives. The doctors and nurses are being more than caregivers to your daughter—they are helping carry you. This is incredible in this culture. God *is already* making good out of a horrible situation. You are safe in His hands and your testimony and peace are touching lives in extraordinary ways.

We pray daily for the culture here to see and understand a God that does not sit on a throne and figure out ways to make it difficult to come to Him, but instead a God that is a Good Shepherd, who wept, laughed, shouted for joy, and desires to walk intimately with each of us. Thank you for courageously being that light.

Picture this: Wendy and me in a hallway of a hospital in Spain at 10:30 a.m., touching and kissing our daughter one last time before the nurses and doctors take her to the operating room. At the same time, God's people are woken from their sleep in the middle of the night, 3:30 a.m., to climb out of bed and drop to their knees in prayer for Maggie.

What a beautiful triangle: our faithful friends, family, and brothers and sisters in Christ praying for Maggie overseas; our heavenly Father answering those prayers and pouring His power down like a beam on Maggie; and the doctors, us, and new friends in Spain completing the triangle. What a perfect illustration of the power of prayer, God's love, and the connection of the body of believers!

We had a great support team in Seville. There were twelve of us in the waiting area. As the time passed and Maggie hadn't gone down to surgery yet, someone suggested we hold hands and pray. As soon as we did, I got the call that Maggie was ready to go and that Wendy and I could see her one last time. After seeing Maggie, we went back and had a beautiful prayer gathering as she entered into surgery.

Lord, Do Your Thing!

by Tad Weiss, June 12, 2014

Maggie just went into surgery. She is in the best hands—our Father and the surgeons and doctors He has provided. Pray and wait with patience.

We are at peace and are surrounded by a loving group of new Christian friends. We just prayed and these words were spoken, "Lord, do Your thing!" We are surrounded by all of you back home and around the world. We are surrounded by God.

The time in the waiting room flew by. Wendy knit a blanket and talked with our new friends. I talked with them also and read messages on Caring-Bridge. We talked about our church and pulled up the service from the previous Sunday on my laptop. We were not anxious or nervous. God had surrounded us with friends, prayer warriors around the globe, and total peace.

And then the phone rang. Although there had been peace in the waiting, our excitement jumped when we went to the phone.

All the news was good!

A huge burden was lifted from us. This was the happiest we had been in all our time in Spain.

The walk back to our hotel room was the first time we allowed ourselves to think about the future with Maggie back home. Our time in the room was lighter and happier. Wendy watched some music videos that had been sent to her. I watched the family movie from our ski trip in March.

I was at peace that we would probably be able to do that again as a family.

SUCCESSFUL SURGERY!!! PRAISE GOD!!!!!!

by Tad Weiss, June 12, 2014

Maggie went in for surgery at 10:30 a.m. She came out at 1:00 p.m. The surgeon said it went as well as possible. The bone was perfectly reset. Maggie continues to exceed all expectations. We are not surprised in the healing powers of Jesus!

Paul and Peggy Borowski and family, June 12, 2014

Great news on the surgery! We, like thousands of others who have posted here, have experienced an entire range of emotions. I have cried, prayed, and been completely humbled by your faith in God and by the awesomeness of His healing hands!

Bonnie and Tom Gasper and kids, June 12, 2014

Thank You to our almighty God who wakes His people on the other side of the pond to pray too (I knew exactly why I was awakened at 1:53 a.m. and 3:30 a.m.). We eagerly await the moment you both get to hear your sweet daughter's voice.

At our nighttime visit, another couple—Juan Carlos and Ana—from a local church in Seville came to meet us, as well as Jaime from CIEE. The people of this city overwhelmed us with their love and support.

The doctors had taken Maggie off the sedation, but she was still on a lot of pain meds, so she slept for the first fifteen minutes of our visit. Then we played the Matthew recording again and sure enough, she started opening her eyes! We could see she was working so hard, and she got them halfway open. What a joy to see. We didn't need any more confirmation tonight that Maggie would recover, and that moment sent us home in happiness.

Wendy and I talked about joy and happiness a lot that day. Our joy was unchanging, and it came from God with the assurance that our sins are forgiven and that we will live with Him in heaven for eternity. That will not change.

We had great joy throughout that week as we saw God face to face. Happiness was abundant also. We could not have been happier with the surgery or Maggie's progress.

Joy and Happiness

by Tad Weiss, June 12, 2014

What a joyful and happy day! As you know, Maggie's surgery was successful. We had been told that it would likely take three to four hours, two hours at the least. From the time we kissed Maggie as she went down to surgery, to the time we got the phone call that all went well and we could see the surgeon, was two-and-a-half hours.

It takes some time to get ready and to do post-op. So she was right around the two-hour mark for the surgery. Maggie has always exceeded expectations, and we are so thankful that she continues to do so in her recovery!

We are so happy, but God doesn't promise us that we will be happy every day. We live in a fallen world. Don't base your faith in God on how happy you are today. Instead abide in Him, stay connected to Him, and you will find the joy and the strength to face each day.

"[Jesus said] I am the vine; you are the branches. If a man remains in me and I in Him, he will bear much fruit; apart from me you can do nothing . . . if you remain in me and my words remain in you, ask whatever you wish and it will be given you . . . I have told you this so that my joy may be in you and that your joy may be complete. My command is this: love each other as I have loved you. Greater love has no one than this, that he lay down his life for his friends" (John 15:5,7,11–13).

We believe in the power of prayer and cannot thank you enough for your support of Maggie. My favorite response today from someone reading the news of the successful surgery was, "Praise God. Still praying!" Keep on praying for our precious daughter.

Over the last week you have seen many pictures of Maggie in the hospital, broken but still beautiful. We also wanted to share a picture of her from happier times. Today we have great hope, happiness, and joy for the future that lies ahead for Maggie, and for all of us. God bless you all!

Laura, John, Logan, and Miriam Gilbertson, June 12, 2014

Wendy, you were one of the first people I met at Westwood when you were Logan's Sunday school teacher. I remember I was having a hard time leaving him, and you gave me a confident smile and said, "Our kids are stronger than we give them credit for." Maggie is one strong woman and she is blessed to have you by her side demonstrating the strength that comes from hope and faith in Jesus Christ. Our family continues to pray for you, and we send our love.

During one of our doctor visits, Dr. Flores provided more information about Maggie's accident. Everything they could see told them the left side of her body and back took the brunt of the impact from the bus. All her major injuries were on her left side, and she had a minor fracture in her left cheekbone. It appeared that her head hit the windshield of the bus, which shattered from the collision.

We were told by a visitor that the first drug test given to the bus driver tested positive for cocaine, but the second and more thorough test was negative. The driver had had a clean driving record for fifteen years, and he was very upset about the accident.

There were four witnesses to the accident, but they didn't agree on what had happened. We felt no anger toward the bus driver, and we prayed that the truth would come out. If the bus driver wasn't at fault, he should be exonerated and relieved of the guilt he was feeling. If he was at fault, we hoped that changes would be made to make the city streets safer. Either way, he was forgiven by us.

The legal system was very different in Spain compared to the US. This would easily have been a million-dollar settlement back home, but Spain didn't work that way. God had blessed us financially, and that was simply not a concern. Our most fervent prayer and desire was to have our daughter back.

CHAPTER NINE

Day 9—June 13, 2014

Wendy and I were learning that the Spanish people had a difficult time dealing with tragedy. You could see in their faces and eyes how sorry they were that this happened to Maggie. They did everything they could to make the situation as right as possible. We believed that most Spanish people had a difficult time understanding how God could take a tragic event and turn it into good.

For my part, I was seeing some good already. After receiving an email of support, it became totally clear to me that it was time to reconcile with a friend.

Reconciliation

by Tad Weiss, June 13, 2014

Good morning to everyone back in the States, and good afternoon to our friends here in Spain as we reach siesta time. Wendy and I aren't quite on that program yet. You do need to get out of the heat though; it will be 100 degrees today!

Maggie had a restful night and looked great at our visit this morning! We could see her full body for the first time. She was breathing peacefully.

We believe that Maggie needs deep, peaceful rest, which she is getting. God gave us the confirmation we needed yesterday after the surgery when she opened her eyes for us. We are trusting in His perfect timing for her healing. Do not fear! That is the most repeated command in the Bible. We are telling Maggie, "Do not fear when you awake." God has told us not to fear and to trust completely in Him.

They have fully removed Maggie's sedation. She moves a lot, which is good. She tries to open her eyes but can't quite do it yet. We need to wait with patience to see the extent of the brain injury, as the recovery process is slow. She has started to breathe on her own but still needs the help of the machine.

They should be able to do a CT scan next week. There is a small amount of damage to Maggie's brain, but it is not in a great spot. So it is waiting time. All signs are positive. Do not fear! Patience and trust. *Paciencia y confianza.*

Last night I received an email of encouragement from a friend of mine that I have known for thirty-four years. He has been in contact with us frequently since Maggie's accident, and I've wanted to respond to him but haven't done so yet. There isn't enough time in the day for us to respond to everyone that contacts us, but God was also having me wait to respond.

This very close friend and I had a falling out in the last couple of years. It was over something that seemed very important to both of us at the time. We both have waved the olive branch, but we clearly haven't reconciled. We don't do things together like we used to before the incident.

After reading the email, it became totally clear to me that it is time to reconcile *immediately.*

Why couldn't we reconcile before? For me personally, the issue is pride. My pride would not allow me to ask for complete and total forgiveness until he asked me first. Pride is not from God. Through Maggie's accident, my pride is gone. It is time to forgive and be forgiven, to move on, to reconcile.

One of the most repeated phrases in your CaringBridge replies is, "If there is anything we can do for you, just let us know." We are learning to take you up on these offers! So here is what you can do for us. If there is someone in your life that you need to reconcile with, no matter how big or small the injustice is, immediately call them. Ask for total forgiveness, and forgive them also. Throw away your pride. It does not matter who was right or wrong. Do what you need to do to reconcile the relationship, and let God handle the rest.

In the book of Matthew, Jesus tells us that the second greatest commandment is to love your neighbor as yourself. In 1 Corinthians 13:4–7 we are taught what love looks like: "Love is patient, love is kind. It does not envy, it does not boast, it is not proud. It is not rude, it is not self-seeking, it is not easily angered, it keeps no record of wrongs. Love does not delight in evil but rejoices with the truth. It always protects, always trusts, always hopes, always perseveres."

Honor God today by reconciling a relationship. Then when Maggie comes home, you can tell her how her great suffering was the catalyst for the restored relationship. Each of us can play our part in turning Maggie's accident from a tragic event to an event that unleashed God's love around the world.

"'Teacher, which is the greatest commandment in the Law?' Jesus replied, 'Love the Lord your God with all your heart and with all your soul and with all your mind. This is the first and greatest commandment. And the second is like it: Love your neighbor as yourself.' All the Law and the Prophets hang on these two commandments" (Matthew 22:36–40).

Denise Zerr, June 13, 2014

Julie and I were just having a conversation about your beautiful post about mending fences and letting go of pride. We absolutely agree and I will take your message to heart and repair a friendship I have lost, as a testament to your words.

Through Maggie's accident, God revealed to me that a friendship is far more important than pride. My friend and I were both able to forgive, forget, and reconcile. We heard from many others that they had reconciled relationships too.

At our afternoon doctor visit, we had Rocio from CIEE with us to interpret, and we met Dr. Amaya for the first time. She was the first female doctor we had met with. I could see the bond between her and Wendy—two mothers caring for Maggie at the same time. It was beautiful to see.

It was the first time Wendy cried in the medical update meetings, but they were tears of joy for the astounding care Maggie was receiving.

Goodnight From Seville

by Tad Weiss, June 13, 2014

This update will be short, but it carries continued good news on Maggie's progress.

We could tell the nurses were excited and wanted us to talk to Maggie to see if she responded to our voices. It took a little while, but she did! She squeezed our hands very strongly. She was moving a lot. She opened her eyes a little. Wendy could see her pupils and she could see Maggie in there trying to connect with us. She is such a fighter, and it all was very encouraging.

As the effects of the sedation are wearing off, we're starting to get our Maggie back. The stitches in the sides of her head have been removed. There are a lot of scabs, but they will fall away. She looked absolutely beautiful. She looks fit and strong. We absolutely cannot believe that she has no fractures in her arms and legs. Her body is healing quickly. God produced a miracle to keep her alive, and He is doing it again with her healing. Thank You, God!

We have been talking so much about faith, patience, and trust. This afternoon some fear started creeping back in. You would think we would have learned this by now, but when we ask the doctors to predict the future, they give us an honest answer. Sometimes we don't like the answer. My question to-day was, with the results and activity they're seeing, did they think it would lead to a speedy recovery of her mind? The answer was no. Everything they are seeing is positive, but they simply won't know how her brain is recovering until they can see how she comes around and how the brain scans look next week. Even the scans won't show that everything is fine, just that there isn't major concern, and we need to be patient.

Back in the hotel before our visit with Maggie tonight, we talked about why we were feeling fear. We went to Scripture and did a little study on "patience." On the way back to the hospital, we are determined to not speculate anymore! God is in charge, and His timing is perfect!! He knows what is best for Maggie; we don't. This total trust thing is easier said than done.

Wendy and I had a nice dinner tonight. Our appetites are returning; some normalcy is creeping back in amid the chaos. Spain is playing the Netherlands in World Cup soccer in Brazil. We will stay in our room and avoid the craziness. Thank you for all your prayers and posts. God bless you!

"Be joyful in hope, patient in affliction, faithful in prayer" (Romans 12:12).

CHAPTER TEN

Day 10—June 14, 2014

A fter our little dip in trust the previous afternoon, we woke up feeling stronger. We had a good night's rest—seven hours of deep sleep. Ready to take on the new day.

Brief Medical Update

by Tad Weiss, Jun 14, 2014

It's hard to believe that it's day ten. Everything is coming at us so fast, and the time is going by quickly. Each day holds twenty-four hours of healing for Maggie, but Wendy and I sure appreciate that the time is flying.

Maggie is doing great! She slept peacefully through the night. At our visit this morning, she was very active. But the sedation is still wearing off and she's on a lot of pain meds, so we will wait patiently for her to open her eyes and fully recognize us.

The best connection with Maggie comes from holding her hand. She squeezes my hand strongly with a firm grip.

Maggie is such a fighter!! She squeezes our hands more at certain moments—when she hears our voices, the *Choral Benediction*, certain words from Scripture. What an encouragement! Praise God!!

God and all of you have walked us through some moments of doubt in the last few days. We come out the other side stronger, with more trust, more patience. At this moment we are at total peace with God's timing and His plan. Pray that we will maintain this peace throughout Maggie's journey.

"Rejoice in the Lord always. I will say it again: Rejoice! Let your gentleness be evident to all. The Lord is near. Do not be anxious about anything, but in everything, by prayer and petition, with thanksgiving, present your requests to God. And the peace of God, which transcends all understanding, will guard your hearts and your minds in Christ Jesus" (Philippians 4:4–7).

It never fails to amaze me how God can speak to us through Scripture, often reinforcing the message by placing the same verse in our path over and over.

Joelle Syverson, June 14, 2014

As I was reading your post, I knew the exact verse I wanted to include and sure enough I get to the end, and it is the Scripture already on your heart. It is one of my favorites and always puts things back into perspective for me when I am reminded to not be anxious about anything. A good friend and pastor once told me try to avoid the "what ifs." Life is filled with enough uncertainty that when we start to say, "what if," it only robs us of the joy we could be experiencing in that moment, causing us to worry about something that may never happen.

Nothing had been "normal" for Wendy or me in the ten days since Maggie's accident. But we established a routine:

We woke up each morning sometime between 6:00 and 7:00 a.m. I think we made it all the way to the 7:15 a.m. alarm once, back on day four, when we had literally passed out from exhaustion. We started each day in prayer. One of the lessons I learned was the need to pray with my wife, to hold her hand, and to start the day talking with God. I'm sorry, God, that I hadn't been doing this before. I then went to get us a cup of coffee. We looked through all the replies to our CaringBridge posts for encouragement. Then we showered and headed down to breakfast.

The Marriott had a nice continental breakfast that opened at eight o'clock. The hostess knew us by this time and didn't need to ask our room number. Then we were off to the hospital for our 8:30 morning visit with Maggie.

We were in a busy section of Seville in the southern part of the country. The first few days were perfect weather, but by this time it was getting hot—over a hundred degrees. It was dry, like the desert in summer. We didn't know how people wore pants in that weather!

Our walk to the hospital was an adventure in faith. This was a very busy city. Our five-block walk took us just under ten minutes. We didn't fully understand how the traffic lights worked. It seemed like automobiles had the right of way, and the sidewalks were right by the street.

The bus that hit Maggie was a city bus. These buses are red, and they are everywhere. On a normal walk to the hospital or back to our room, ten of them would pass us, sometimes just five feet away and traveling at least 30 miles per hour. We tried to block this out, holding hands tightly.

Wendy and I knew we couldn't get through this without each other. I didn't think we could even walk to the hospital safely without each other. We waited for the pedestrian signal to turn green, looked every possible direction, and crossed quickly.

The UCI is right above the emergency room entrance at the hospital. On almost every walk, there was a siren blaring—an ambulance leaving the hospital or returning with a new patient. We prayed for the person in the back of the ambulance. It had been our daughter just ten days ago. The reminders of the accident were in our face every day . . . every walk to or from the hospital, six times per day.

We prayed and talked as we walked. It took us four days to even notice our surroundings. There were flowers and plants around us and a beautiful old church right across the street. We began to appreciate details as the walk became normal for us.

When we arrived at the UCI waiting room, we were greeted by our missionary friends, Carey and Sharon, and someone from CIEE. What a comfort to see a familiar face. Carey and Sharon prayed with us daily.

CIEE was indispensable to us. We had met many of their staff. They were our interpreters and constant companions. Someone from CIEE was with us at every visit and every doctor meeting. These people had dropped everything to support us, and we couldn't have navigated a foreign country without them.

We met new friends daily . . . brothers and sisters in Christ who came to the hospital to show their support, families that heard of Maggie and wanted to see her. Frank was one such friend who showed up regularly to assure us that Maggie would be okay. He said that Maggie's healing was a miracle. She did in one week what can take a month. We felt loved by the people of Seville, and we loved them back.

For the most part, the nurses didn't speak English, but the love and care they provided said what words cannot. They provided assurance to us that Maggie was doing great, and that she was strong. They could say things the doctors couldn't say.

The other patients touched us too. Alberto was a twenty-year-old young man who had also been hit by a vehicle, three days before Maggie. We walked alongside his parents, Luis and Fina. We watched them care for Alberto and celebrated when he sat up, spoke, and left the UCI. We developed a special bond as we went through the same tragedy at the same time.

The man in the room next to Maggie's looked like he'd had his legs amputated at the knee. Each day I waved to him, and he waved back, and we gave each other the thumbs-up. I could see his family and friends peeking in our window. *What is going on in that room? Why are they praying and singing?*

The lady directly across from Maggie was close to ninety. She looked like she was moments from death, but she was still there every day when we came back. *Would she recover, or was this simply hospice?* I prayed that she knew Jesus.

After our morning visits with Maggie, we'd go back to the hotel and post to CaringBridge and read more replies. We read each and every message and comment. We loved them all! There's strength in numbers, and these words, prayers, and Scripture verses lifted us and sustained us.

Afternoons were typically spent having a light lunch, responding to emails, and occasional phone calls to take care of business in Spain before heading back to the hospital for our meeting with the doctor.

Friendly, familiar faces smiled when we walked by the front desk of the hotel. We'd update them on Maggie's progress. Many of them expressed they were happy for us and said that we were "lucky." We decided that "lucky" for a Spaniard was the same as "blessed" to us. We knew that we were blessed.

Back at the hospital for our afternoon meeting was when we needed our CIEE translators the most. Morgan, Rocio, Madeline, Helena, and Elena were with us for various visits. The doctors spoke in Spanish very quickly. Our interpreter listened intently, then gave us the update. Sometimes they talked back and forth for a minute, but the translation to us took only about ten seconds.

What were they saying that we couldn't understand? Surely, we were missing something.

No, this was a time to trust. We learned that our interpreters were telling us the truth and not hiding anything from us, but they were also skilled in how they relayed the information. We learned to trust them and the doctors and not to ask the questions that couldn't be answered at that time.

Returning to the hotel for an afternoon break was typically filled with more posting and reading on CaringBridge, but one day we went to the pool.

It felt weird to sit by the swimming pool in the hot summer heat. This was not a vacation. But the water was soothing, and the warmth of the sun felt good.

Back to the hospital for our evening visit with Maggie. "Spanish time" was like "island time." It would happen when it happened. Some evenings we arrived at 6:30 p.m. and waltzed right in. Other times we had to wait until 8:00 p.m. That was okay, as it gave us time to visit with our friends and learn about their lives. We were learning patience. We learned we were there for other purposes beyond caring for Maggie.

On the way home at night, we'd stop for *tapas* at one of the local restaurants. Tapas would be similar to ordering a number of appetizers in the States . . . small plates of foods to share that are brought out slowly, one or two at a time. The evening meal was a time to sit, relax, talk, and enjoy the company of family or friends. We liked the size of the portions and the pace of the meal—smaller and slower, relax and enjoy.

On this particular evening, Wendy's phone rang, showing an unknown number. We never answered these at home. She picked up to a telemarketer from the States. It was bizarre to me that these calls came through as if we were at home.

Without missing a beat, Wendy said, "I'm very sorry, but I can't talk now. Our daughter has been in an accident, and we're in Spain. But you can follow her story by visiting CaringBridge.org. Just search for Maggie Weiss!"

I snickered. Who knew? Maybe the telemarketer would come to faith in Jesus after visiting Maggie's site. This happened again, and I laughed both times. God has a sense of humor, and Wendy didn't miss an opportunity!

Back to our hotel room, usually late around 9:00 p.m. We'd call home and FaceTime with our family. And we were addicted to reading messages on Caring-Bridge and relied on them as a lifeline for encouragement.

We finished up with the last post of the day.

I Lift My Eyes . . .

by Wendy Weiss, June 14, 2014

Just a little update after our visit with Maggie this evening. She is trying so hard to "lift her eyes!" She'd had a bath by the time we saw her; she looked so good. Her wounds are healing; she has cuts above both eyes that look much better.

She was sleeping when we got there, but as we talked, sang, prayed, and read Scripture to her, she started waking up. It was the *Choral Benediction* that really woke her up tonight. We play that *every* time we see her; she really responded to it tonight!

Maggie is stronger on her left side than her right, which is apparently normal; her left hand was squeezing our hands hard. She did not want to let go. Her left leg moves, even hanging almost off the bed. She turned her head toward the sound of her daddy's voice. It was precious to see. She seems at peace, not laboring against the breathing apparatus or fighting the tubes. They have, however, restrained her arms, so she cannot pull the tubes out if she wakes up.

As we were getting ready to leave, we quietly stood and watched her, so she would have time to settle down and go back to sleep. We pray for another restful, healing night for our darling Maggie.

Tad and I are in a good place tonight. Thanks for praying for our son, Peter, while he took his ACT; he thought it went well. We feel loved and supported, by you and by our new *familia* here. Tad and I are lifting our eyes to God in gratitude for another good day!

"I lift my eyes to the hills—
where does my help come from?
My help comes from the Lord,
the Maker of heaven and earth" (Psalm 121:1-2).

Frank Mina, June 14, 2014

Another burning hot day today here in southern Spain; type of heat that slowly kills you, but all this doesn't have any meaning compared to the happiness and joy I get deep inside my soul and heart each time I read your updates on your brave and strong Maggie. She has become a powerful and beautiful icon for many people and how you can trust in God and He will never let you down.

Liz and Scott Turner, June 14, 2014

I just have to comment to let you know we are addicted to CaringBridge! Not just because we are so interested in knowing how to pray more specifically for Maggie, but because of the encouragement we get by watching God do something supernatural, right before our eyes . . . virtually anyway. As we pray that Maggie will be fully restored, we pray that hearts will be transformed by your story! Ephesians 2:6–10

Bonnie and Tom Gasper and kids, June 14, 2014

Thanking God for you all every day and for your posts. This is a rich journey . . . which is just like God. In the midst of tragedy, He is doing something new, powerful . . . purposeful. Thank you for your honesty, Tad. There will be far reaching impact. Praying God will let you see it this side of eternity. As for Maggie exceeding expectations, I am not surprised. Underneath that sweet countenance resides a very determined and indomitable spirit. God has wired her perfectly for the task at hand.

Then we let the body of believers take over. We fell asleep, resting in the arms of our Lord and Savior. Maggie needed to rest. We needed to rest. We looked forward to a new day and all the marvelous miracles God would show us. We were excited. We were patient.

CHAPTER ELEVEN

Day 11—June 15, 2014

Todd Rooke was so locked in with me. He had encouraged me in my communication and seemed to know what I'd be going through each day before it happened. If I hadn't known it was the power of the Holy Spirit, I would have been scared!

In an email, he advised me to journal everything going on around us—all the things that didn't make into the CaringBridge posts. I would have thought I wouldn't forget the God sightings and the mystifying things happening around me but, in his words, "The velocity of change in flight is high and it will get higher." Being able to see how God worked was a gift, both in this battle and for future battles.

I had some constant companions over these eleven days checking up on me each day and offering me continual encouragement and support: Kevin Cashman, Jeff Jarnes, Bret Abbott, Vibhu Sharma.

There were three kinds of support that really stood out. The first was the Christ-follower who knew Scripture and how to apply it. The second was the person who had been through the fire in their own life and who could empathize. And the third was the constant companion who showed up each day to provide support.

Todd was all three. He emailed me a story of a man who fell into a deep pit. A fireman walked by, saw him, and went to get a ladder. An outdoorsman walked by, saw him, and went to get a rope. A third man walked by, saw him, backed up a few steps, and jumped into the pit with him.

"What are you doing?" the man asked. "You don't have a rope or a ladder. How are you going to help me?"

"I don't know," he said, "but I've been here before, and I know we'll get out together."

Rest

by Wendy Weiss, June 15, 2014

Happy Father's Day to all you daddies, but especially our dads, Wayne and Bernie. We wish so much that we could all be together. We look forward to a big celebration and family reunion when we bring Maggie back home to Minnesota.

Tad and I rested well last night; we slept until the alarm went off at 7:15. That is only the second time that's happened since we arrived; what a blessing good rest is! Jaime from CIEE and his wife, Paqui, were waiting for us at the hospital.

Maggie was also resting well as we arrived for the visit. Tad and I like to visualize Maggie's bed as God's mighty right hand and that Maggie is resting comfortably in His hand of power and healing.

I sang "Good Morning, God" to Maggie as well as "God is So Good." Maggie was a littler quieter than she was last night, but she had similar responses to our voices and videos. Her pulse goes up when she hears our voices. She continues to try to open her eyes. We were told that yesterday, as they were bathing her, they found a little wound on her head that needed stitches. She is on some additional painkillers and antibiotics as a result of this wound. We continue to pray that nothing will escape the attention of Maggie's doctors and caregivers, and we are grateful to know that this prayer continues to be answered!

Maggie instinctively wants to hold hands with us. If we take our hand away, she reaches for it, then wraps her hand around it when she feels we are near. She continues to turn her head toward the sound of Tad's voice.

We told the nurses last night to call her "Maggie" or "Mags" ("Mags" is actually easier for the Spanish to pronounce). She almost never hears anyone call her "Margaret," so if the nurses call her that, I am afraid she will think she is in trouble! It was a blessing to hear her sweet nurse talking to her in English, calling her "Maggie" this morning!

When we came out of the UCI ward, Carey and Sharon were waiting for us, so we also got to talk to and pray with them. Sharon is getting ready for a trip back to the States on Tuesday. I am excited for her that she gets to see two of her daughters and her granddaughter, as well as many other beloved family members at a wedding, but I will miss her. She has been a great support to Tad and me. Carey will still be here; sorry for him that he is not going with Sharon, but selfishly glad to have him here.

Time for us to rest at the hotel while you are also sleeping at home!

"He who dwells in the shelter of the Most High will rest in the shadow of the Almighty. I will say of the Lord, 'He is my Refuge and my Fortress, my God, in whom I trust'" (Psalm 91:1–2).

Julie, Kip, and Kelsey Kaufmann, June 15, 2014

Happy Father's Day, Tad! Maggie will always be your little girl. Continued prayers and love from us!

A Happy Father's Day!

by Tad Weiss, June 15, 2014

Happy Father's Day to all the dads back in the States! We understand it's raining back home, and it's a hundred degrees right now in Seville, so we can't go outside either, but for different reasons.

We visited with Dr. Flores at 2:00, along with Morgan from CIEE. We love her; she is a strong and steady woman, and she has been a great comfort to us.

Dr. Flores is the doctor we have seen most often. He understands our questions but usually answers in Spanish, and then Morgan translates. Maggie's progress is great! She is breathing spontaneously on her own. The breathing tube is still in but should come out soon. They have weaned her off the strong painkillers from the surgery. They will see how she progresses without the morphine. Maggie is a *campeón*—a champion!

A friend has been emailing me regularly with what is on his heart, and he seems to sense where I'm at and what I need. He has talked about *Trust* (capital T) being a "muscle": the more you exercise it the stronger it gets. We have had a lot of opportunity to exercise in this fashion over the last eleven days! Both Wendy and I have Trust muscles that are getting stronger!! We told Dr. Flores that we Trust him and his team completely, and he senses that we do; you can see it in his eyes. They don't usually get this Trust from Americans. We told him that they will know when it is best for Maggie to move out of the UCI, when it is best for her to come home, and that we will not rush that process.

I've mentioned that we've learned over these eleven days what questions to ask our doctors, and more importantly what questions not to ask. We try very hard not to ask the questions that can't be answered at this time. The answers to those questions always lead to doubt, fear, and worry. So don't ask the question! That is Trust. Trust the doctors. Trust that God is in charge of all of the details. God will let us know when Maggie's brain injury is healed. God will let us know when we can come home. He alone knows the answers and He will let us know in His perfect timing. Our job is to be here for Maggie, love her and pray for her, keep all of you updated on her progress, spend our free time meeting new friends, spread God's love, and Trust. With a capital "T." We hope that your

Trust muscle is getting stronger too through Maggie's journey!

It has been a happy Father's Day! Just seeing Maggie continuing to heal and holding my hand, knowing and trusting that God has got Maggie and us covered, it is a happy day. But it by no means is complete.

Peter, I miss you, buddy! We are so proud of you, and we know you are doing great. Stay strong, we'll make up for it together when Maggie, Mom, and I get home. Be patient; it won't be long. We are proud of you!

Dad, it is strange with you being in Minnesota and me not there with you. Thanks for always being there for me, just like you and Mom are there for Peter right now. I love you, you're the best!

To Wendy's dad, Wayne, we always spend Father's Day together watching the last round of the US Open. I'm sorry I can't be there with you to watch it, but we'll get back on our routine next year. Watch the last round for me, and I'll check up on the scores online.

I don't cry a lot. I've certainly shed some tears over here in Spain. They have a word in Spanish—*desahogarse*—which means you are "undrowning" yourself. I undrowned myself this morning. I think I was a little vulnerable due to it being Father's Day. And I read four posts in a row from Sue and TK, Jennifer, Smitty and Beth, and Patti. And then the Bible verse from the Quernemoens on "rejoice in our suffering." Five posts in a row and it hit me hard. A good couple of minutes of sobbing and letting it flow, no way to hold it back, don't even try. I undrowned myself. They were tears of joy, not of sadness.

How do you "rejoice in your suffering?" That doesn't make any sense. Suffering is an intense word, extreme sadness, and hardship. Suffering is bad. No one wants to go through it or wish it upon anyone. And I'm supposed to rejoice in it? There's only one way. Jesus is the one who turns things upside down. He brings life through His death. The least among you is the greatest. The King is the servant. Only through Him can we rejoice and be glad in our suffering. He is the Way!

When you're drowning and you can't pull yourself out of the water, there's only one thing you can do. Reach out to the One who walks on water. Jesus will save you. He saved Maggie. He has saved me.

God bless you, and Happy Father's Day!

"We also rejoice in our sufferings, because we know that suffering produces perseverance; perseverance, character; and character, hope. And hope does not disappoint us, because God has poured out His love into our hearts, by the Holy Spirit, whom He has given us" (Romans 5:3–5).

CHAPTER TWELVE

Day 12—June 16, 2014

We had a powerful prayer circle after our evening visit with Maggie the night before. In the circle was Miha (born in Romania), Christy (a new friend from North Carolina), Angela (also from the US), Jorge (from CIEE in Seville), Henry (a pastor from Nigeria), Wendy, and me.

We were struck by Angela and Henry's impassioned prayers for Maggie's "immediate" healing. We'd been reading and hearing that word a lot. Wendy and I hadn't been praying often for immediate healing of Maggie. It seemed to be a contradiction to pray for immediate healing and patience in the healing process at the same time.

At our morning visit with Maggie, she was more active than when we'd seen her the night before. Her right eye was half open for most of the visit but her left eye was closed. We could see the pupil of her eye following, looking, searching.

We went through our normal routines, and we concluded our visit in prayer. But this time we fervently asked God to heal Maggie immediately. Her right eye opened wider, and her left eye opened for about ten seconds before closing again.

I Am Changed

by Tad Weiss, June 16, 2014

God wants us to come to Him with our prayers and petitions. God answers all prayers. With some the answer is yes, with some it's yes but not right now, and with some the answer is no. But He hears and answers our prayer. So we ask you to pray for Maggie today, for immediate healing. And also pray that Wendy and I will continue to have patience and trust in God's perfect timing.

I am sharing what God is putting on my heart during a very emotional and intense experience. This morning when I woke up at 5:00 a.m., my brain turned on and God started filling it with thoughts. Those thoughts are what I've tried to type out here.

I consider myself a regular guy. I do not have any theological training, other than what I've gained from the Bible studies

I've been in and from going to church. My wife comes up with all the Bible verses in these posts because she knows them and where to find them. The reason you haven't read any spiritual posts from me before June 6 is because I haven't written any. It feels good to me to "cut open a vein." It is helping me heal and make sense of this. I hope there is something in here for you too.

Before the apostle Paul's conversion, he was a mean guy. He was a Pharisee who thought he was doing God's will by memorizing all of God's laws. He persecuted Christians fervently.

As Paul neared Damascus on his journey, God struck him down with a bright light and blinded him. Ananias touched Paul and the scales were removed from his eyes. Paul could see again, very clearly. God called him to spread the gospel of Jesus Christ to the Gentiles.

Paul endured suffering, hardship, imprisonment, and beatings, yet he faithfully spread God's Word around the world. He was changed from a judgmental Pharisee to the greatest evangelist for Jesus Christ that the world has ever seen.

God didn't strike me down with a bright light, but you have to admit that how he opened my eyes is pretty dramatic. My daughter, whom I love dearly, got hit by a bus, 4,300 miles from home. In one phone call, my life was turned upside down. This was my "Paul" moment.

On one level, I'm very saddened that so much pain had to happen to my daughter to open my eyes. That is a hard one to take. But I'm also humbled and encouraged that God loves me so much that He will do whatever it takes to draw me closer to Him.

My faith journey has been periods of closeness to God, followed by periods of drifting away. God, with His patience and kindness, always welcomes me back. I come back a little stronger, a little closer. And then I drift away again.

Why do I do this, God? What is my problem? I have known there are areas in my life that need improvement—where I can walk more closely with God. But I have resisted making the change. I know I should pray with my wife, love her, and support her more fully. I know I should be a better witness to my kids. I can support those going through hardship better, more like you have supported us these past twelve days. I believe that you need to know Jesus to go to heaven, yet I'm afraid to tell the gospel story for fear of being ridiculed. This is really hard to say, but my past behavior and my lack of witness says that I'm ashamed of the gospel. That is someone else's job, I'm not gifted in that area; when I try, it never works. I'll just stop trying. You get the idea. I needed to change.

One of the overwhelming things about the last twelve days is how God has opened my eyes to see so many things *so clearly.* Have you ever had a "mountaintop" experience, where you feel so close to God, so energized, so excited? Well, I've been on one of those for the last twelve days. I don't want it to stop.

Have you been changed by Maggie's accident and our journey? If you feel that you have, or maybe you think so but you're not sure, lean into it. It is God drawing you closer to Him. That is what He so deeply desires for you and for me. Lean into it. Do not be afraid.

I don't want any responses to this post saying, "Don't be so hard on yourself." It's okay. I don't need therapy. Posting to CaringBridge and reading your words of encouragement is my therapy. God hit me with a sledgehammer right between the eyes because that is what I needed to see Him so clearly! Praise God!! But what Wendy and I would love to hear at some point in the future is that God ministered to you through Maggie and this accident. That you were able to draw closer to God because of Maggie's accident. That the love of God and the reputation of Jesus Christ was magnified through our precious daughter.

"I am not ashamed of the gospel, because it is the power of God for the salvation of everyone who believes: first for the Jew, then for the Gentile. For in the gospel a righteousness from God is revealed, a righteousness that is by faith from first to last, just as it is written: 'The righteous will live by faith'" (Romans 1:16–17).

Niki Klein, June 16, 2014

What God has revealed to you has truly inspired both Matt and me. We thank you for opening your heart and sharing that with us. It has inspired us to wake up each day, live for Jesus, love our children more, witness to others, share the love of Jesus, and pray for others in need. As I washed dishes this morning, I was thinking Maggie's verse for now is Psalm 46:10. "Be still and know that I am God." She is being quiet and still, resting on the promises of God while the two of you are proclaiming them to everyone listening!

Judith Thomas, June 15, 2014

Maggie's former English teacher here. I'm on vacation in Venice. This morning about 3:00 or so, I think God's spirit filled up this tiny hotel room and I just couldn't stop praying for Maggie's complete restoration. I don't remember if the word "immediate" was a part of it, but it had that very urgent and complete sense about it. I've been praying for her and you all but this morning it was stronger and almost poured out, as if I wasn't the one doing the praying or the thinking of the prayer. Make of it what you will—just know that here, in Italy, God is stirring a heart to urgently pray.

Today, Wendy and I met with Carlos from Garrigues and attorneys from RZS, the local firm that specializes in this type of accident. They'd hired a technical expert who had reconstructed the accident using data collected from the police and interviews of eyewitnesses the day after the accident. The report showed that the bus was traveling at 60 kilometers per hour (37 miles per hour) at the time of impact, double the speed limit of 30 kph. This didn't match up with what Carlos had previously told us—that Maggie had been thrown "four to five meters" by the impact.

The report said Maggie had traveled twenty-three meters in the air, bounced off a bike rack, and ended up twenty-five meters from the point of impact! We already felt that God had protected Maggie and saved her life, but now there was no doubt—no other explanation for why she was still alive.

Carlos sheltered us from this information when we first met him, as he knew we weren't ready to hear it.

We also saw pictures of the accident site . . . the bus with its cracked windshield, the impact point, and ending position for Maggie on the *Torneo*. The graphic details were hard to see and hear.

The bus was articulated—essentially two buses connected. It weighed over twenty tons. The dedicated bus/taxi/motorcycle lane was only 3.6 meters wide from curb to curb, leaving little room on either side of the bus.

The bus driver admitted to being behind schedule and distracted, looking to his left before the impact and not straight ahead. He honked his horn but did not apply the brakes before hitting Maggie. He stopped thirty-three meters from the point of impact, or eight meters past where Maggie lay on the side of the road. He had somehow managed to avoid running over

her as he slowed down after the impact—no small feat considering the narrow lane and the width of the bus.

We were told that after stopping the bus, he came out screaming, "I've killed her, I've killed her!"

Four eyewitnesses were at the scene of the accident, but none of them saw the full event clearly since it happened so quickly. Two of them

said Maggie's crossing light was green, and two said it was red. One who said the light was red also claimed he heard the bus driver honk his horn. He speculated that Maggie was wearing headphones and probably couldn't hear the horn.

We knew this was wrong! Maggie never wore headphones when she ran, and they didn't recover any headphones at the accident scene. Her headphones were later found in her bedroom. I was incensed that this would be in the preliminary report from our law firm who was supposed to be representing us. We were all in favor of a fair report but not false speculation that would hurt our case.

We also didn't agree that Maggie crossed the lane when her light was red. It's a natural response to defend your child, but Maggie was always a rule follower, and we didn't believe that was what happened. This question would never get answered for us.

The conclusions from the preliminary report were that Maggie probably crossed the bus lane when her light was red and was likely distracted by wearing headphones and didn't look to her left before crossing the lane. It also was concluded that the bus driver was traveling 60 kilometers per hour in a zone designated as 30 kilometers per hour, eliminating the possibility that he could slow down in time to prevent the accident . . . joint responsibility for the accident.

We told the attorneys we didn't agree with part of their conclusion and that speculating and concluding Maggie was partly responsible seemed like a poor legal strategy. As we had been warned and were now finding out, the legal system in Spain is very different from the legal system in the US. We were being drawn into another battle—one we didn't care to enter but were forced to, so we could protect our daughter legally.

Brief Maggie Update
by Tad Weiss, June 16, 2014

Hello to everyone, it is after 1:00 p.m. here in Seville and it has been a busy day.

Our 2:00 p.m. doctor visit started at 3:05 p.m. Dr. Marin said Maggie is recovering quite well. They have removed the heavy painkillers. She is beginning to open her eyes. She needs more time for the sedation and painkillers to wear off, and then she should respond more.

Progress will be slow. She is improving from a respiratory point of view and breathing without support. The surgeons are happy with the results of her pelvic surgery. All news is positive, and Maggie is doing a great job. Thank you, God!

At our evening visit, both of Maggie's eyes were open when we walked in the room! The healing process is phenomenal to witness. We played a new video for her from Grandpa Wayne and Grandma Pat. They talked about how she was running a race and winning . . . her eyes opened wider, and both of her legs started moving; she was running the race!

It has been a long day and we are ready for bed. We love you all so much and can't begin to describe what your support and love means to us!

"For God did not give us a spirit of timidity, but a spirit of power, of love and of self-discipline" (2 Timothy 1:7).

CHAPTER THIRTEEN

Day 13—June 17, 2014

Morgan Reiss had been doing a great job coordinating the sharing of medical information with the various insurance companies that were involved. Her latest email to them shared the following:

> Since Friday's operation, Maggie has not been administered sedation, and they took her off the morphine-based painkillers yesterday. They are very pleased with her progress and anticipate more activity from Maggie in the coming days. She has opened her eyes and tried to focus. She follows the sound of her father's voice and tries to track where it is coming from. Her heartbeat accelerates when the parents are there and speaking with her. She is moving more (yawning, coughing, squeezing her parents' hands, shrugging), although she currently has limited movement on her right side. The drain from the pelvic surgery has been removed. Maggie is now spontaneously breathing (off assisted breathing) and the breathing tube will likely be removed soon.
>
> You can contact the parents directly regarding the issue of medical evacuation/repatriation or any related decisions, although they are quite comfortable following the local medical team's recommendation, which is that once Maggie is out of the UCI and under observation for a short time she could safely return to the US. Nobody is giving exact dates, but more than a week and less than a month, according to Dr. Flores. My best guess is that we are looking at around two weeks.

After sending this concise summary to the interested parties, Morgan emailed me, asking me to confirm who EIAA and Navigators represented. We had more insurance companies involved than I could keep track of. In addition to EIAA, all CIEE students were covered by iNext, which was underwritten by Travel Guard. Then there was our primary health insurance through PreferredOne and Maphre, the insurance company for the bus company.

After some emails back and forth, we received word that Maggie was covered by the EIAA policy's foreign protection coverage portion for emergencies up to $100,000 USD for medical and up to $1,000,000 USD for medical repatriation. There was also coverage for one parent to fly home in economy class seating with the patient. Our attorneys were gathering the various policies, and we were hoping they could sort it out.

Homesick
by Tad Weiss, June 17, 2014

For our morning visit with Maggie, Carmen from CIEE joined us in the UCI, and Miha and Mel waited outside. Both of Maggie's eyes are open now!!

She responds to the messages from you that we share with her. We play the *Choral Benediction* on every visit. She loves it and becomes very active when she hears it; it is beautiful to see.

She has both her feet off the bed and she kicked off the "shoe" that was on her left foot. Her legs are very active. We think in her mind that she is out for a run, doing her summer training. That is what she loves to do. Nothing will hold this girl down!

We met with Dr. Flores at around 3:00. Maggie is breathing on her own. Her neurological evaluation is positive; she has an intent to be alert and to follow movement. The steps will be small but they all mark progress, and we have seen them every visit. The doctor said that Maggie may be able to leave the UCI soon! That was a surprise to us, and we were thrilled to hear it.

I've written about many of the God moments we've had on this journey. Many of them are profound and take us to the deepest places of struggle, fear, faith, and hope. Some are flat-out silly. We think they're all from God.

Back in February, we lost our black lab, Carly. She was ten years old and the best dog in the world for us, and we miss her! We had decided not to get another dog right away, even though we've had a black lab for as long as we've been married. Wendy's and my first black lab was a wedding present from one of our neighbors! We love dogs, and particularly labs. They are a perfect picture of unconditional love and companionship to us. But we were going to wait to get another dog. Life is just easier without taking care of a dog.

On the walk to the hospital this morning, there was a man walking a five-month-old chocolate lab puppy. The puppy was carrying a crushed-up water bottle for his bone. He was as cute as can be. I'm trying to be open to all of God's promptings in this journey. This one was crystal clear. Maggie needs a puppy, and she will get one!!

Last night, I awoke in the middle of the night. It is very dark in our hotel room. I lay in bed for a couple of minutes, confused. I knew I wasn't at home. I was becoming afraid. I got out of bed and went into the bathroom and found my phone. 1:57 a.m. There was a text on my phone from Peter that I hadn't seen. It all came back to me, where I was, what I was doing. I felt peaceful again, very quickly, and I went back to sleep.

This is day thirteen in our journey, and we can't believe how fast it is going. It feels like day five to us.

Yesterday was the first day that we've thought about going home. Believe me, we want to go home. But with everything we're dealing with here, it just wasn't something we even thought about. Too many other things are keeping our attention.

We talked with Peter on the phone, and we miss him dearly. My mom sends us pictures of Wendy's flowers in bloom, and I know she misses seeing that happen. Going to church online helps, but it's not the same as being with all of you in person. The best months of the year in Minnesota are starting right now. We want to share them at home with you. Yes, we are getting homesick.

There is a great story in the Bible about being homesick, the parable of the prodigal son, found in Luke 15:11–32. This is a different kind of homesick. One son messed up big time. He blew his inheritance and lost everything his father had given him. When he was at the end of his rope, he humbly went home seeking forgiveness. His father welcomed him with open arms, forgiving his past sins, rejoicing in the return of his son. Our God is a God of second chances.

If you are missing "home," missing being with God the Father, know that He will welcome you back with open arms. Your sins will be forgiven, and your life will be enriched when you truly go home to God.

We think we'll get an idea later this week of how long we'll be in Spain. We are trying not to get ahead of that—just trusting in God's timing. But we are homesick. We miss you all and are so looking forward to getting Maggie back in Minnesota.

"Now we know that if the earthly tent we live in is destroyed, we have a building from God, an eternal house in heaven, not built by human hands" (2 Corinthians 5:1).

Todd had emailed me with the advice to be ready to advocate for Maggie. The email arrived right before our meeting with the attorneys the day before, and he was spot on. He didn't know about the meeting or why we would need to advocate for her. Clearly God was guiding him in his prayers, and he was obedient. I don't know much about the gift of prophecy, but he consistently "saw the future," and it is cool to have him on our side.

Todd emailed me and suggested I investigate Angel MedFlight[4] for Maggie's transportation home. I looked them up on the internet and discovered they're an international air ambulance service arranging private flights to transport patients from one hospital to another. God was telling him that Maggie's rehabilitation and resources would be better in the US and that I should push for this sooner rather than later.

It was the first I'd heard of such a service, but we'd need to pray on that one. We had been working so hard on patience and trust, and this seemed to be going against that approach. Based on Maggie's current condition, Wendy and I had our doubts that we were only two weeks out from bringing her home.

Eyes Wide Open!

by Tad Weiss, June 17, 2014

Our evening visit with Maggie was nothing short of miraculous! When we walked into the UCI, we could see Maggie's eyes open from across the hall. She looks absolutely amazing! Your prayers for immediate healing are being answered right before our very eyes!!

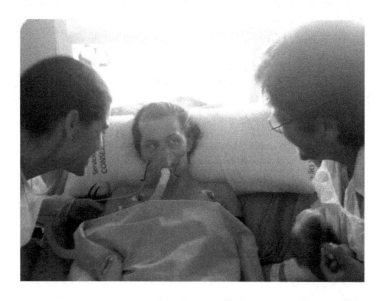

We have seen steady improvement from Maggie every day,

but today was the biggest change by far. Her eyes move and follow us, and she is very alert. She looks like she's exercising, her legs move so much. She smiled numerous times. What a joy to see our daughter smile, to know that her beautiful spirit is shining through.

We had a Power Team visit tonight. Our friend Carey, who has been with us almost every day, got to see the dramatic improvement in person. MariLo, a nurse at the hospital who attends a church that has supported us, did a healing prayer and anointed Maggie with oil. Madeline has been such a steady and encouraging rock of support for us. She gave Maggie a Spanish lesson and she said that Maggie got straight A's! And Madeline's daughter Sara, who is sixteen, came in and held Maggie's hand. You could see the special connection between the two of them—two young girls who love Jesus and His healing touch! Chari also came in to pray for Maggie.

Our precious Maggie is being healed right before our eyes. Your prayers for "immediate healing" were heard by God and He answered yes!

Just as Maggie's eyes were wide open tonight, Wendy's and my eyes are wide open to the glories of God and His healing powers. We hope your eyes are wide open to the healing powers of our Lord and Savior! Trust in Him; He is the way, the truth, and the life!!

"One thing I do know, I was blind but now I see" (John 9:25).

Kim Flemmer, June 18, 2014

The first thing I am anxious to do every morning is read your posts. It seems your lives have intentionally led you to this very moment in time. God has *great* plans for you and your family, through this horrific accident, the wonderful new friends you have made, the doctors' perfect care, and support from people all over the world and Maggie's phenomenal healing! "This is my command—be strong and courageous! Do not be afraid or discouraged. For the Lord your God is with you wherever you go" (Joshua 1:9).

Beth and Todd Smits, June 17, 2014

Wow, Tad, pictures say a thousand words . . . You can really *see* Maggie in the photos tonight! Thanks to God, your team of doctors and nurses, your *familias,* new and old, and all the people around the world (literally) lifting up prayers to God.

Frank Mina, June 17, 2014

I can´t express with words what I am feeling right now reading and seeing this. Thank You God!! She looks so amazing.
Remember the first day we met and I told you she is going to
make it for sure! But man, this girl is so strong I never thought
she would run this marathon so fast!

Heather Durenberger, June 17, 2014

Praise God. She is back. Her eyes shine. And God's people said
amen!

CHAPTER FOURTEEN

Day 14—June 18, 2014

Wendy and I met with two police officers at the hospital. We signed a document to initiate a complaint. The police report would be the main document used in the proceeding, and it wasn't finished yet. Maggie's case had been very public, and the bus company had agreed to cover Maggie's medical expenses in Spain.

This seemed like an admission of guilt to us, but it was more a sign of how the Spanish legal system is different from the US. They wanted Maggie to sign a power of attorney, but she wasn't going to be able to do that for some time. We were told that we'd probably need to travel back to Spain to testify at some point in the future.

I emailed one of our attorneys at RZS and told them about Frank Mina. He and his girlfriend were runners, and he had tried to contact us early on right after the accident. Frank lived two blocks from the accident site, and they had filed a complaint with the city two weeks before Maggie's accident. They had almost been hit by a bus while out for a run, and in his complaint, he stated that the buses often travel in excess of 90 kph. They knew an accident was going to happen, and their worst fears were realized with Maggie.

Frank agreed to meet with our attorneys, who felt this complaint was a very important issue in our favor.

The People of Seville
by Tad Weiss, June 18, 2014

We had a good night's rest and went to see Maggie for our morning visit. We usually wait to see her, as all of the patients in the UCI ward need to be stable before we can go in. This morning, we arrived at 8:25 and walked right in, which was a treat.

God continues to heal Maggie immediately. We have been warned that there will be times when it appears that Maggie is not progressing or has even taken a step backward, but this hasn't happened yet. Thank You, God!

Maggie's eyes are open, and she follows our voices and movements. Her legs are very active. It is very clear to us that Maggie is going to need to learn *paciencia* along with us. She tries to climb out of bed. She wants to go for a run.

We can practically hear her saying, "I've been in this bed for almost two weeks; let's get up and do something!"

We think her pelvic injury may be a provision to make her be still and let her brain heal completely. She's not going to be able to walk or run for a while, but we firmly believe those abilities will return to her soon. So we're all going to need to work on the patience thing.

For the first time, we think, Maggie responded to a command. I asked her to squeeze my hand and she did! Just another sign that God is healing her perfectly and according to His plan.

The first day we arrived in Spain was June 6. I remember very clearly thinking on that day, *I have to get my daughter out of this city and back to the United States as soon as possible.*

The very next day, our first full day in Seville, that thought changed. Everyone we ran into told us how great the hospital and doctors were—the best place for her in all southern Spain, maybe the whole country. Okay, she can get the care she needs here. I knew we needed a strong, solid support person in the city to help us with the language and to organize everything. Morgan was firm and steady, talking with us during the flights over, driving us to the hospital, translating for us, getting us set up in the hotel. She was that answer to prayer.

Visitors started arriving from all over Seville. Word was out that an American couple had arrived in Spain and they needed help. Carey and Sharon showed up and they have walked beside us every single day. We always have someone with us for the hospital visits, and we've had as many as six people with us sometimes.

At first, only one person could come into the UCI with us. The others would wait outside and pray. So many people changed their days, their routines to be with us and comfort us. Now we can take multiple people into the UCI with us, and we are so happy to share Maggie's progress with them.

The doctors and nurses here are fantastic! At first, we struggled with getting the medical updates through an interpreter. We now realize it was a blessing in disguise. We are confident that our interpreters are giving us the truth, but they are also able to translate the doctor's information in a way that gives us more peace. You can see that the doctors and nurses are touched by Maggie. We believe Maggie's lead doctor was moved when Wendy told him, "We trust you. We know that she is in the best hands here in Seville."

The same goes for Carlos, an attorney we were put in touch with. Carlos is here for us as a friend. He is not "on the clock." He has given us great wisdom and counsel. I know I'm using the word "amazing" a lot, but God has put all the right people in place, at just the right time, to support Wendy and me fully. He is in charge of *all* the details.

The staff at the AC Marriott is great! We had a funny moment two days ago when we walked by the front desk and Sofia sheepishly told us we needed to make a payment on our bill. We had passed the 1,500-euro mark on our eleventh day, and that was the limit before they put the charge through. This is not a hotel that normally has guests for eleven days. These are tough times in Spain, economically. It is not uncommon for a guest to try to skip out on their bill. We gladly made the payment, and we most likely will get reimbursed for all of it. The people at the front desk are so kind. They ask us how Maggie is doing, and we show them the pictures. They have made our stay comfortable and have supported us with everything we've needed, which has been a lot.

Mercedes serves us at dinner, and it has been fun to get to know her. She laughs at my weak attempts to order in Spanish. We love her and all our new friends at the hotel!

We have met with the police three times as a part of the investigation. Felix was one of the first officers on the scene of Maggie's accident, and he has been at all three meetings. He thinks of Maggie every day. He was so happy when we shared her progress with him yesterday. They continue to assure us that they are doing their job, that they don't listen to the gossip that is flying around in the Spanish newspapers and on the radio. They will investigate and report the facts to the judge. We trust that they will do a great job. We tell them that all we want is for the truth to come out, whatever that may be.

We hear many stories of how God is using Maggie's accident to minister to the people of Seville. The hard part of thanking the people here is that there is no way to do it completely. We hesitate to name anyone because we can't name them all. We love you all and you have touched us deeply. The people here are beautiful, filled with love and compassion. They have *mucho ánimo.* There is a reason so many young Americans come to Seville and end up marrying someone from here.

Wendy and I are so blessed by all the new friends we have made here. We will go home but you will not leave our hearts. We will be back to see you, and it will be a glorious celebration! And you are welcome to come visit us in Minnesota at any time. Just be prepared if you come in the winter; you might not like it!

God has this unbelievable way of turning things upside down. In less than two weeks, I have gone from thinking I want out of here ASAP to knowing that we are in the right place at the right time. The love of Jesus Christ has no borders. The people of this city have touched us deeply. We are changed; we are brothers and sisters for life. Thank you from the bottom of our hearts, and God bless you all!

"For our citizenship is in heaven, from which also we eagerly wait for a Savior, the Lord Jesus Christ, who, by the power that enables him to bring everything under his control, will transform our lowly bodies so that they will be like his glorious body" (Philippians 3:20–21).

Susan Olson, June 18, 2014

Blessings to all the supporters you have around you! I marvel at your patience and am so grateful for you that you have this astounding network, around the world, praying and holding and helping you in this journey.

Sharon Owen, June 18, 2014

Yeah! I'm over here now but my heart is in Seville. Our prayer is that no one who comes to read this blog or who meets you in Seville will be able to say anything less than that God *does* exist and He *does* hear and respond to His children who love and follow Him wholeheartedly.

FMSC Packing Event for Maggie

by Tad Weiss, June 18, 2014

Feed My Starving Children[5] is an organization that has blessed our family throughout the years. I served on the board for seven years, and our family has packed food at the Chanhassen site on many occasions. As most of you know, FMSC packs food through volunteers and then ships it to starving children around the world. I know of no other organization that is the hands and feet of Jesus more than FMSC.

Many of you have asked how you can help us while we're over here in Spain with Maggie. My company, Modus Advisors, has scheduled a food packing event for next Thursday, June 26, from 6:00 to 7:30 p.m., at the Chanhassen site. It doesn't look like Maggie, Wendy, and I will be there for the event, but we want it to go on! So we've changed the event from the Modus packing event to the Maggie Weiss Packing Event. Can you guys do us a huge favor and fill up all the volunteer slots?

CHAPTER FIFTEEN

Day 15—June 19, 2014

W e were told that Maggie should be able to move out of the UCI to *planta*, the recovery area of the hospital, in two to three days.

Scripture, Song and . . . Exercise!
by Tad Weiss, Jun 19, 2014

What a beautiful morning it is here. After a heat wave that took us into the 100s, we are back into the low 80s and it's welcome. Cool in the mornings, comfortable in the afternoons. We hear that our wet spring continues in Minnesota, but we're just about to hit summer, so hopefully we will begin to dry out back home.

Thursdays are big days for us. Maggie's accident happened exactly two weeks ago on a Thursday. Her successful pelvic surgery was last Thursday. And Wendy and I are feeling a change, a shift, on this Thursday.

Last night, we were talking about how tired we were and we needed to get more rest. We've been running on adrenaline for two straight weeks. You can't keep going at that pace forever without a crash. Wendy recognized this, and we went to bed at 10:00 p.m. last night. We slept soundly until 7:00 a.m., a full nine hours. We awoke refreshed and excited to see what God has in store for us today.

We had a truly astonishing visit with Maggie this morning. Her eyes were wide open when we walked into the UCI, and she smiled a lot. We have been praying for peace for Maggie—that she won't be confused or afraid as she regains full consciousness. You can see this peace in her face; God has answered our prayers once again.

Maggie is a runner and a fighter! When she gets excited on our visits, she grabs our hands tightly and pulls herself up, trying to climb out of bed, stand up, walk, and run. But God knows it isn't time for her to run or even stand up right now.

We firmly believe that she needs to be still for her brain to heal completely and perfectly. We will not rush this.

There is something about a traumatic event that opens your eyes to the truth of Scripture and the power of God. One of the many blessings of Maggie's accident is that my eyes have been truly opened to the power of Scripture.

Are the verses we're posting coming alive for you? Do they make total sense to you like they do for me? I hope so. The verses you send us are such a comfort. God is prompting you to send us those verses; we read them all and they bring us comfort, peace, hope, patience, and faith.

As many of you know, Wendy is very versed in Scripture. She studies God's Word diligently and faithfully every day. It is the first place she goes in the morning, and I see her reading God's Word throughout the day. What an example for me and our children—one that I didn't fully grasp until now.

She is the children's supervisor for BSF in Chanhassen. What a group of faithful women who gather every week to study God's Word. They have all tapped into the power of the Bible. Wendy has not been changed by Maggie's accident as much as I have. She was already locked into the power of God, the Holy Spirit, and God's written Word in the Bible. I knew all these things too, but I didn't truly *know* them. I now know them; they have been burned upon my soul. What a power to carry with me throughout each day!

I love sports and exercise. My dad was a basketball and tennis coach, and as kids, Matt, Julie, and I grew up with the "keys to the gym." I have participated in many sports throughout my life, and I exercise regularly, six days per week. Many of you have sent us messages reminding us to take care of ourselves. My friend, Billy, a regular exercise partner, encouraged me to continue to exercise. I hadn't exercised for two weeks! So I took his advice yesterday afternoon, put on my workout clothes, grabbed my iPhone and headphones, and went up to the Marriott workout room.

This is your typical hotel exercise room. A bike, treadmill, weight machine, and a few dumbbells. I jumped on the bike, and the timer was set for 21:00 for some reason. That would do. I didn't have much more time than that anyway.

So I start pedaling and turned on some music. The song that was on was "I Will Lift my Eyes"[6] by Bebo Norman. Okay, I'd go with that. The words amazed me . . . lifting his eyes to the God who made the mountains he can't climb, the God who calms the waters of the raging sea.

So there I was in a workout room in the AC Marriott in Seville—just me, God, Bebo, and the bike—pedaling hard, arms uplifted, crying my eyes out, sweating, singing, praising God. What if someone walks by and sees me? *I don't care!!* Praise God! He has met me completely, fully at my darkest hour.

God, I need You now. Calm my fear, take my doubt. I can't climb the mountain on my own. The ocean is raging around me. You are the Healer; take this hurt from me. Only You can. I will lift my eyes to You!

Wow, that was great, God. What should I listen to now?

Third Day is one of my favorite bands. Talented musicians, a little southern-based influence, Mac Powell's deep and beautiful voice. Wendy has always said she feels it is how God will sound when we hear Him sing in heaven.

The first song that pops up is "Born in Bethlehem."[7] This is a Christmas song, but it is one of my favorites and I listen to it year-round.

Great, we're staying with Third Day. Next up, "Show Me Your Glory."[8] The song tells of seeing God's glory and being in His presence; exactly what I've been experiencing the last two weeks.

Mac, did you write these words just for me?

Next up, "Cry Out to Jesus."[9] Pull up the words to this song. It is about Jesus's healing power in whatever circumstance you're in. Death of a loved one, addiction, a broken marriage, an illness, an accident. Jesus is there to help you through whatever is hurting you.

And I finished my workout with "I Believe."[10] I believe in faith, hope, and love. I believe in Jesus.

Wow! The most intense workout/worship experience of my life. I went to the pool to let God's soothing waters pour over me.

Scripture will come alive for you if you crack open the Bible, pray, and meditate on God's Word. This has been so clearly revealed to me over the past two weeks. Music is one of God's gifts to us, and a Christian artist can pull together God's Word and music to speak to us in awe-inspiring ways.

"Speak to one another with psalms, hymns, and spiritual songs. Sing and make music in your heart to the Lord, always giving thanks to God the Father for everything, in the name of our Lord Jesus Christ" (Ephesians 5:19).

Sarie Anderson, June 19, 2014

We have very good Spanish friends in Madrid who are struggling to make sense of why their sixteen-year-old daughter has to face cancer (for the second time). I am going to forward your CaringBridge site to them, as I think it will give them the perspective of how you, as Christians, can face this kind of tragedy, and the *hope* you have in the midst of it.

We look forward to meeting you in Minnesota when you bring Maggie home. So thankful for the many people in Seville who have won a place in your hearts. After seventeen years in Spain, we left a *big* part of our hearts there when we left last week. We trust God will take us back after a year in the US. *Un abrazo fuerte!*

Maggie Update

by Tad Weiss, June 19, 2014

The doctor says that Maggie continues to be stable, with no fever and no complications. They're going to remove the staples from her pelvic surgery tomorrow. They continue to be pleased with her progress!

At tonight's visit, it became clear that Maggie is going to need a big dose of patience. Maybe that's why God has been training Wendy and me so diligently in this area. Maggie is still not communicating, and she responds sporadically to our prompts. This is a normal part of the process; brain injuries like hers take time to heal.

But man, is that girl active! She's driving the nurses crazy because she pulls at her hand and leg restraints and tries to get out of bed. It is great to be with her and to talk and pray with her. But we spent much of the visit tonight telling her to lie down, rest, and heal. We think this will become easier when she can understand what we're saying more fully. Our Maggie has much spirit or *mucho ánimo!* A little too much *ánimo* at the moment.

"Peace I leave with you; my peace I give you. I do not give to you as the world gives. Do not let your hearts be troubled and do not be afraid" (John 14:27).

Karen (Franz) Haley, June 19, 2014

I felt such sadness when I first learned of Maggie's accident, but reading all your reports, I've been nothing but inspired. None of us know God's full purpose in allowing this to happen, but the good that has come from it has been powerful. Tad, I praise God that you have so humbly allowed yourself to learn and grow in your faith! Wendy, you are such an awesome mom and wife. I see the joy that you both have in spite of the circumstances. God is glorified. Maggie is blessed. Praying for her continued healing.

CHAPTER SIXTEEN

Day 16—June 20, 2014

During our daily update with Dr. Flores on day sixteen, a Friday, he indicated that Maggie would be able to move out of the UCI on Monday. From there, the doctors would then decide when Maggie could travel home, likely seven to ten days after the move.

Dr. Flores had the best handle on Maggie's situation, and we loved visiting with him. He said the more time we spent with Maggie, the better. As her parents, we had the best chance of connecting with her, and we'd have more time to do that with the move to *planta*. The recovery area of the hospital would allow us to be with Maggie around the clock, rather than the two, thirty- to sixty-minute daily visits in the UCI.

God Answers Prayer!
by Tad Weiss, June 20, 2014

Wendy and I had another good night's rest, and we went to see Maggie. The UCI has been calmer lately, and we've been able to get in and see her pretty quickly.

When we walked in, we could see Maggie across the hall, her right leg bent and working back and forth, doing some leg exercises. She was working out! She was very happy to see us, with a huge smile! We can tell that she is more attentive, and everything is healing.

As soon as I got my gown on and could go into the room, I held her hand and asked her to squeeze it . . . and she did! She also smiles when we ask her to!!

Her brain is healing perfectly, with God's perfect timing. Small, steady progress on each visit. No, change that: *big* steady progress on each visit! It is *so clear* that God is in control of her healing. *Thank You, God for answering our prayers!!*

In addition to our prayer for immediate healing, we asked that you pray for Maggie to have patience. She needs to be still and rest. The nurses told us that she slept for an hour and a half last night, not very much.

God is answering our prayers, your prayers for Maggie!

"Delight yourself in the Lord and He will give you the desires of your heart" (Psalm 37:4).

Sue Favorite, June 20, 2014

"From the lips of children and infants you have ordained praise" (Matthew 21:16). I know VBS is close to your hearts. I wanted to share with you last night's God moment. Miss Danise shared with the seven hundred-plus children a little of Maggie's story and we all prayed for Maggie. While this was happening, God moved in these children to pray with their still, quiet voices. Praise God!

Wendy and I received a nice email from Megan and Michaela and the St. Olaf cross-country and track teams. They'd been following along and sharing stories of Maggie's friendliness, kindness, and fierce spirit. They'd been talking with the coach, Chris Daymont, and were making preliminary plans to sponsor a 5K race in Maggie's honor on September 14 at St. Olaf.

We would have loved nothing more than for all of us to be there and to give thanks for Maggie's healing, whatever that might look like.

How Far We've Come

by Tad Weiss, June 20, 2014

Maggie is progressing nicely. She is now fully conscious but is not verbal yet; that will come, and her progress is normal for a diffuse brain trauma.

The current plan is that Maggie will move out of the UCI and go into *planta* (a regular hospital floor) on Monday. We are very excited for this move, but we will miss Dr. Flores. He has been a kind, patient, talented doctor for Maggie and for us. We cannot thank him and the other doctors enough for how skillfully they have cared for our daughter.

Maggie was sleeping when we arrived tonight, but the nurses wanted us to interact with her. She is very responsive and was peaceful for the first twenty minutes or so. She is trying to say some words, but they can't come out yet.

Toward the end of the visit, she started to get more active. This is hard, as we can tell she wants out of that bed! She's been stuck in it for over two weeks, and she is ready to move, but her body isn't.

So once again we ask that you pray for continued immediate healing of Maggie's body and brain. Also that she will get a great night's sleep, and let her body and mind heal.

Before our visit with Dr. Flores this afternoon, we had some time with Morgan from CIEE. She was there to translate for us, but we've also grown to appreciate her medical knowledge. She isn't formally trained, but she has learned a lot from being thrust into these situations. We were talking about two weeks ago, our first day in Spain. We didn't have very much information. We weren't thinking about her coming home, going back to school, or running again. We just wanted our daughter to live.

We hadn't set up Maggie's CaringBridge site and hadn't relayed any information back home. Word had already gotten around about Maggie, but you knew less than we did. That was where we were two weeks ago.

Look at where we are today! Maggie is not only alive, but she is thriving. What a truly miraculous recovery! How far she has come in two short weeks! All thanks be to God!!

Wendy and I spend our days visiting Maggie, visiting her doctors, and reading and posting on CaringBridge. We have gotten into a comfortable routine.

We felt so at peace that we went into the city today to shop for a few things and to go to the site where Maggie's accident occurred. We went running in a park today and have tried a couple of restaurants in the area. We are very settled in, as much as you can be in a foreign city. We have more friends here than any place else except home.

I'm also struck by the changes that have happened to me in two short weeks. Before this happened, I didn't talk about Jesus very openly and certainly not to strangers. I didn't understand the profound truth of Scripture and how it could comfort me and impact my day so meaningfully. I had no idea how many friends I had or how much they cared for me. I thought I knew how *my wife* needed to change to make our marriage better. I did not know a single person in Spain. I knew that God wanted more for me, but I didn't know how to find out what.

Now, I can't stop typing on CaringBridge. I tell everyone who will listen about the wondrous healing powers of Jesus Christ. God's Word has been revealed to me and I can clearly see how immersing myself in it will lead to a richer, fuller life. I have hundreds of friends who care for my daughter, my wife, and for me. I think I know what *I* need to change to make my marriage better. I can conservatively say I have fifty new friends in Seville, many of whom I will stay in contact with after we go home. Most importantly though, I know how God wants me to live the rest of my life.

One thing that has always puzzled me is funerals, particularly when someone has died well before their time. We see death up close and personal, and it makes us realize that life on earth is short, and we need to reevaluate our own priorities. We think about how we spend our time and the need to focus on the things that are truly important: faith, family, and friends.

We think, *Okay, God. This time I'm really going to make a change.*

Then this thing called "life" comes along: work, school, kids, laundry, cooking, cleaning, hobbies. The whole list of the stuff we do. Those things start grabbing our attention, and we quickly forget about that little conversation we had with God. How long does it take to revert to our old ways? A day, three days. For most of us, a week at the most.

What has happened to you over the past two weeks? Are you feeling something stirring inside of you, asking you to change? If you are, it may be God calling you to a richer, fuller life. If He is calling you, don't run away from Him. If you don't know about Jesus or what to do next, talk to a pastor or a Christian friend. You can find both at a church; that is where they hang out!

If you already have a faith in Jesus but feel God calling you to go deeper, find a friend that has a more mature faith. One thing I have learned the past two weeks is you can't do it alone! Trust me on this. I've been trying for way too long. You need someone to walk beside you, to hold you accountable.

Since the accident, our almighty God has been doing His thing, and the love of Jesus Christ is spreading. I thank God that today is not two weeks ago. We have come a very long way in a short period of time. Thank You, God!

"A friend loves at all times" (Proverbs 17:17).

Ann Renfroe, June 20, 2014

Thank you for the devotional Tad, your new calling! It feels like you wrote this for me. I lost a dear friend on Monday. It was sudden and they don't know why. She left behind a husband and three sweet children. Your updates serve three great purposes—we know what to thank the Lord for and what to pray for and are reminded of God's upper story—the bigger picture. Jesus is all we can trust in completely. Jesus is the big picture!

Roxanne Martin, June 20, 2014

Thank you for sharing your walk with the Lord. It is very raw and convicting for me. No matter how hard I try to have a closer relationship with the Lord, it's confounding what knocks at the door. We know it's the devil knocking. Since Maggie's accident, I have spent more time in the Word than ever.

Paul and Peggy Borowski and family, June 20, 2014

This post made me laugh out loud! You probably know by now that those of us back home have clung to virtually every word you've posted along this incredible journey! I love that you post as often as you do, because we get to share in your ups, downs, and everything in between. Keep the faith and keep posting!

CHAPTER SEVENTEEN

Day 17—June 21, 2014

At our morning visit, Jaime from CIEE and his wife, Paqui, greeted us at the hospital and came into the UCI with us to see Maggie. Maggie looked very well rested. Our prayers for a calm night were answered.

She continued to squeeze our hands, smile, and respond occasionally. We could see her trying to get a word out, but it just wasn't time yet. The big improvement was that she seemed more at peace, which helped Wendy and me to rest in that peace too.

Maggie seemed to be on track to leave the UCI on Monday, two days away, and then our routine would change. We prayed that she'd begin to speak and process what she had been through.

Changes were coming—good changes—in God's perfect plan for Maggie's complete healing.

My Job, God's Job
by Tad Weiss, Jun 21, 2014

We love the weekends here. The walk to the hospital is quieter, less busy. We hope you have a great weekend back home and that you continue to dry out!

We've had a few moments in the last twenty-four hours where the six-month timeframe has come up. At our visit with Dr. Flores yesterday, when we were talking about changing to a new doctor on *planta*, Wendy said we would be back with Maggie to visit him when she is whole. Dr. Flores said to wait until Christmas; that would be the time, six months from now.

This morning with Jaime, we talked about Michael Schumacher, the former Formula One racecar world champion. Six months ago, he fell while skiing and hit his head on a rock. He was wearing a helmet that probably saved his life. He just came out of a coma this week, six months later, and they still don't know what his future looks like.

Dr. Flores thinks Maggie has the potential to be completely healed in six months.

What a total and complete miracle and picture of immediate healing! Thank You, God!!

One of the things that's been on my mind lately is discerning between what is my job and what is God's job. I've been learning the things I need to do with my time every day. But I've also been learning what not to do. Learning the lessons on what not to do has been the more painful part. Once I try to jump over into doing someone else's job, or doing God's job, it usually leads to impatience, anxiety, and fear.

My Job

- Love, care, and pray for my daughter. Read Scripture to her, pray with her, talk with her, laugh with her, get her to smile.
- Take care of, pray for, and love my wife. Make sure she is getting her rest and staying strong.
- Take care of my son, as best I can from far away, and give thanks that all of you have wrapped your arms around him while we're away from him.
- Write on CaringBridge so you can stay updated on Maggie's progress and our journey; stay in contact with family and friends, as needed.
- Read all your responses. They sustain me. Read Scripture and listen to music that honors God, encourages and uplifts me, and gives me strength for the day.
- Trust God. He has a perfect plan for Maggie's healing and for me.
- Rest and exercise so I can stay strong for Maggie and Wendy.
- Have an attitude of gratitude in all things. Look for the good, eyes wide open for the many ways God works in our lives and shows us His love.

Not My Job

- To speculate on the future or timetable for Maggie's healing. Every time I do this, it leads to worry and anxiety. Only God knows the answer, and He will reveal it at the right time.
- To be fearful. God doesn't want me to be afraid, and that is why it is commanded more often than anything else in the Bible! *Do not be afraid, Tad. I've got this, can't you see that?* Yes, I can see it clearly, God, thank You!
- To ask for answers that the doctors don't have. This ties directly in with the first one, but instead of me speculating, I'm asking someone to speculate for me, since they're

smarter than me. Our doctors have been very clear in telling us what they know and what they don't. I've learned what questions not to ask throughout this journey. Once again, God is in charge of that.

- To hold on to bitterness, anger, or impatience. God is teaching me to let it go. Believe me, I still have my moments! But He is faithful and just and will relieve me of these feelings if I ask him to.

As you go about your day, maybe you can make a list of what God wants you to be in charge of and to do on this day. Also make a list of the things you're doing that aren't in your department. Give them over to God, and He will take care of them and give you peace.

Wendy and I want to finish this post with a picture of Maggie and her brother, Peter, or "little Petey" as Maggie likes to call him.

"Little Petey" is now 6'2" and weighs 190 pounds, so he isn't so little anymore. Peter is playing in a basketball tournament with the Minnetonka team at the University of Wisconsin, Madison, this weekend.

We love and miss you, Peter!

"'For my thoughts are not your thoughts, neither are your ways my ways,' declares the Lord. 'As the heavens are higher than the earth, so are my ways higher than your ways and my thoughts than your thoughts'" (Isaiah 55:8–9).

At our two o'clock doctor visit with Morgan and Dr. Amaya, it struck us that these visits had become shorter and much more joyful.

Maggie was still on track to move out of the UCI on Monday. Her pelvis was healing, and it was okay that she was moving her legs around like she was doing Zumba in bed. The doctor felt strongly that one of us should be with Maggie at all times in *planta*, and Wendy and I couldn't wait! She told us to get our rest now.

Remember Alberto? He had been hit by a truck three days before Maggie's accident and had also been in a coma. We'd started running into his parents, Luis and Fina, in the UCI waiting area. Wendy had connected with them—one of her specialties! Luis spoke only a little English, but we connected closely with them.

They were always three days ahead of us in the recovery process. Alberto progressed nicely. After about a week, he had come out of his coma. We would peek into his UCI room, and he would wave to us.

When we left the doctor's office, we saw Alberto and his parents outside the entrance to the hospital. We hadn't seen them for five days or so as they were in *planta* and we were still in the UCI.

What a joyful celebration we had. Alberto was standing outside the hospital in his gown with a neck brace on. He was talking and smiling, ready to go home as soon as they'd let him! Hugs and kisses all around. We were so happy for them. We showed them pictures and videos of Maggie, and they celebrated her progress with us.

I shook Alberto's hand, and he told me, "We are young, and we can heal quickly from these accidents. Your daughter will be just like me in a few days!"

Wow!! We saw with our own eyes what the healing process looks like. They were such an encouragement to us.

VBS

by Tad Weiss, Jun 21, 2014

At our evening visit, Maggie looked rested and very peaceful. Carey and Madeline were with us. We played Maggie the video from the Westwood Vacation Bible School that finished this Thursday.

When Maggie heard seven hundred kids screaming, "Maggie, Jesus loves you!" it was the first time we've seen real emotion from her. She choked up and looked like she was going to cry! It was so beautiful. Thank you Danise, Westwood, and all the kids at VBS. You truly made our day!

"Jesus said, 'Let the little children come to me, and do not hinder them, for the kingdom of heaven belongs to such as these'" (Matthew 19:14).

CHAPTER EIGHTEEN

Day 18—June 22, 2014

Wendy and I made our forty-ninth walk to the hospital for our morning visit—a five-block walk, forty-nine round trips.

When we were let into the UCI, Maggie was sleeping. We asked the nurse if we should wake her, as she hadn't been sleeping much.

Through our interpreter, Nancy, the nurse, said, "Yes, we want you to wake her. Ask her to smile, grip your hand, and talk. Ask her if she is hungry—whether she would like some yogurt."

Wendy woke Maggie up by singing "Good Morning, God," "God is So Good," and "Jesus Loves Me." Maggie slowly awoke and smiled at us. We gave her a couple of minutes to fully wake up, then asked her to squeeze our hands, which she did. Then the miracle of Jesus's healing powers was revealed to us again.

Wendy asked her, "Are you hungry?"

Barely above a whisper, Maggie answered, "Yes."

Wendy and I shared a look, and then Wendy sputtered out, "D-do you want some yogurt?"

Again, Maggie spoke. "Yes."

"I love you." Wendy could barely contain the tears. "Do you love Mommy?"

To that, Maggie nodded.

Not wanting to be left out, I chimed in. "Can you say 'Daddy'?"

A small smile played on her lips before she said, "Daddy."

We witnessed a miracle right before our eyes. Jesus healed our daughter. He made the mute speak again (Mark 7:37)! Huge smiles spread across our faces. I could do nothing but lift my hands and give thanks to God.

We spent forty-five minutes with Maggie. She needed to rest, but I finally hit on a question that got her talking again.

Half joking, I asked, "Can you teach Daddy to speak Spanish?"

She gave me a look that I wasn't quite sure how to read. "S-sure."

As Wendy chuckled, I pictured Maggie mentally adding, "I'll do it, but it's not going to be easy!"

Turning serious, Wendy grasped Maggie's hand. "Do you understand you were in an accident?"

Maggie closed her eyes. "Yes."

Wendy ran a hand over Maggie's forehead. "Do you know that you're okay?"

Opening her eyes again, Maggie seemed to consider the question. "No."

That tore at my heart. I had to ease her pain, so I asked, "Do you believe that Jesus loves you and He will heal you?"

Maggie looked at me with glistening eyes. "Yes."

Sensing that she wanted to tell us something more, we both bent in closer.

With a voice that we could barely hear, Maggie uttered, "Twenty-nine days."

Frowning, Wendy shook her head. "You've only been in the hospital for seventeen days. Are you telling us you'll be ready to go home after twenty-nine?"

Looking impatient, Maggie said with more force, "Twenty-*eight*."

"Okay, honey." A soft smile replaced Wendy's frown. "We think you're right. We will go home after twenty-eight days."

The nurse came in to tell us it was time to go.

The last thing Maggie said to us was, "Stay."

Although it was hard to leave our daughter's side after that, we told her she needed to rest, and we did too. We would be back to see her soon. In fact, the nurse told us to come back at noon and they would get us into the UCI to see her again. This was exactly the interaction they wanted to see. Maggie knew and trusted her parents the most, and we could bring this part of her healing out better than the nurses or doctors could.

What an unforgettable, awesome, magnificent visit. *Thank You, God!* Could anyone deny the healing power of Jesus? Could anyone deny the power of the body of believers coming together in prayer, love, and support? Or that God can take a tragic accident and turn it upside down, spreading the love of Jesus Christ around the world? *No!* This cannot be denied. It was a miracle for all to see.

The Healing of the Mute

by Tad Weiss, June 22, 2014

Maggie is speaking! Praise be to God!!

"Then Jesus left the vicinity of Tyre and went through Sidon, down to the Sea of Galilee and into the region of the Decapolis. There some people brought to him a man who was deaf and could hardly talk, and they begged him to place his hand on the man.

"After he took him aside, away from the crowd, Jesus put his fingers into the man's ears. Then he spit and touched the man's tongue. He looked up to heaven and with a deep sigh said to him 'Ephphatha!' (be opened). At this, the man's ears were opened, his tongue was loosened and he began to speak plainly.

"Jesus commanded them not to tell anyone. But the more he did so, the more they kept talking about it. People were overwhelmed with amazement. 'He has done everything well,' they said. 'He even makes the deaf hear and the mute speak'" (Mark 7:31–37).

You have been so faithful to God, to Maggie, and to us through your love, support, and prayers. We have some specific prayer requests:

- That Maggie will not be afraid. We know our daughter, and we can sense that she is going to feel sadness and guilt as she starts to understand what happened.
- That we will "hold it together" in our time with Maggie (particularly her dad!). We need to be positive and encouraging. Tears, even tears of joy, may make her feel sad and we don't think that is the right emotion for her to have at this time.
- That Maggie will continue the path of steady healing according to God's perfect timing, and that she will move to *planta* on Monday.

Many of you have asked us to tell you if you can do anything for us. Wendy and I are learning to ask! We have a couple things we would like you to do for Maggie:

Go to church and give thanks to God for the marvelous immediate healing He is performing in Maggie.

While you're there, if you don't know Jesus, ask a pastor or someone you trust to help you learn about this Jesus guy, the One who walks on water and heals the sick. You have heard and seen His wondrous love and healing power. Take the first step in getting to know Him and what He can do to bring power, love, and healing to you.

For those of you that already know Jesus, ask Him to heal you. We have a very big God who can help us through whatever trials we are facing. Ask Him to heal you, and you will grow closer to Him through your submission and dependence on Him.

We have previously asked you to tell us about how you're seeing God do a simple or astounding work in your life through Maggie's accident, and many of you have done that. Our second request is this:

Write down how you are seeing God in new ways through Maggie's accident.

It could be through you, or it could be in how it has impacted someone else. Big or small, it doesn't matter. Write it down, and do not forget it. We want to be able to share with Maggie how God used her accident to spread the love of Jesus Christ around the world.

"And all these things, whatsoever you shall ask in prayer, believing, you shall receive" (Matthew 21:22).

Barbara Chresand, June 22, 2014

Such fabulous news!! Our lives here in the US run by your posts. We wake up to see your morning post, check in throughout the day (each check prompts more prayers), then we don't go to bed without checking for any last post. I told another former Chapel Hill Academy (CHA) school worker about your journey with Maggie and the thing she remembered instantly were the fabulous "Maggie hugs" that she was always so generous in giving. She has such a loving heart! Thank you for your wonderfully detailed updates!

Chelsea Lee, June 22, 2014

Praise You, Lord!! I am just amazed! By the title of the post, I was thinking "Could it be that she is speaking?" then thought maybe it was going to be a prayer request for speech. But no, like you say, Jesus is healing her immediately, right before your eyes.

Steve Durham, June 22, 2014

We don't know you but are family in Christ. Praise God for His healing touch. We believe in miracles.

My friend Todd emailed with thanks and praise to Jesus for Maggie's healing. He was praying for special provisions as we changed rooms in the hospital and that there would be comfortable, reclining chairs or sleeping accommodations for Wendy and me. That thought hadn't crossed our minds. We were just excited to be able to be with Maggie throughout the day.

We won't go through life without encountering a medical challenge, personally or with a family member. That is the fallen world we live in. We all need an anchor for life's most difficult moments.

The Anchor Holds

by Wendy Weiss, June 22, 2014

We had been told to come back and see Maggie at noon today. When we showed up (armed with our Google-translated Spanish, explaining why we were there), they told us we could not see her just then, to go back to the hotel and wait. They said they'd call us before the two o'clock doctor visit; this didn't happen, but we were not discouraged.

At the consultation, Dr. Marin spoke English with us, though Morgan was also there to translate. Can I just take a minute to tell you how much we have come to love and trust Morgan? We got to meet her husband and two kids last night—what treasures they all are! We are truly *eternally* grateful for Morgan!

Dr. Marin needed to be updated regarding what Maggie had said to us this morning, and he laughed with us at our favorite "sure" response in regard to teaching Tad Spanish. We still giggle when we think of that response. She is obviously processing and not simply responding. She always has been a very honest person. Even in this situation, she remains honest!

Dr. Marin gave us some new information. Maggie ate both yogurt and rice today! This is phenomenal news, because the sooner she eats and drinks, the sooner she can get the feeding tube out. Dr. Marin said it is normal that she would feel discomfort, not only from being intubated but also because she has been inactive for so long. My friend Heather also pointed out to me that the last thing she was doing before the accident was running, so this is what she is still trying to do. I had not thought of that, and it makes sense. No wonder she is running in bed!

We got called back to the hospital, as we were "going to church" in our hotel room via livestream. They allowed us to sit with Maggie for a full two hours. She is talking quite a bit more, though it is barely a whisper and takes great effort to say one, two, or at most, three words. Sometimes she makes sense and sometimes not, but she does answer us.

In trying to ascertain exactly how lucid she was, we asked her some questions:

"What is the name of your brother?"
She correctly answered. "Pete."
"What is the name of your boyfriend?"
She correctly answered. "Matthew."
But then, "Where do you go to college?"
To that, she answered, "I don't know."

The nurse fed her a yogurt while we were there. She seemed to enjoy it. She responds well to touch, likes to hold hands, enjoys having her forehead, neck, legs, and feet massaged. She is still occasionally restless, moving her legs and trying to sit up. Tad played some music for her, and she visibly relaxed. We look forward to being with her all the time when she moves to *planta.*

The Bible I am primarily using here in Spain is the one Tad and I gave Maggie when she entered junior high at Chapel Hill Academy. Through high school, she used different Bibles for her devotions. During her senior year in high school, I took this Bible back, with the intention of reading it and marking it up for her. I presented it to her on her eighteenth birthday, although it wasn't (and still isn't) completely "finished." The cool thing is that I am recording in this Bible all the verses and thoughts that many of you are sharing with us on this journey.

Our new friend Carey shared a verse that resonated with me about the "anchor that holds," and when I referenced it in Maggie's Bible, I saw that she had highlighted it while she was in junior high:

"God did this so that, by unchangeable things in which it is impossible for God to lie, we who have fled to take hold of the hope offered to us may be greatly encouraged. We have this hope as an anchor for the soul, firm and secure. It enters the inner sanctuary behind the curtain, where Jesus, who went before us, has entered on our behalf. He has become a high priest forever in the order of Melchizedek" (Hebrews 6:18–20).

I am so grateful that the anchor truly does hold! When the storm came, my Anchor in Jesus held. Praise God!

In addition to our faith in Jesus Christ, you are all definitely part of our "anchor" as well!

Susan Olson, June 22, 2014

Wendy, it is such a miracle to view the photos you've posted as a slideshow. At the beginning you see this battered person in bed, unrecognizable, with tubes and bandages. And quite quickly there is this unbelievable transformation! The tubes and bandages come off, the person is revealed as a beautiful girl, her eyes focus more and more, she looks more awake and cognizant, and she is smiling and running! It made me cry with joy to see the changes occur. Blessings to you, Mom!

CHAPTER NINETEEN

Day 19—June 23, 2014

W endy and I packed up to go to the hospital hoping and praying that Maggie would move to *planta*.

On our walk there (number fifty-two), we prayed that God would give us the words to comfort Maggie, teach her patience, and help her to not be afraid or feel any sadness or guilt. She loved to please us, and we thought she would feel she'd let us down.

Of course, nothing could have been further from the truth. Just knowing that our daughter was alive and recovering was all we needed. But we didn't feel it was the time to tell her all the details of the accident, which could have given her the perspective we had and kept her from some of these feelings. That was our dilemma.

Renew Your Mind

by Tad Weiss, June 23, 2014

When we walked into the UCI, Maggie started waking up from a light sleep.

She said, "Good morning."

When Carey came in and said it was good to see her, she replied, "It is good to see you too."

Sweet Maggie, just like before. Wendy thought that Maggie looked sad. We prayed with her, read Scripture, and comforted her. God answered our prayers again. He gave us the right words. Maggie's sadness seemed to go away, and she fell into a deep, peaceful sleep.

Early in our journey, I received messages from God in the middle of the night or early in the morning. They became some of the posts I've written. It was very exciting to feel that God was revealing things to me, but it also was exhausting! I wasn't sleeping much and had been running on adrenaline. Thankfully, God has allowed me to get more sleep in the last ten days. He knew I needed it!

Many of the things I've written about more recently have come to me through your posts. Today's post is specifically inspired by Patty Sheridan discussing her faith journey and from a devotion shared by Julia Sharma.

"The mind" has been on my mind lately. Maggie had a beautiful mind before her accident. She knew in her mind that Jesus loves her and that He is the Way. She is very intelligent, and she excelled in academics. She had street smarts too. She has a great mind, and she uses it well. We are so encouraged to see her mind coming back to how it was before the accident. That has been one of our most fervent prayers, higher than the healing of her body, which we've prayed for a lot too.

Wendy and I have been in a small group the last few months that is studying The Daniel Plan. This study covers the five F's: Food, Fitness, Faith, Friends, and Focus. The section on Focus really intrigued me. We can control what happens in our mind—what we focus on—and that in turn can control our thoughts, our moods, and our actions. Here's an example:

You're driving on Highway 5, and a speeding car zips around you, no turn signal, dives back in front of you, and makes you slam on your brakes. Five miles later, they're still right in front of you, or maybe even behind you. All their reckless driving did absolutely no good and served no purpose.

How did you choose to react? Did you honk your horn, let out a stream of obscenities, and think terrible thoughts about the person and how they irretrievably ruined your day?

Did you know that you can choose to have a different thought? You could instead say, "Lord, I'm sorry that this person is in such a hurry. I hope it has nothing to do with a serious event. I pray that You will bring peace to them. I forgive them, it really isn't a big deal, I will arrive at my destination a few seconds later and I know You will redeem the time. I pray for their safety. Go in peace."

That may sound silly, but try it next time. See if you don't feel better, more peaceful, closer to God.

We can choose what we think about. We can choose thoughts that draw us closer to God or that take us further from God. The more we choose the thoughts that bring us closer to God, the more joyful, hopeful, peaceful, and faithful we become. These are all good things!

We've received many emails and replies that tell us about how Maggie's accident has been the catalyst to draw you closer to God. We can't begin to tell you how we rejoice over this. Many of you have read a verse of Scripture that has spoken to you directly, or prayed more often or more fervently, or read something on this site that touched you deeply. That is God talking to you, tugging at your heart, whispering in your ear.

But I also know there are many of you reading this that are feeling God speaking to you—feeling that same tug, that same whisper—but you are choosing to ignore Him. I know this because that was me nineteen days ago. I knew that God was calling me to more, to a richer and fuller life through Him, but I chose to ignore Him. I was using my mind and making a conscious decision to ignore God.

I don't take this lightly, and I know it isn't easy to turn to God instead of away from Him. It is our natural inclination—its accurate definition is sin. We are all sinners. We are all seduced by the things of this world that are designed to draw us away from God. But true life comes when we are obedient to God, when we answer His call. Do not be afraid! If you turn to God, it doesn't mean you have to give up all the great things in this life that you enjoy. He wants us to enjoy the good things of this world. Just trust and know that when you turn toward Him, when you answer His call, your life will be renewed and enriched in ways that you can't even imagine.

"Do not conform any longer to the pattern of this world, but be transformed by the renewing of your mind. Then you will be able to test and approve what God's will is—His good, pleasing, and perfect will" (Romans 12:2).

Colleen McCormick, June 23, 2014

Each day I am inspired by your family's courage and response to Maggie's accident. This particular post I have reread several times because it speaks very directly to me.

Recently I had something that I really wanted to happen, and it didn't. I know it wasn't meant to be at this time. God has a different plan and that is okay. I know this in my head, but it was not in my heart.

It's like a bridge. God has a plan for me on one side, but I have been firmly planted on the other side where I think things should go as I see fit. Your post has helped me walk across the bridge. Not ignoring God's whisper to me is the answer. Turning to Him will make for a more peaceful life—the life He wants me to live. Thank you for the help. I needed it.

I received an email from Pat Swanke, a friend at Feed My Starving Children, about the example Maggie has been so far in her recovery. Maggie needed to rest and be patient, a difficult task due to her nature, but she also lacked the ability to fully comprehend what had happened. With an inner trust in God, which developed in Maggie over the years, she was able to lean on Him without thinking. Pat related how we had so much to learn from the example of the children, as told in Matthew 18:1–4:

Who is greatest in the kingdom of heaven? He called a little child and had him stand among them. And He said, "I tell you the truth, unless you change and become like little children, you will never enter the kingdom of heaven. Therefore, whoever humbles himself like this child is the greatest in the kingdom of heaven."

In 1 Corinthians 1:25, Paul says, "For the foolishness of God is wiser than human wisdom, and the weakness of God is stronger than human strength." It is human nature to applaud and idolize the achievements of man. We marvel at our ability to create buildings, iPhones, and electric vehicles without stopping to compare it to God's creation . . . the heavens, earth, and all living creatures. Which is harder to create—a computer or the mind that makes it happen? Children get it because they don't overthink it. The "wisdom" of the world elevates man over God. We hoped that Maggie's accident could help us see the foolishness of this thinking.

It brought Wendy and me great comfort to think that God was using Maggie for a divine purpose. Was it possible that Maggie had to go through a terrible accident for a part of God's ultimate plan to be fulfilled?

Our longtime friend Bonnie Gasper sent a note telling us of a Bible passage that spoke to her as something very important for Maggie as she continued to heal and to grasp the opportunity that God had given her.

"Hardships are necessities, the difficulties of life that come our way, difficulties we can't righteously escape. They fall to us as our natural lot in life and become a platform, an arena to appropriate and display the sufficiency of His grace. You have been given an arena, sweet Maggie . . . one that spans the ocean."

A Big Day

by Tad Weiss, June 23, 2014

I'm writing to you from our new home in *planta*. We just moved Maggie down about an hour ago and are settling into our new room. We can already tell that Maggie likes the new surroundings. She is much more at peace without the bustle and the noise of the UCI. We have a private room, which is a real blessing. We are getting settled in and will make this home for the next week or so.

Maggie's feeding tube has been removed. The only thing she's hooked up to now is a solution for hydration. The UCI called us around 1:30 to come over and feed Maggie. She has a big appetite. Wendy fed her lunch and then worked on her hair. She needed a bit of a haircut and to get rid of some snarls. Maggie loved the attention, and it was a sweet moment to see her fall asleep while Wendy was cutting and combing her hair.

Maggie was very happy to see two old friends who weren't allowed in the UCI: Bun-Bun and blankie. Both have been with her since early childhood and Maggie gave us a big smile when we pulled them out.

It will take a little time to figure out our routine and the visitation schedule. We can't have any visitors today, but there were five people who showed up at 6:30. We couldn't get the word out soon enough.

Maggie's new doctor, Dr. Falcon, came to see her this evening. She is a young woman, and she speaks English well, so that is a real blessing. Maggie is answering questions in English and in Spanish; this is a truly bilingual recovery! Maggie can't answer all the questions, but she is starting to piece everything together.

We were a little nervous moving to *planta*—kind of like bringing that first child home. But those concerns were quickly alleviated. Now we need to come up with the right activities to keep her occupied and to continue the healing process. I know one thing for sure—we'll be reading a lot of Caring-Bridge messages to her!

"Save us, Lord our God, and gather us from the nations, that we may give thanks to your holy name and glory in your praise" (Psalm 106:47).

Mary Kay Fuhrmann, June 23, 2014

Chip and I are following the progress every moment of the day! We so appreciate your postings and feel connected thanks to you. We were at church last Sunday and they prayed for immediate healing for Maggie. It's working!! I personally want to thank you for posting your journey with Jesus, and to quote Matthew 5:13. "Don't hide your light! Let it shine for all; let your good deeds glow for all to see, so that they will praise your heavenly Father."

Sherri Higdon, June 23, 2014

Wow Maggie! We are watching God heal you! It is growing our faith! I have been reading the updates and often share the news with my kids. Now they come up to me throughout the day and ask, "Mom, are there any new Maggie updates yet?" One day I read to Lana, and as she heard that you were able to eat yogurt, she was so excited that she ran and said, "Graham and Boden, Maggie is eating!!"

CHAPTER TWENTY

Day 20—June 24, 2014

A s predicted, our routine changed as we left the UCI, and this was good.

I went back to the hotel to get a few things, and Wendy stayed with Maggie. I returned to the hospital to take the night shift so Wendy could sleep in the hotel. Moms are so good at that healing thing, and I wanted Wendy to be rested for the day, as I thought it would be a full one.

So Maggie and I got to spend the night together in a private room on the second floor of the Virgen del Rocía hospital in Seville.

Our room was right above the entrance to the UCI on the main floor, and two floors above the emergency room entrance. We had the windows open; it was a nice night for sleeping. The sounds of the city and the hospital filled the air: ambulances coming in with new patients, taxi drivers talking with each other as they waited for a fare, and other conversations from the street.

Maggie was very restless and agitated as I tried to get her to go to sleep at around 11:00. She had been lying in a bed for nineteen full days and she was sick of it! She wanted to get up . . . to walk, to run. She rolled to her right, then to her left and pulled herself up for a couple of seconds, then she lay back down. She kicked her legs in the air up and around and then repeated the process. I searched for words to calm and comfort her. She fell asleep for five minutes, then awakened again three separate times.

Finally at 12:45 a.m. she fell into a deep sleep that lasted until 3:00 a.m. We talked for a while, and she relaxed. She fell asleep again at 4:15 a.m. for an hour. She dozed off, in and out of sleep, and so did I.

The nurses came at 6:00 a.m. to change her bedding, and she fell back asleep. Wendy came at around 8:00 a.m. and took over. Maggie was happy to see her; she was rested and ready for breakfast. I went back to the hotel to eat and sleep.

This would be our new routine. At least one of us would be with Maggie around the clock.

Reliving Maggie's Childhood

by Tad Weiss, June 24, 2014

Last night took me back to when Maggie was a little girl. When you're living through those days, you want them to end, and when they're gone, you want them back. In a very strange way, one of the blessings for us is we do get to relive those days for a short time.

We read to her from the Bible, just like we did when she was five. We hold her hand at night and comfort her so she can fall asleep. We sing to her; Wendy dug out the Mockingbird song from the archives, "Hush little Maggie don't say a word, mamma's gonna buy you a mockingbird. And if that mockingbird won't sing, mamma's gonna buy you a diamond ring. And if that diamond ring turns to brass . . ." I loved singing that song to Maggie.

I sang "Jesus Loves You" to her last night, over and over. This one helped her fall asleep. It is a miracle that the sound of my voice singing anything can make her fall asleep. Maybe it is the right incentive to sleep and not be able to hear my off-key songs!

Maggie is anxious and afraid at night, just like when she was little, but for different reasons. We search for the right words that will comfort her. It usually takes patience and time and the constant presence of a parent, combined with the accumulating need for sleep. The simple words seem to be the best.

"I love you, Maggie."

"I love you too," comes back. Just the words I need to hear.

It is hard to be patient, I pray that her pain will go away, that she will find peace. It's hard to see her in pain, just like when she was five years old. The "owwies" are a little bigger this time.

In the middle of the night, sometime around 4:00, I got the sense that she was starting to put some key pieces together. Yes, she understood she had been in an accident. She understood she was getting better. That she needed to keep her legs still and close her eyes to fall asleep. That sleeping was the best way for her to heal and make the pain go away. Yes, she knows that Jesus loves her and is healing her. I pray that she will continue to gain that understanding today and that it will comfort her.

Although there were many things last night that took me back to when Maggie was five years old, there clearly are signs that she is on the road to a full recovery. Some of the things she says are profound.

Yesterday, she said, "I know there are a lot of *Sevillenos* that want to visit me."

I had to ask Wendy what a *Sevilleno* was. It is a person from Seville!

She told us, "I am very frustrated!" Pieces of the answers she is looking for are there, but they can't quite fit together at this moment.

In the middle of the night, I asked her how she was feeling. I'm not going to print her answer, but suffice to say it was very honest. It made me sad, but it also made me laugh. Our daughter is nothing if not honest.

You're probably expecting the "live every day to its fullest" words of wisdom now, and they certainly would be true. Maggie didn't sign up for this, and Wendy and I didn't plan on a month-long trip to Spain this summer. Life certainly can throw you a curveball. But instead I'm going to go to the Bible, to the truth, to leave with you a few thoughts for today. Many of you have shared these two passages with us over the last nineteen days, and they are words for us all to live by today and tomorrow:

"Therefore, I tell you, do not worry about your life, what you will eat or drink; or about your body, what you will wear. Is not life more than food, and the body more than clothes? Look at the birds of the air; they do not sow or reap or store away in barns, and yet your heavenly Father feeds them. Are you not much more valuable than they? Can any one of you by worrying add a single hour to your life?" (Matthew 6:25–27).

"'For I know the plans I have for you,' declares the Lord, 'plans to prosper you and not to harm you, plans to give you hope and a future'" (Jeremiah 29:11).

These words apply to Maggie, to me, and to you. Do not worry about the future. God is already there, and He has great plans to prosper us, to protect us, to give us hope and a future. Thank You, God; we will live today boldly for You.

Megan, Jason, Justin, and Ava, June 24, 2014

Your post today made me stop and think. We are in the exact stage you refer to, with our own babies. And on the days that seem endless, this reminds me to take a step back and remember that each day is a gift.

Madeline Marfe, June 24, 2014

Maggie U Betcha! You're going to be all well . . . *paciencia*.
U Betcha us *Sevillenos* want to visit you all the time . . .
U Betcha we will keep praying for your healing and peace of mind.

Te quiero . . . Una Sevillena y Neo Yorkina

Mary Schmidt, June 24, 2014

Reading today's post, I thought about a marathon. As you know, once you get to mile twenty, and twenty-one, it is the real test of your ability to continue moving forward. So, you are on day twenty and you are moving forward. These are the hard, dig-down miles. We are on the side of the road with our cow bells cheering you on!

We received word from Morgan Reiss that the Hospital Universitario del Rocio informed her that Maphre (the bus insurance company) would cover Maggie's medical expenses until she would be discharged. We weren't worried about the medical expenses, and we trusted God that it would get worked out. But with two-plus weeks in the ICU, life-saving equipment and care, and multiple procedures, it was a comfort to know that the bus company was stepping up so soon.

Morgan continued to do an incredible job coordinating on the insurance side. Here's her update to FrontierMEDEX, the travel insurance company, on Maggie's status and our move to *planta* from June 20:

> Maggie is awake and at times quite alert, looking at her parents, smiling, moving quite a lot, and even following basic commands. The doctors are pleased with her steady and rapid recovery. They caution that this will be an "ongoing process" after such a head injury. It could take as long as six months to fully assess and understand the consequences.
>
> Maggie's parents are thrilled, not just with her daily progress. They were told that once Maggie was transferred from the ICU and spent several days under observation, a medical evacuation could likely occur. They do not wish to move Maggie while any risk remains, but they are starting to get excited about the prospect of taking her home. Now might be a good time to begin this conversation with Maggie's doctors.

A Full Day in Planta
by Tad Weiss, June 24, 2014

Maggie was sleeping peacefully at 8:00 this morning when Wendy came to relieve me. I went back to the hotel to rest, and Maggie continued to sleep off and on throughout the morning.

Maggie had a bath, and new doctors and a physical therapist came in to do a full evaluation. They put her through the paces, asking her questions in English and Spanish, also testing her reflexes and range of motion. Wendy was there to repeat the questions when the Spanish accent was a little tough for Maggie to understand. The questions she answered she generally got right, but often she just does not answer. She did not know the year. We know this is normal; she occasionally makes sense, but often seems eager to say something that comes out gibberish. Overall, she seems more settled and at peace, knowing that either Wendy or I are here with her.

Maggie had pain in her right arm when the physical therapist was working with her today, so she had two additional X-rays to determine whether she has broken bones in her elbow and shoulder. I imagine we will get the results tomorrow. We had thought it was amazing that she hadn't broken any bones in her arms or legs, considering how far she was thrown.

Meanwhile, back in the hotel, I was getting a nap in when the bat phone went off. It tends to go off at very inopportune times, like during a nap. It was our health insurance liaison working on some details for our eventual return, so it was an important call but not the best timing.

I hit the wall this afternoon and had a minor meltdown. Fortunately, Wendy held the team together. It is funny how these hit us. We were both so strong during Maggie's pelvic surgery, but then on the first day in *planta*, her first day out of the UCI with no tubes and no monitors, I crash.

I'm sure it was a combination of factors, one being the lack of sleep. But our new routine has its challenges too. While Maggie was in the UCI, our main stress was mental, and the physical demands weren't that hard. Now we've switched over to the physical demands and we're probably not in great shape. But I'll get a good night's sleep tonight, and Wendy is strong and ready for the night. We do welcome your prayers, that we'll get enough sleep and have the stamina to care for Maggie around the clock. Many of you already anticipated this need for us.

Maggie is catching up on her sleep and making great strides. She knew where she went to high school and to college today, which she didn't know yesterday. You can see her consistently putting more of the pieces together, and we've been told by a few of you that everything she's experiencing is normal. God allows certain parts of her memory to come back sooner while other parts need more time. He has the perfect plan for her healing, and we have no fear regarding this.

I walk by the UCI waiting area often and see all the people waiting to be with their loved ones. We were in that group for eighteen days. I'm glad we no longer have to do that, but my heart aches for the people waiting. You can see the pain and worry on their faces. My eyes have been opened to the pain and suffering in the world, and I hope to do a better job of comforting and encouraging others when we return. You all have been the perfect example of how to do that, so thank you once again!

Please pray that Maggie's immediate healing would continue at such a pace that by Friday we can start to plan our return to Minnesota for the following week. We'll be here as long as we need to be to ensure Maggie can return safely, but we are sure hoping that day is in the near future.

"This is what the Lord says: 'Stand at the crossroads and look; ask for the ancient paths, ask where the good way is, and walk in it, and you will find rest for your souls'" (Jeremiah 6:16).

Sarie Anderson, June 24, 2014

I know what it is like to be in *planta* in a hospital in Spain, as I have been hospitalized twice and my husband spent eight days in the hospital this past spring. They really do expect the family to do a lot of the care for the patient. The Lord impressed upon my heart to pray for you during these days as you tag team in caring for Maggie. As a result, you will have very little time together. This is a new scenario for you to adjust to and I wanted to let you know that I am specifically praying for you both in this. The first seventeen days were intense, and you could spend much of it together to pray, process, and simply be together. This will now be harder, and though you want nothing more than to care for beautiful Maggie, I am praying you can still find time to be together, as you will need this.

CHAPTER TWENTY-ONE

Day 21—June 25, 2014

Morgan emailed St. Olaf and emphasized how Wendy and I were both needed on a permanent basis to care for Maggie, taking shifts to calm, encourage, feed, prompt, and stimulate her. She stated that we were the primary and often times only people on hand to provide Maggie with full-time care and attention, which the doctors had stated was fundamental for her progress.

Morgan pushed this reality, as she had been told that the family companion benefit for Maggie's return (airfare, hotel, and food) was limited to just one family member, but in past cases where FrontierMEDEX had assisted, it had been possible to arrange for two family members when that level of care was necessary. She reached out to St. Olaf (the policyholder) to see if they could be of assistance to help make this happen.

The initial response from FrontierMEDEX was that we had coverage for one economy class ticket, plus $5,000 of incidental expenses, capped at $300 per day. We couldn't see how flying Maggie back on a commercial flight would work. We were going to need some divine intervention around this one.

Healing Rain

by Tad Weiss, June 25, 2014

Wendy spent the night with Maggie and didn't sleep. Maggie would sleep for ten minutes, then wake up and need a hug or a squeeze of the hand from her mommy. Ten minutes of sleep, five minutes awake, all through the night. We are so thankful we can be here around the clock to give her those hugs.

Right before her accident, Maggie told us in a phone call that she needed a hug. We've got some catching up to do, Maggie!

Maggie's physical therapist, Toni, came this morning. Toni gave Maggie a shower for the first time, and you could tell that Maggie loved it! The warm, healing water pouring over her, soothing her body, cleansing her skin, washing her hair. Healing rain. We put her back to bed and Toni worked with her on her range of motion. There is some pain when she extends her right arm at the elbow, and we found out from the doctor later in the morning that she has a small fracture.

Dr. Flores, one of the main UCI doctors, stopped by to see how Maggie is doing. The *planta* rehabilitation doctors are in charge now but he still checks in on her. I met with one of Maggie's new doctors and everyone is pleased with her progress.

Maggie has a big appetite and is eating very well. Last night, she ate all her dinner, except the okra.

Wendy said, "It looks horrible, but let's try it."

Maggie ate a bite, got a pained look on her face, and said, "It tastes horrible too!"

So, Maggie's taste buds are working, and she's able to tell us what she likes and doesn't like.

One of our challenges is comforting Maggie throughout the day. For the first two weeks, she was insulated from the pain by being unconscious and through various medications and pain-killers, but those protections are now gone. She gets a concerned look on her face frequently, and we need to tell her constantly that she's okay, that she's healing and getting better each day. She doesn't have the perspective we do, and she is in pain.

As my friend Bret reminded me, she did get hit by a bus. She has multiple broken bones that are healing. She had stitches in multiple places, and she's got a lot of road rash that is slowly healing. And her brain isn't fully healed to be able to process and to understand that the healing is all good.

So today we're praying for God's healing rain to continue throughout the day. A few of you have referenced the song "Healing Rain"[11] by Michael W. Smith.

Lord, we pray that Your healing rain will fall on Maggie. Help her to not feel pain or be afraid. Help her body and brain continue the immediate healing You have provided to her, and to us. Keep showing us Your miracles, Lord, and give us the faith and strength for this new day. We know that You, Lord Jesus, have the power to heal Maggie immediately. We have seen it with our own eyes. Our hope, our faith, our trust is in You. Amen.

"So Jesus went with him. A large crowd followed and pressed around him. And a woman was there who had been subject to bleeding for twelve years. She had suffered a great deal under the care of many doctors and had spent all she had, yet instead of getting better she grew worse. When she heard about Jesus, she came up behind him in the crowd and touched his cloak, because she thought, 'If I just touch his clothes, I will be healed.' Immediately her bleeding stopped and she felt in her body that she was freed from her suffering" (Mark 5:24–29).

Mark and Diane Sahr, June 25, 2014

So inspired by how God is healing Maggie! Her progress can only be attributed to God's love and her family's encouragement and faith. I am amazed and have never seen such fast progress in my years of working in neuro and rehab units.

When we left for Spain, my seventy-six-year-old parents, Kay and Bernie, dropped everything and flew from their home in Florida to Minnesota to be with Peter.

Dad was showing signs of early dementia, so Mom had her hands full. She wrote to me about how she was convicted by a recent post that she was wishing away moments in life. Moments added together become a period of time. Then we look back on our life and wonder why we didn't appreciate all those times.

She was getting that opportunity, holding hands with Dad as they walked together from our house to the town of Victoria to go to get a cup of coffee. He was a little unsteady, but she enjoyed the moments, knowing they wouldn't last forever and they likely wouldn't get easier. It warmed my heart that she was enjoying those walks and not wishing them away.

Take Action or Trust?

by Tad Weiss, June 25, 2014

Maggie's second full day in *planta* has been a busy one. In addition to her shower, physical therapy, and doctor visit this morning, she's had a couple of snacks and two full meals. She is very hungry and is doing a great job eating. The saline solution IV was removed this morning, so she is no longer hooked up to anything, which is a huge blessing.

It was confirmed this morning that she has a small fracture in her elbow, and the doctors are determining when that can be fixed. She also had a slight fever, but it has reduced throughout the day with medication. That may be why she had such a hard time sleeping last night. Maggie has been more peaceful today, sleeping quite a bit between interruptions.

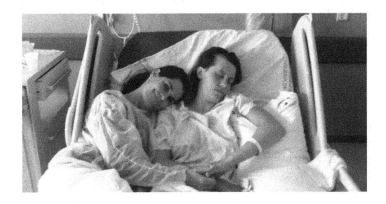

It will be dinnertime soon. They don't even start thinking about dinner in Spain until 8:00 p.m., and that applies to the hospital too. Wendy will go back to the hotel room to get a good night's sleep, and Maggie and I will hang out here for the night.

The Spanish economy is in recession and has been since 2008. The unemployment rate is 30 percent, and the unemployment rate for those under age thirty-five is 60 percent. The country is under forced austerity measures as the high level of social programs and welfare can't be sustained. We're at a public hospital, one of the best in all of Spain, and we are very fortunate to be here. But the cost cuts are hitting here as well. We feel very blessed that Maggie has received the professional care that she has throughout this process, and the doctors and nurses have been incredible. We are ready to come home, though, as soon as Maggie is able to travel.

This leads into the issue Wendy and I are dealing with today, as we seek to discern the best time to bring Maggie home. It is a complicated decision, and it is not totally ours to make. When do we take action and try to get the outcome we feel is best, and when do we leave it up to others? And where does trusting God fit into this? We want to trust God with all our decisions, but we can't just crawl into the fetal position and wait. God gave us a brain for a reason, and He wants us to use it.

How do we know when to act and when to back off and trust? And when we do decide to act, we certainly want to make a wise decision. How do we develop wisdom that will help us not only know when to act, but to make wise decisions when we do? Oh, to have the wisdom of Solomon for making life's most difficult decisions!

Wendy and I have tried to offer everything up to God in prayer first. May Thy will be done, not our own. We certainly know what we want, but we also know that God's ways are higher than ours. We tell God what we think is best, and those end up being many of our prayer requests. But we trust that He knows what is best for us and what is part of His plan, and those are the things He can make happen.

Next, we try to keep our eyes open to what is in His will. He will put the people in place and help make the events happen that are in line with His will. Wendy calls it "God pouring grease on the highway." It's a great comfort when what we're asking for is in line with His plan and happens quickly.

If, on the other hand, we start running into roadblocks, that can often mean that what we think we want is not in His will. It doesn't always play out that simply, but when we put this into practice, we usually find the results end up being in our best interests long-term.

Everyone would like to have wisdom when they make decisions. How do you develop wisdom, preferably without going through a lot of pain and hardship along the way? There's a lot written about this in the Bible. The whole book of Proverbs is from Solomon and is devoted to wisdom. God asked Solomon what he most desired, and Solomon answered that he wanted the wisdom to make wise decisions. God granted it to him.

I spent some time today in Proverbs chapter 3, titled "Further Benefits of Wisdom." Yes, the chapter outlines many of the benefits from gaining wisdom, but I want to know: How do I get wisdom? That can be found in the chapter too, and here are a few of the lessons God gave to Solomon, and to us:

- Do not forget My teaching.

- Let love and faithfulness never leave you.

- Trust in the Lord with all your heart.

- Lean not on your own understanding.

- In all your ways acknowledge Him.

- Honor the Lord with your wealth.

- Do not resist the Lord's discipline.

The instructions we need are in there—everything we need to know and do. So then what? Well, how do you get good at anything? The more you follow God's instructions and practice them daily, the more wisdom you will have.

I'm looking forward to studying His Word deeply in the months and years ahead. The Bible is a living, breathing book that is there for all of us to access. I know that by reading and studying God's teaching, I'll be better able to make decisions in all areas of my life that will benefit others, benefit me, and glorify Him.

"And I have filled him with the Spirit of God, with wisdom, with understanding, with knowledge and with all kinds of skills" (Exodus 31:3).

Leslie Connelly, June 25, 2014

Wendy, I bet you have wanted to crawl into bed next to Maggie since day one! I'm so very happy you have finally been able to do it!! Thanks, Tad, for snapping the photo for all of us moms who have been yearning for Wendy to be able to do this.

There was so much we would have liked to have said in our CaringBridge posts that we couldn't. I guess you could say we hit our breaking point. We were so excited for Maggie to be out of the UCI, but Wendy and I felt like two novices being asked to provide a high level of medical care for Maggie. We didn't have the knowledge or skill, and we were physically and emotionally at a tipping point.

A therapist came once a day, but she was spread way too thin. She showed us what we needed to do for the day ahead. Maggie needed a lot of attention, and it routinely took the staff forty-five minutes to respond to a call for help. We fed her all her meals. Maggie got very agitated, moving her arms and legs and trying to get out of bed. We had to hold her down and tell her she couldn't get up, which she didn't understand.

Wendy removed three stitches from Maggie, changed her, showered her, and changed her bedding. Maggie's days and nights were flipped; she slept a little during the day and then was awake most of the night.

When the physical therapist began to suspect that Maggie had a broken elbow, twenty days after the accident, I went down with Maggie to have an MRI. She had to lie still while the images were being taken, and she couldn't do it. The noise of the machine was loud, and Maggie freaked out. After fifteen minutes of trying to get her to remain motionless, they gave up. Maggie looked shell-shocked.

I met with one of the doctors who had been talking with Navigators about Maggie's transport back home. He said that Maggie should have the surgery on her elbow before going home, and it would take time to schedule the procedure. He also said she would be able to fly home sitting up in a couple of weeks. The comment struck me as odd. Why did he care about Maggie sitting up on the flight home? It became apparent to me that this was the approach the insurance company wanted to take, as a commercial flight home would be much less expensive than a private medical evacuation.

I talked with Wendy, and she agreed that I should call Navigators and lay out our case for why Maggie needed to be flown home. The EIAA insurance policy with Navigators had a $1,000,000 benefit for medical repatriation. It was my job to make the case that it was medically necessary for Maggie to be flown home immediately.

God had blessed me with a logical mind, but my wife and friends would say it didn't always make me fun to deal with. I had the ability to lay out a convincing argument and the stubbornness to persist until I got what I felt was right. I put on my "trial attorney hat" and wrote out all the reasons why now was the time for Maggie to fly home.

I went back to the hotel room with my page full of notes ready to call Navigators and plead our case. This was going to be a slam dunk.

The manager I reached at Navigators was kind but professional. I walked her through all the reasons why Maggie needed an immediate medical evacuation on a private air ambulance. I threw everything at her—the staffing level in *planta*, the care we had to provide, the need for ongoing medical attention and expertise, injuries that were now being discovered twenty days after the accident, and the need to start her rehabilitation now rather than in a couple of weeks.

Despite my best effort, I could tell by her response that my prodigious, logical argument was going nowhere.

With all my talking points exhausted, the conversation was about to end, and not in our favor. With God's prompting, I took a different approach, one I had not thought of or planned out.

I asked the manager if she had children, and she said, "Yes."

I paused. "Can you imagine what it's like to change the diaper of your nineteen-year-old daughter because no one is there to help you, while she's squirming and struggling to get out of bed to try and walk . . .?" Then I broke down. Sobbing on the phone, I was unable to continue.

"It's okay, take your time." Her tone had softened. "I'm here to help . . ."

After two minutes of trying to regain my composure, I was able to mumble, "Our daughter needs to come home now."

A moment passed. Then, "You're right." I heard her swallow. "We will make that happen."

CHAPTER TWENTY-TWO

Day 22—June 26, 2014

Midafternoon, Maggie was sleeping peacefully. She had a shower and a session with her physical therapist, met with the doctors, and had breakfast and lunch. She could drink water now, which was another step of progress. She'd been able to drink juice and thickened water from a spoon but was now able to drink water from a cup without coughing.

So it was a busy first half of the day, and she rested while I wrote.

A Different Routine

by Tad Weiss, June 26, 2014

Good morning to you all in Minnesota. It is a little after 2:00 p.m. here in Seville.

The big news from today is that Maggie can sit up in a chair! This is great progress and another step in her healing. The only problem is that it gets her that much closer to standing up, which she desperately wants to do. We need for her brain to keep healing so she can fully understand the things she can and can't do, but we're not there yet.

Alberto gets to go home today, praise God! We had a nice celebration and farewell with him and his mom, Fina. Alberto has been a huge blessing to us as he entered the UCI three days ahead of Maggie. It has been such an encouragement to see his healing and to know that Maggie is on the same path.

I told Alberto that Maggie is not sleeping during the night, and he said he has the same issue. Maggie doesn't sleep much all night long, maybe one to two hours total through many short naps. Then during the day, she has more activity, and she sleeps a lot more. The tag teaming Wendy and I are doing is an absolute necessity. The one who sleeps at the hotel is rested and sharp, and the one who pulls the all-nighter with Maggie is in a funk. I don't think we could do this without each other.

I am going to try to visit a Christian school that's being built in Seville. Our new friends, Carey and Sharon, are involved in it. Maggie and Peter both attended Chapel Hill Academy (CHA) in Chanhassen from kindergarten through eighth grade, and CHA was a huge blessing in our lives. Faith in God is declining in Spain and all of Europe, and Christian education can help reverse the trend. Wendy and I would like to see the school in person and see if there's anything we can do to help them expand the school.

I saw the chocolate lab puppy again as I was walking back to the hotel this morning. I can't remember the day of the initial meeting with him, but he helped inspire my promise to Maggie that I would get her a puppy when we got back home. I sure hope I read that sign correctly because now I'm committed. If it wasn't from God, I'm sure He's having a good laugh right now.

"I thank my God every time I remember you. In all my prayers for all of you, I always pray with joy because of your partnership in the gospel from the first day until now, being confident of this, that He who began a good work in you will carry it on to completion until the day of Christ Jesus" (Philippians 1:3–6).

Before I called CIEE, I had a conversation with Kathy Tuma, associate director of international and off-campus studies at St. Olaf. I outlined all our concerns, and she promised to contact CIEE as well to advocate for us. She emailed later that she had been in contact with CIEE and that everyone seemed on board in getting Maggie home as quickly as possible. We still needed approval from the doctor that Maggie could travel. Kathy didn't think Monday was reasonable, as it was only four days away, but sometime early the next week was looking possible for us to fly Maggie home.

Thankful hearts

by Tad Weiss, June 26, 2014

It was three weeks ago today that Maggie's accident occurred.

If I'm ever feeling down, I just take myself back to those first few days. What an unbelievable recovery she has made in a short period of time! It is only through God's protection that her life was saved, and through the miracle of His healing powers that she has come so far so fast.

There are many things we relay to you that may sound like we're worried about certain aspects of her recovery. We aren't. We know that God is in control of all the details and the timing of when certain events will take place. God designed our bodies to function, and He also designed how they are to heal.

Today was a great day in *planta* room 122. Although we didn't get much sleep last night, Maggie was awake for most of the day today. That bodes well for the nighttime, and I hope and pray that both Maggie and Wendy will get some good rest tonight. The morning hours at the hospital are filled with a shower, rehabilitation, breakfast, and doctor visits. The afternoon is lunch, some visitors, and various activities to keep Maggie occupied. Maggie and I watched our spring break ski video. She seems to like watching and listening to the music and seeing the action. We talk a lot about future ski trips, and I believe I'll be fighting to keep up with her again in no time.

It has now been two weeks since Maggie's pelvic surgery, which also is hard to believe. We were told that she'd be able to walk on one leg with crutches four weeks after the surgery, so we're halfway there if that prediction is accurate.

Watching her brain heal is fascinating. One example: we go skiing in Jackson Hole, Wyoming, regularly. I asked Maggie where we ski, and she didn't know the answer. Then I asked her what ski runs she likes, and she correctly rattled off two of them, one of which was very obscure.

Each day more and more comes back. It is hard to get her to talk sometimes, but I can get her working through numbers or the alphabet easily. And when she has visitors, she always will say hello and thank you to them. The sweet, considerate, and caring side of Maggie can't be held back by any brain trauma! We know that God will heal her brain completely according to His perfect plan.

As our friend Alberto told me, "We are young. We recover from these types of things quickly!"

"Rooted and built up in him, strengthened in the faith as you were taught, and overflowing with thankfulness" (Colossians 2:7).

My company had scheduled a food packing event at Feed My Starving Children (FMSC) for Thursday, June 26, before Maggie's accident happened. The team at the office went ahead with the event and over one hundred people showed up to pack food and to pray for Maggie. Mark Crea, CEO at FMSC, was there, as were Peter, my parents, and many friends. It brought us great joy that the event continued in our absence.

I received an email from our case manager, Corinne, at FrontierMEDEX that Dr. Templeman at Hennepin County Medical Center (HCMC) had accepted Maggie as a patient upon her return. Dr. Templeman is one of the premier orthopedic surgeons in the country, and we have our friends, the Durenburgers, to thank for helping make this happen. Corinne also said they were checking the availability of air ambulance providers and the earliest availability would be in one week, July 1.

PART TWO

GOING HOME

CHAPTER TWENTY-THREE

Day 23—June 27, 2014

Wendy "slept" with Maggie Thursday night... not a lot of sleep, short little bursts followed by time awake. I arrived a little after 8:00 Friday morning—day twenty-three—and took over, and Wendy went back to the hotel for a quick nap.

Life Is Better with You!

by Tad Weiss, June 27, 2014

Maggie continues to heal very quickly. She is rolling over onto her stomach and answering more and more questions. She likes to count with me, and we made it up to thirty-five today before she got tired and decided the game was over. We watched a video and listened to music.

She has been very fidgety, a combination of being confined to the bed and frustration of not being able to put to words all of her thoughts. The physical therapist, Toni, arrived just in time (an immediate answer to my prayer!) to give Maggie a shower and to comfort her. Wendy was back at noon to feed Maggie and to adjust her bed just right.

It appears that our travel back to Minnesota is coming together! We still have some details to figure out. We ask you to fervently pray that all will come together for our travel back home, that Maggie will be strong enough, and that Wendy and I will be able to get everything wrapped up on this end before we leave. God has been answering those prayers, and we are very encouraged and ready to come home!

I've mentioned in a few posts that we like to go to Jackson Hole, Wyoming. When we were out there in late March, Maggie and I went to a Michael Franti and Spearhead concert. The resort does an end-of-the-season concert to celebrate the ski season, and Michael Franti was the headliner.

We didn't know much about him other than a few songs.

He's from San Francisco and has a "Jesus" look to him, in my opinion. His music is a combination of reggae, hip-hop, and contemporary music. He also has a very socially conscious and loving view of all humanity. We loved seeing him in concert, and he immediately became one of my favorite artists.

One of the songs he sang is titled "Life Is Better with You."[12] The song is about a special relationship between two people and I think of Wendy every time I hear the song. There are many verses that I just love; one says that nobody does that thing you do better than you.

Many of you know this, but the "thing" that Wendy does is serve others. She serves her family and children in big ways and little ways. She has faithfully served God and our kids while they were at Chapel Hill Academy and Minnetonka High School by volunteering at the school. She served as the leader of WATCH, a youth program at Westwood Community Church, and she also serves in the nursery. She is currently a high school small group leader at Westwood, and she pours her heart and soul into those girls. She is the children's supervisor for BSF, leading a program that teaches two hundred young children about God and the Bible while their moms and grandmas study the Word. I'll stop there, but you get the idea. She loves children, she loves to serve, and she is very good at it.

There have been times when I wished my wife would serve less. I'd like to see her spend more time at home or more time taking care of herself. Some of this is selfishly motivated. But I think over time I've become more comfortable with the idea that she has been called by God to serve. He has blessed her with many talents to use in this purpose, and she has answered the call faithfully. I am so blessed to be married to a woman that loves God first, loves me and our family second, and loves all of you as well.

When her time on earth is done, I know that Jesus's first words for Wendy will be, "Well done, my good and faithful servant."

It has been an honor to walk through this journey with her over the past few weeks, and I know our marriage will be enriched from it. Wendy, life is truly better with you!

As I've been listening to this song a lot with Maggie over the past week, it dawned on me that "Life Is Better with You" could really be a song about the relationship we can have individually with Jesus. I don't think that Michael Franti wrote it with this in mind, but it works perfectly. Life is better with Jesus. He is the way, the truth, and the life. We all need Him, and most of us have tried to find life's answers in other ways only to come up empty handed. He is the only way that we can find true peace, complete joy, and happiness in our lives. He is the path to eternal life. There are many times when we all feel alone, but He will always be there with us if we simply ask Him to. Thank You, Jesus. I'm not afraid to be alone. Life is better with You!

"Each of you should use whatever gift you have received to serve others, as faithful stewards of God's grace in its various forms" (1 Peter 4:10).

Midmorning, I received a call from Morgan that an air ambulance had been found for Maggie, and they would be coming to get her that night. I couldn't believe it! I called Wendy, and she started packing up the hotel room—our home for the last three weeks.

The itinerary came in from FrontierMEDEX at around 11:00 a.m.:

Air Ambulance arrive: Seville, Spain 23:50, local time
Ground Ambulance arrive: Virgen del Rocio, 2:00 a.m., local time
Air Ambulance depart: Seville, Spain 3:00 a.m., local time

The medical air transport team would land in twelve hours and arrive at the hospital soon after that. Maggie and I were scheduled for the following flights, five in all:

Seville to Karlsruhe/Baden, Germany, arrive 5:00 a.m., local time
Karlsruhe/Baden to Keflavik, Iceland, arrive 8:15 a.m., local time
Keflavik to Goose Bay, Canada, arrive 9:35 a.m., local time
Goose Bay to Hamilton, Ontario, Canada, arrive 12:15 p.m., local time
Hamilton to Minneapolis, arrive 1:45 p.m., local time

I could accompany Maggie on the plane and take my briefcase; that was it. Wendy would fly back tomorrow with all of Maggie's luggage and ours from Seville to Barcelona to Amsterdam to Minneapolis.

We had the rest of the day to pack and tie up loose ends. I worked feverishly to get all the Spanish medical records to the doctors, via Dropbox, who would be waiting for us in Minneapolis. The language barrier made this tough. I received an email from Dr. Templeman saying not to worry. They would take their own X-rays once Maggie arrived, and they would be ready and waiting for us to arrive in Minneapolis.

We also had a few hours to see our friends from Seville one last time. Word got out quickly, and we had a blessed gathering with Morgan, Jorge, Paqui, Jaime, Madeline, Sara, and Miha.

At around 9:00 p.m., Wendy kissed us goodbye and went back to the hotel to finish packing and to try and get some sleep before her flight the next morning. Morgan, Maggie, and I were in the hospital room, waiting for the air ambulance team to arrive. We had thought there was a chance to go home in four days, and suddenly today was the day!

I was tired but incredibly excited, unsure of what this experience was going to look like, but trusting that God was in charge of all the details.

I couldn't help but smile when I remembered Maggie's claim that she'd be ready to go home after twenty-eight days. She'd beaten even her own prediction and was going home on day twenty-three!

Coming Home!
by Tad Weiss, June 27, 2014

It is with great joy that I can tell you we are coming home!

Travel plans have come together very quickly. Only one of us can fly with Maggie on the way back, along with a medical team and the pilots. I will stay with Maggie, and Wendy has a commercial flight booked for Saturday morning.

Our plane will make a few stops for refueling and arrive in Minneapolis on Saturday afternoon. Maggie will be transferred directly to the hospital. Wendy's commercial flight will arrive a few hours later.

God is so good, and He has answered so many of our prayers throughout this journey. We have many people to thank but there isn't time to do an adequate job.

We look forward to celebrating with you in person. We'll try to keep CaringBridge updated, but there will be a gap in our posts for a while.

God's team, His angel army has rallied around Maggie and our family. Bless you and keep praying!!

"For whoever wants to save their life will lose it, but whoever loses their life for me will find it" (Matthew 16:25).

Cassie Allen, June 27, 2014

Seriously?! What an *awesome* God we serve! Thank You, Lord! *So so so* happy!

Frank Mina, June 27, 2014

Have a beautiful trip back home and we will never forget all of you, Tad, Wendy, and Maggie . . . God bless you all!

Madeline Marfe, June 27, 2014

Gracias Padre Nuestro, thank You our Father for giving Tad and Wendy and Maggie all the energy, peace, and wisdom through Your powerful love. May Maggie feel peace and awareness of how near she is getting to all her loved ones in Minnesota. We love her in Seville very much, but her home is with you there, so we *Sevillenos* are passing the baton to you, her dear family and friends in Minnesota.

The transport team showed up at our hospital room on time. At 11:30 p.m., Dr. Evelyn and nurse Harald arrived, along with three of the Spanish nurses from the hospital. It felt like the cavalry had just walked in. The doctor and nurse were a German crew, but they spoke English flawlessly. This wasn't their hospital, but they were in charge now, and they took control of the situation. They started measuring Maggie's vitals and getting her ready to transport. They issued directions, and everyone jumped into action.

The ground ambulance arrived at 2:00 a.m. We left the room and worked our way down to the ground level, where Maggie was loaded into the back of the ambulance along with the medical team. I rode up front with the ambulance driver.

We drove from the hospital through the city. The lights of the ambulance were on, but there was no need for the siren, as the streets were quiet.

I love the *Bourne* movies with Matt Damon, and I felt like I was in one of those films, riding in an ambulance at night with foreign traffic signs.

We drove to the private part of the airport. The ambulance driver, doctor, and I went inside to show our identification and papers. We were let through and drove onto the airfield toward the plane.

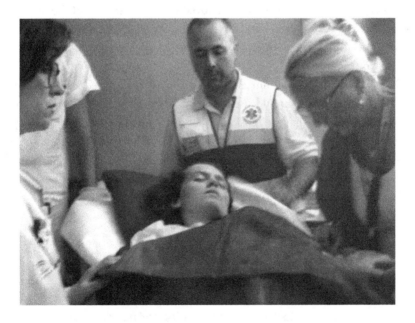

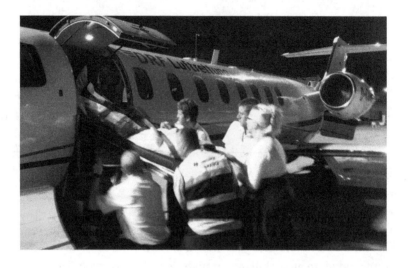

The Lear 45 was a beautiful plane and waited for us on the runway. The medical team, pilots, and ambulance driver all loaded Maggie's stretcher onboard. I was told to climb aboard, head to the back, and buckle in. There were two leather chairs for me to spread out. The seats had been removed in the midsection of the plane, making room for Maggie's stretcher and all the medical equipment needed for the flight.

Within minutes, the plane taxied to the runway, and we took off on the first leg of our journey.

Once we were in the air, nurse Harald asked me if I needed a shot of whiskey! I said no but that I really could use a beer. There was no beverage service on this flight though. I'm sure that the tension, excitement, and fatigue of our journey were written across my face, but I was too amped up to sleep on the first leg of the flight.

We had an hour and a half layover in Germany. It was 5:00 a.m., so there wasn't much activity at the hangar. I went into the lounge, poured a cup of coffee, and shot off a quick CaringBridge post.

Maggie Is in Very Good Hands!

by Tad Weiss, Jun 27, 2014

Maggie and I are in Karlsruhe Baden, Germany for a refuel stop. Just wanted to send a quick picture that she is in very good hands.

We have a doctor and nurse caring for her on each leg of the journey. Thank You, God, for orchestrating such unbelievable care and talented people to take care of Maggie!

A few minutes later, a guy showed up with a gift for me—a German beer! Harald remembered our conversation, and I just smiled and laughed. Why not? I was along for the ride at this point.

CHAPTER TWENTY-FOUR

Day 24—June 28, 2014

Wendy's travel followed a more conventional but challenging route. She was up at 4:00 a.m. for her 7:00 a.m. flight from Seville to Barcelona. She had five suitcases total—the two small ones we had brought and Maggie's three larger ones. She checked three bags and carried on two.

She had a long layover in Barcelona and went to get a cup of coffee and something to eat. The Holy Spirit told her to get moving for her next flight, which seemed odd since she had a few hours, but she obeyed.

Navigating a foreign airport, she determined she needed to get in line for a kiosk. It was a long line, and when she got to the front, she was told she had to go to another line to pay a tariff for having too many bags. She was the fifth person in that line.

Air France was on strike, and within minutes the line grew from five people to over two hundred! To make matters worse, the line wasn't moving. Wendy started to panic that she would miss her flight and turned around to talk with a man behind her. He asked the people in front if Wendy could jump the line. She quickly paid her tariff, ran back to the gate, checked in, and made her flight to Amsterdam.

Wendy picked up the three bags she had checked and had to juggle five suitcases through the Amsterdam airport. They didn't post the gate numbers on the digital boards, and she didn't know what to do. A quick prayer, and she saw a kiosk that had the information she needed.

At the gate, the agent put her through the wringer. Why did she have so many bags? Why was her flight booked late yesterday? Was she fleeing the country? She explained the situation, which you couldn't make up, and the agent let her through.

When Wendy boarded the plane, a flight attendant had heard her story and gave her a big hug.

Just as she was settling in, she looked up to see some friends of ours, Jim and Kathy Thomsen, who were returning from a trip to Europe. They'd been following our story on CaringBridge and suspected that Wendy might be on their flight.

Once they had landed in Minneapolis, they helped Wendy get through customs and retrieve her bags. A couple of friends picked her up at the airport, and she made it home Saturday evening.

Back in Minnesota!
by Tad Weiss, June 28, 2014

Maggie, Wendy, and I are all back in Minnesota! Wendy's commercial flight from Amsterdam just landed and she is at home.

Maggie and I landed at the MSP airport around 2:00 p.m. and were brought to Hennepin County Medical Center. We've been settling in and meeting the new nurses and doctors.

The care that Maggie received on her flights was fantastic. She handled the travel very well and slept for the majority of the fourteen hours of flight time. It's hard to believe we were in our hospital room in Seville twenty-four hours ago. Thank you so much for all your thoughts and prayers, specifically for our safe travel back home and for Maggie's healing. We know we have a long road ahead for her recovery, but we are so thankful we can continue the journey here in Minnesota. The last forty-eight hours have been a whirlwind and we're all hoping to get a good night's rest. Maggie is sleeping peacefully now, and we hope that will continue through the night.

"Give thanks to the Lord, for he is good; his love endures forever" (1 Chronicles 16:34).

Rob Reiskytl, June 28, 2014

Welcome home to all of you!! I'm sure it is with mixed emotions that you left Seville and all the wonderful new friends God brought into your life. We are so glad your travels went smoothly and that Maggie made it without complications. We look forward to seeing how God will continue to use the situation to bring glory to His name.

CHAPTER TWENTY-FIVE

Day 25—June 29, 2014

Back home, we were grateful to be in great and capable hands at Hennepin County Medical Center (HCMC). The medical team was fantastic, and it was a relief not to need an interpreter. We were in the absolute best place for Maggie's recovery and rehabilitation.

A Huge Team Effort

by Tad Weiss, June 29, 2014

Good morning to you all from Minneapolis! It feels good to type those words. And yes, it feels a bit strange too. We spent over three weeks in Seville, Spain. Maggie, Wendy, and I were incredibly loved and cared for by the people of Seville. They have become our friends for life, and we already miss them. We will see them sometime soon under happier circumstances. But it does feel marvelous to be back in Minnesota!

Maggie had a lot of visitors on her last day in Seville. As she said a few days ago, "There are a lot of *Sevillenos* that want to visit me!"

Maggie's travel back home was "room to room," from the hospital room in Seville to her new room at HCMC in Minneapolis. A doctor and nurse from Germany met us in our hospital room late Friday night and took over Maggie's care. From there it was an ambulance ride to the Seville airport and loading Maggie onto the plane.

The company that flew the first four legs for us was DRF Luftrettung. Along with the medical team were two pilots, Mags, and me. The first leg was a little out of the way but that was to DRF's headquarters, where we switched flight crews. The plane had a four-and-a-half-hour range, and the flight crews are also restricted as to the amount of time they can be on duty. The first crew flew in from somewhere to meet us, handled the transfer from the hospital, and then the first leg of the journey. They had completed a full day.

Once we landed in Baden, Maggie stayed on the plane with a medical team member, and I hung out in the hangar for an hour and a half. It was 5:30 a.m., and I hadn't slept since Thursday night. I checked in with Wendy and figured out how to make a CaringBridge post on my iPhone.

We took off again, this time heading to Lefkavik, Iceland, a three-and-a-half-hour flight. Maggie and I slept the entire way.

We flew to Iceland and had a forty-five-minute stop to re-fuel. Then on to Goose Bay in Newfoundland, also a three-and-a-half-hour flight that we slept quite a bit on.

In Goose Bay, there was a Russian flight crew on the ground with a huge transport plane. One of the guys spoke English and I asked him what they were transporting: four helicopters from the US to Turkey. Now that is a big plane!

Another forty-five-minute refueling stop and on to Hamil-ton Ontario, Canada, near Detroit. In Hamilton, we changed planes and transport companies. We switched to a company called Latitude from Canada for the last flight to Minneapolis. This required a switch of aircraft as well as crew. The flight into Minneapolis was short, about an hour and a half.

We were met by a Health East ambulance that drove us to HCMC. We arrived at HCMC twenty-two hours after leaving the hospital room in Seville. It is hard to put to words the pro-fessionalism and care of the air ambulance crews. They handle extremely difficult situations with grace and skill.

I haven't talked to Wendy much, but she landed on time in Minneapolis at around 7:00 p.m. She had all of Maggie's lug-gage for a two-month stay in Spain as well as our luggage, so she was juggling a lot. She ran into our friends Jim and Kathy on the flight, and they helped her get through customs. She said she didn't think she could have done it on her own. Just another example of God arranging a "coincidence" at just the right time. Wendy went home to sleep and is on her way to the hospital now.

Since we've been at HCMC, I think I've talked to ten dif-ferent doctors. Maggie had X-rays taken of her pelvis and arm. I just received an update that she's on the back end of the timeframe that trauma doctors work with, as her accident was over twenty-five days ago. They are reviewing all the records and scans from Spain to see if any additional work needs to be done, but we are likely moving into the rehabilitation phase. Maggie is speaking a lot more today, but her instincts still tell her to rip out the tubes and get out of bed. Even with her hands restrained, she has ripped out three IVs! She is sneaky and just a little naughty! The medical staff is realizing that they will have their hands full. But each day brings better understanding of the situation and her condition, so we are hopeful that this will translate into more cooperation very soon.

I was talking with Maggie early this morning and she asked me what injuries she needed to be afraid of. I asked her if she remembered the most often spoken instruction Jesus gave us.

I said, "Do not . . ."

And she said, ". . . be afraid."

I'm sure today will be a busy day with the doctors and hospital staff. I hope to go see Peter play basketball at the U of M with his Minnetonka teammates. I haven't seen my buddy for twenty-five days. We'll start to figure out the schedule here at HCMC and will keep you updated. We will let you know when Maggie will be able to accept visitors and what the hours are.

Many of you have asked how you can help us. For now, continue keeping Maggie and us in your thoughts and prayers. Jesus is healing Maggie; let Him heal you today too. Your prayers are being answered, so keep praying!

"Jesus went throughout Galilee, teaching in their synagogues, proclaiming the good news of the kingdom, and healing every disease and sickness among the people" (Matthew 4:23).

Joelle Syverson, June 29, 2014

We are so grateful for God's provision in all the details of bringing the three of you back to Minnesota safely!! This story continues to unfold before our eyes of a faithful God who heals, is sovereign, trustworthy, merciful, and loving, and is in control! We have a larger glimpse of God's kingdom at work in our own lives because of all of you.

Ann Lavelle, June 29, 2014

Now begins the work of God in Minneapolis!!! Thanks for the updates. We continue to pray for Maggie! We thank God for His angels from Seville to MSP to HCMC.

Wendy slept at our house for the first time in almost a month, while I stayed with Maggie at HCMC. I was sleeping in a chair when a team of six doctors came in the room and flipped on the light to start checking on Maggie. They were all in different stages of their careers, but it was an impressive show of the medical system in the US.

Wendy came down in the morning with my mom and dad, which freed me to go see Peter with my parents.

Pete was going into his senior year of high school, and he played on the Minnetonka basketball team. As with most high-level sports these days, the season becomes year-round. He was playing a game that summer day with his teammates at the University of Minnesota, only a ten-minute drive from the hospital. I couldn't wait to see him and to watch some basketball, one of my favorite things to do!

It was a few minutes until game time when I walked into the gym with my mom and dad. The guys were going through a layup line, getting loose for the game. Peter saw me and came over to give me the biggest hug ever—a full minute just squeezing each other so hard. I'm sure some people in the stands wondered what we were doing, but we didn't care. I told him how much I loved him and to go play a great game, then sat down to watch.

I wish I could say that the previous twenty-six days had refined me as it relates to watching a basketball game, but it hadn't! I quickly returned to being a homer parent and letting the referees know all the mistakes they were making. But it felt so good to see my son play, to watch the team, and to have my first glimpse of normal in a long time.

They won the game, which made it even better.

CHAPTER TWENTY-SIX

Day 26—June 30, 2014

We had a fantastic first full day in Minnesota. Maggie was doing great, and it was easy to see that her recovery would be accelerated by being back home. The medical team at HCMC was so thorough and skilled; it was truly a blessing to see a team at full strength taking care of Maggie.

The word *team* kept coming up. There had been so many teams taking care of our daughter. She'd been seen by no less than ten different doctors. Every possible specialty that could come into play had checked her out. There were the obvious ones—the trauma team and the neurology team. Yesterday she was also checked out by an occupational therapist and a speech pathologist, as well as an ear-nose-throat physician. I felt comfort that she was in the care of so many experts as she began the journey of her recovery at home.

Reunion

by Tad Weiss, June 30, 2014

Today they did a swallow X-ray (with barium) to make sure all the fluids Maggie consumes are going to the right place. Praise God, we had good results. There is a small amount of fluid leaking into her airway when she swallows, but more viscous fluids and solids go down just fine. This basically means she does not require surgery to repair anything.

The other part of Maggie's recovery that we are incredibly pleased with is how well she's received family and a few visitors. We didn't know how she'd react. Would she remember all the important people in her life when she saw them again? Would she be sad or confused? She was visited by Peter, Matthew, both sets of grandparents, aunts, uncles, cousins, and two dear friends from St. Olaf. The visits were great for Maggie and for all of us.

Back on day thirteen, our post was titled "Homesick" and I'm truly amazed that I can write about a homecoming reunion with family and friends less than two weeks later. I remember day thirteen clearly; it was the first time we'd gotten our heads above water enough to even think that we might be able to come home. Thank God for answered prayer and for a very quick return home for Maggie, Wendy, and me.

We are in for a long period of rehabilitation, but we are overjoyed with the progress Maggie makes every day. We specifically ask that you pray the following:

- Praises for the good news regarding bones knitting together, elbow and throat not needing surgery, and overall progression of (immediate) healing.
- Continued patience, rest, and healing; understanding of what she can and cannot do.
- Continued "team" wisdom and discernment regarding care and treatment.
- That Maggie will continue to get into an "awake during the day with small naps, and sleeping at night" schedule, and that we would be able to rest well, so we can effectively care for her.

Jill Sievers, June 30, 2014

Thank you for your words and wisdom through your journey and highlighting what we should be focusing on in our own lives. This is going to be a very special book one day. Praying for your specific requests.

As happy as we were to just move on, we still had business to attend to in Spain.

In addition to corresponding with Morgan, I had an email string going with both Javier at RZS and Carlos at Garrigues. Javier needed information on the insurance policy with EIAA Navigators, and I was requesting digital images of the accident scene from Carlos.

CHAPTER TWENTY-SEVEN

Day 27—July 1, 2014

Maggie had another good day as she continued to adjust at HCMC. We received a number of visits throughout the days from various doctors, and we started to talk about what her rehabilitation would look like.

Her elbow did not need surgery, so that was a praise! They removed the cast on her arm and replaced it with a brace, which was much more comfortable.

When she drank water, some of it went down the wrong tube and made her cough. She also spoke in a whisper, so they wanted to do a throat test to make sure nothing was wrong. For this test, they had her drink barium, allowing them to see where the fluid was going on the scan. It tastes bad and most people take their time and fight it.

The nurse looked a little sheepish as she held out the glass. "Sorry, but we need you to drink this . . ."

Before she could even get the words out, Maggie grabbed the glass and slammed it down.

The medical team just started laughing. That's our Maggie! We weren't concerned that she'd resist doing her rehabilitation; she'd probably do double what they asked her to do. That girl has *mucho ánimo!*

The neurologist talked with us about brain trauma and what we could expect. We had literally seen improvement in Maggie's condition every day, which made it easier for us to envision total healing in the future. Steady improvement wasn't normal, and we'd been warned to expect good days and bad days, but we loved seeing the improvement.

I prayed with Maggie, and when I was done, I asked if she wanted to add anything.

She said yes. After taking a moment, she carefully said, "I want to make a difference and to honor and glorify God."

I had to stop and think. I really didn't recall either of us saying that to her recently, so she wasn't repeating something we'd told her.

Our dear Maggie was indeed making a difference, as well as honoring and glorifying God!

Immediate Healing

by Tad Weiss, July 1, 2014

Back on day twelve, after one of our evening visits with Maggie, we had a powerful prayer circle. Only one person could go into the UCI with us to translate, but three others waited out in the waiting area. We gathered in a circle to pray, as was our custom. We all took turns, and I continued to ask for patience and trust in God's timing for Maggie's healing.

During the prayer, Henry, a pastor from Nigeria, took over. Man, could that guy pray. I was overcome with the intensity and the fervor with which he prayed. He was the first one to pray for "immediate healing."

"Jesus, You are the one who can heal this girl, and we pray that You heal her immediately! We trust You Father, we know You can do this, so please do it!!"

Angela, a woman of God from the same church, took over. "Lord Jesus, we know that You can do this, and we fervently and humbly ask that You heal this girl immediately!!"

My hair was on end. Yes, this is how you pray!!

Wow! That was it!! Why don't we pray for immediate healing? If God can create the world in six days, and raise His Son Jesus from the dead, He certainly can heal our daughter immediately.

The reason I hadn't thought to ask for immediate healing is I knew the process was going to take time. And we also were learning that patience thing. It seemed contradictory to ask for immediate healing and at the same time pray for patience. But it became clear to me at that prayer circle that we should pray for both, and we did. God has answered our prayers right before our eyes, and the healing of Maggie has been nothing short of a miracle!

When we think of immediate healing we think in terms of the Bible stories.

Jesus touches the blind man and he can see. He touches the lame and they can walk, right away. In all these stories, the healing is immediate. It happens instantly. When we started this prayer, Maggie didn't jump out of bed and put on her running shoes. She also didn't return to full brain capacity right away. So how can this be answered prayer? Was her healing immediate, or was God's answer to our prayer request a "no" or a "not yet"?

I strongly believe God's answer was and is yes, and her healing is immediate, according to God's perfect timing. We have seen daily progress that shows us that Maggie is healing, and we are confident she will return to 100 percent in both her body and brain.

The healing process needs to be a slow one though. Would we rather she jump out of bed today, regain 80 percent of her abilities, and we're done? Or would we rather be patient, let the healing process run its course, and have her regain 100 percent of her function? Would we rather she regain 80 percent of her brain function immediately and be done? Or would we rather be patient, go through the rehabilitation process, and have her mind be 100 percent again? The answer is obvious. We want our daughter to be 100 percent in both body and mind. God and the doctors are performing that healing before our eyes for Maggie, and He is doing it immediately. The process has started!

When we pray to God about anything, we think we know what we want for the answer. But God's ways are higher than ours, and His knowledge of what is best for us greatly exceeds any knowledge we can have. We need to trust that He knows what is best for us.

How many times have I prayed for something I wanted to be different in my life, and when it didn't happen in a few days, a week, or a month, I simply gave up and quit doing the things I could do to help make it happen. I just wouldn't give God the time to make the change, according to His timing. It had to be on my timetable.

When we pray to God, we should bring all our heart's desires to Him. He will answer prayers that are in His will, but He also will do it according to the timing that fits His perfect plan. This has been easy for us to see with Maggie. But the same thing applies to all our prayers. Bring your petitions, requests, and prayers to God. Do your part, and make the changes that you need to make to help the change happen. But then trust in God, in His timing, and in His perfect plan. He will answer your prayers at the time that He knows is best.

In my devotion time yesterday, I read from the book *Prayers that Bring Healing*,[13] a gift to Maggie and us from Angela. The intro is titled "Expect to be Healed." It talks about placing a "demand" on the anointing, to push forward to the place where immediate healing can happen and to overcome all the obstacles along the way. Too often we don't receive the healing we so desire because we don't push through the challenges, and we don't truly expect a miracle to happen.

We occasionally get a glimpse or understanding of God's perfect timing. After some time has passed, we can see that God waited for a reason. At the moment it didn't make sense, but time gives us perspective.

When it doesn't seem like God is answering your prayers, *keep praying!* Keep reading the Bible, keep talking with Him, keep worshipping Him, keep making the changes that you know that you need to make. He will reveal to you His good, pleasing, and perfect will. Your prayers will begin to align with this will, and He will answer your prayers.

"As the heavens are higher than the earth, so are my ways higher than your ways and my thoughts than your thoughts" (Isaiah 55:9).

CHAPTER TWENTY-EIGHT

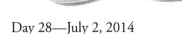

Day 28—July 2, 2014

In an event like we were experiencing, there were many favorite moments, and day twenty-eight held one of them. Maggie was receiving a full range of treatments, one of which was speech therapy.

The therapist started off easy. "Maggie, can you name three colors for me?"

Maggie thought for a while, and then answered, "Blue, red, and black."

"Okay, very good," the therapist replied. "Now name three animals."

Maggie thought hard and answered, "Dog, cat, and horse."

"That's great, Maggie." The therapist continued. "Now this one will be harder. Can you name three countries?"

Maggie scrunched her nose for a couple of seconds, then rattled off: "Albania, Lithuania, and Georgia!"

I about fell out of my chair laughing! It was one of those moments where I knew she was going to make it all the way back.

I Am Yours and You Are Mine
by Tad Weiss, July 2, 2014

Yesterday was a full day of rehab and Maggie did exceptionally well. She did a number of motor skill exercises with the occupational therapist, who left realizing she needed to bring more for Maggie to do.

Next was physical therapy. Maggie was able to sit upright in a wheelchair (and not try to get out!) so she got to go for a ride around the third floor.

Third was speech therapy. Once again, Maggie did a phenomenal job! She was able to answer all of the questions, and some of her answers showed that her great mind is coming back.

It sounds like Maggie will be moving from HCMC to a long-term acute care facility soon. The trauma to her body seems to be under control. Praise God! So now it is time to move on to more intense therapy as the next step in her rehabilitation.

She only has one full-strength limb, as she can't bear weight on her legs, and her elbow fracture needs to heal. So that limits the facilities she can go to, and she will probably move to two more facilities before she can go home.

One of the side effects and challenges of a traumatic brain injury is that the sleep cycle gets out of whack, and Wendy and I have been dealing with this for two weeks now. Maggie is tired at about 10:00 p.m. and seems ready to go to bed. Then she will go through a period of falling asleep for five to ten minutes, and then waking up. She is very restless and not fully aware of everything that is going on. She acts instinctively and not always in her own best interests. So it is a bit of a wrestling match with her, both physically and mentally. She'll be awake for twenty minutes and then doze off again.

The cycle repeats. Last night this went on until midnight, and I hit my breaking point. I can't say that I'm proud of how I acted.

The night nurse came in to save me. She gave Maggie some medication, and then we just waited for her to fall into a deep sleep. That finally happened at 2:00 a.m. She slept until 4:00 a.m., was up for a half hour, then slept till 5:30 a.m.

The nurse watched Maggie while I went down to the Dunn Brothers inside HCMC. Sleep wasn't going to happen, so I thought I might as well get some caffeine. Maggie and I split a blueberry muffin and watched the church service online from a few days ago. After the third song, Maggie fell asleep. After my extra-large coffee, I'm here typing a post to CaringBridge!

Laura Shellum, a friend of Maggie's, recorded the song "Oceans (Where Feet may Fail)" for her. It is a beautiful song, and she has a lovely voice. The song talks about being called into the unknown, trusting God in the parts of life we can't understand or handle in our own strength.

Worship music has this ability to touch you right when you need it. The song described my night last night. I was out in the deep waters with Maggie, and my feet were failing. God was with me in the mystery. I had to call upon Him. If I tried to do it on my own strength, my head would fall beneath the waves; I would drown. With Him, my eyes stayed above the waves, barely. It wasn't pretty. I'm not happy with how I acted, but we got through it.

Today is a new day. The cavalry is on the way; I will get some rest. I will try to act with more patience next time. But through each step of this journey, God, I am Yours, and You are mine.

I've heard from many of you that are going through life's trials right now, just like we are. God never promised us that life would be easy. In fact, He tells us that we will face trials.

These trials seem like a bad thing, but God is using them to perfect us, to draw us closer to Him. All I can say is don't try to go it alone! It doesn't work, and you will drown. Lean on Him through worship, music, prayer, and fellowship. Pray for His will to guide you in how you should act, but then give it all to God.

"Consider it pure joy, my brothers and sisters, whenever you face trials of many kinds, because you know that the testing of your faith produces perseverance. Let perseverance finish its work so that you may be mature and complete, not lacking anything" (James 1:2–4).

Lorinda Barney Donaldson, July 2, 2014

I am speechless, breathless, but in awe of our great God who has carried you and your dear daughter through this deep valley. And yet, it seems as though you've also been on a mountaintop with Him here and there through the journey.

CHAPTER TWENTY-NINE

Day 29—July 3, 2014

O ur stay at HCMC was a short one—only five days. The doctors determined that Maggie had received the necessary surgeries and care in Spain and there was nothing more for them to do. She was fitted for an arm/elbow brace, and her ribs were tightly wrapped. It was time to move on to rehabilitation and therapy, and that would be done at another facility.

As happy as I was to continue making progress, I must admit I was going to miss HCMC. We were in the Vikings Suite, a room usually used for football players recovering from injury. The room was huge. I'm not sure who pulled that string for us, but it was so appreciated and a comfortable place for Maggie to see her first guests.

Wendy and I slept in a reclining chair that turned into a full bed—quite an upgrade from trying to sleep in a chair in Spain next to Maggie's bed. Navigating the hospital and talking with the doctors and nurses in English was a huge stress reliever. The staff was phenomenal, and I was so humbled by the professionalism of all the caregivers who helped us. They truly are saints, and served us so well in our time of need.

Maggie was transported by ambulance from HCMC to Bethesda Hospital in St. Paul. She was wearing her St. Olaf cross-country T-shirt, and one of the EMTs who transported her was also an Ole, so that was a cool connection. We made the twenty-minute drive from Minneapolis to St. Paul and checked in on the fourth floor of Bethesda to the traumatic brain injury unit.

The Lucky Ones

by Tad Weiss, July 3, 2014

Hello to you all from St. Paul. Yes, we moved across the river yesterday.

A little less than three years ago, Maggie and I ran the Twin Cities Marathon together; she was seventeen at the time. When we were at HCMC, we could look out the window and see the old Metrodome site, which was always the starting point for the marathon. Now we've moved over to Bethesda Hospital in St. Paul, and you can look out the window and see the State Capitol, which is the finishing line for the Twin Cities Marathon. How cool is that! God does not miss a single detail in encouraging us. Yes Maggie, you will run that race again someday and there will be thousands and thousands of people cheering you on, just like there are thousands encouraging you in your recovery today!

Wendy had overnight duty last night, and this morning when she texted me, she said, "Take your time and wait for the traffic to clear; all is good here." That is the first time that has happened for either of us!

Maggie has a full day of therapy today: physical, occupational, speech, and transitional recreation. Each session takes a lot of energy, and she usually naps in between. Maggie has a wheelchair she can ride around in, and she went for a stroll with Rachel and Anne today. We are so happy to be at Bethesda, that her physical injuries are healing, and that she is making great progress in healing her brain.

Last night I was driving home from St. Paul and I heard an announcement from Minnesota Adult and Teen Challenge. A young man was talking about his alcohol addiction and how he had tried everything to cure himself. Nothing worked, and he tumbled deeper into dependency and depression. Finally, at rock bottom, through the help of Teen Challenge, he turned his life over to Jesus. He has been freed from his addiction, and has finally found true life—the life God intends for him.

When you hear a message like this, what do you think?

Four weeks ago, to the day, when I received the phone call telling me about Maggie's accident, I hit rock bottom, and it didn't take years of abusive behavior to get me there. It happened in fifteen seconds. But I also had nowhere else to turn.

No one wants to become dependent on alcohol or drugs or have a loved one be involved in a terrible accident. But that young man and I are a couple of the lucky ones. Through different circumstances, we realized the need to depend on Jesus, totally and completely. We had nowhere else to turn. We opened our arms wide and ran full speed to our loving Savior. He took us in, protected us, strengthened us, and carried us through our darkest moments. He will not let us go.

Do you need to go through a traumatic or life-changing event to give yourself to Jesus one hundred percent, totally and unconditionally? No, you don't. I know many people that have gotten there without going through all the pain. And I sincerely hope that everyone else can get there too, without undue suffering and hardship. The Bible tells us that when we let God use our suffering, it can be good for us. It can bring us hope and refine us. It can make us run full speed into the arms of our Father. It did for the young man at Teen Challenge, and it did for me.

One of the challenges of having a successful, prosperous, relatively pain-free life is it can lead us to think we don't need God. We think we can do it on our own. Look at how well things are going! I'm not dependent on anyone. I depend on myself.

In many ways, our great country has been built on and elevates this thinking. But it is a dangerous way to think. We are called to love God above all things, but it is often hard to do through all the temptations and distractions of life. The world we live in celebrates the best and the greatest, no matter what the field. But Jesus said the greatest among us will be our servant. That requires humility, and the recognition that we all are sinners in need of a Savior.

Give that some thought today. Do you really know that you need Jesus in your life? And if you do already know this, have you given yourself wholly and completely to Him? If you haven't, you're in a far worse predicament than the young man at Teen Challenge, or me. God used suffering as a way for us to finally open our eyes to the need to come to Him completely.

We are the "lucky" ones. You can be "lucky" too, without going through the pain. One of the beautiful things about the greatest gift is that it is free. That's the way God works, it is part of His plan, and it has nothing to do with luck. That just made for a good title.

"The greatest among you will be your servant. For those who exalt themselves will be humbled, and those who humble themselves will be exalted" (Matthew 23:11–12).

One of the symptoms of traumatic brain injury is agitation—constant fidgeting, wiggling, and moving. This was a challenge for us as caregivers, especially when Maggie wanted to get out of bed and walk. We could tell her a hundred times throughout the day that she couldn't get up, but the message didn't sink in. For the one on duty, there weren't many moments to relax.

When we first moved to Bethesda, Maggie was sleeping in a "tent" on her bed that prevented her from getting out. That was a help to us, although she wasn't thrilled with it. She graduated to having the tent removed, which felt more normal. Her anxiety and agitation decreased each day, as she became more aware of her body and could communicate her needs—hunger, thirst, and needing to go the bathroom. This was also the first time we could get her into the shower on our own.

All were little victories that continued the healing process.

CHAPTER THIRTY

Day 30—July 4, 2014

Maggie's physical healing was excellent. The doctors were very pleased with her physical condition. There were a lot of wounds that needed to heal, but there had been no complications.

She wouldn't be able to bear weight on her legs for eight weeks, and we were hoping and praying for immediate healing of her right elbow. Once she could use both of her arms, she'd be able to assist more in transferring, and this would create more opportunities for her rehabilitation.

Independence Day

by Tad Weiss, July 4, 2014

Maggie and I had a great night last night. There were a few interruptions, but I would guess she got seven hours of sleep. More importantly, she's sleeping at *night!* That will give her more energy for her rehabilitation today, so we're moving in the right direction in the sleep department.

They have quite a selection of movies at Bethesda, and we're going to watch *Legally Blonde* at some point today. Maggie likes to watch episodes of *The Office* on Netflix, and it is great to see her laughing. We're also able to tool around the hospital floor in a wheelchair and go see the birds and the fish. So there is plenty to do here!

We think we'll be able to watch the fireworks over the State Capitol tonight.

Over the last thirty days, we have certainly had an international experience. The first twenty-four were spent in Spain. On our flight home, a company from Germany and one from Canada handled the flights. Back home, our first stop was at Hennepin County Medical Center.

One of the things that's most striking at HCMC is all the different nationalities represented by the medical staff. This is just a guess, but we had to have direct contact with at least ten medical professionals that were born in a country other than the United States.

Finally, the support network for Maggie on CaringBridge has circled the globe. Among other things, this has truly been an international journey.

We could not be happier to be back in the States, continuing Maggie's recovery in our hometown. We are blessed to have the extraordinary medical care Maggie is receiving. We are blessed by a faith community that supports us completely. We have access to phenomenal resources through friends and connections that can make phenomenal things happen very quickly. We are truly blessed to live in this country!

When it comes to how you view our country, is the glass half full or half empty? You don't have to go far to find out everything that is wrong with the United States. Just open a newspaper, get on the internet, or watch the around-the-clock talk shows. We certainly have problems that need to be fixed. As a country, however, we come at these problems from a position of stupendous strength and with a list of freedoms that were guaranteed by our forefathers over two hundred years ago.

One of these freedoms, provided in the Constitution and the Bill of Rights, is the freedom of religion. Our forefathers chose to not name one specific religion that everyone must follow, and they also provided the freedom to practice no religion. To me, this seems consistent with God giving us free will. We can decide to worship Him or not; it is our choice.

As you celebrate Independence Day and all the freedoms provided in this great country, give some thought to your freedom to follow God. He created the world, and He created you. All He asks in return is that you choose to follow Him, honor Him, and worship Him. Freedom is a great thing, but it also requires us to make the right choices. I choose to follow God, and I hope and pray that you do too.

"Blessed is the nation whose God is the Lord, the people whom he has chosen as his heritage!" (Psalm 33:12).

Gudrun Spitzig, July 4, 2014

So glad that Maggie is improving and back in the States, even though it was a blessing for her to be taken care of by an excellent staff in Spain, a nation that has freedom that should be praised every day; a nation whose God is the Lord. Enjoy Maggie's recovery and celebrate the freedom founded in 1776.

CHAPTER THIRTY-ONE

Day 31—July 5, 2014

Maggie had a lot of visitors on the Fourth of July, and she had a great day. She was able to move around more using the wheelchair. In her speech therapy, she was strong in memory and recall but struggled with concentration and organizing her thoughts.

Each day showed improvement, including improvements in voice strength. She had only been able to speak in a whisper, and now her real voice was starting to reengage.

Maggie asked to use her computer, and she shopped on the Color Run website and picked out some socks all on her own! She also went to her Facebook page for a while. She left no doubt she was on the road to a full recovery!

Maggie, Matthew, and Wendy watched a full Harry Potter movie in a few installments, and then they wrapped up the day watching fireworks over the State Capitol.

Running for Maggie

by Tad Weiss, July 5, 2014

We've been told that when someone has a traumatic brain injury, to be prepared that they will exhibit moments of intense sadness and depression. We have been on the lookout for this with Maggie. She seems to have moments of sadness, but they usually seem short in duration, and it is easy to cheer her up.

Two days ago, I was pushing her around the hospital floor in the wheelchair, and I saw that she was feeling sad.

I asked her what was wrong, and she said, "Am I crippled?"

As you can imagine, the question broke my heart. "No Maggie, you're not crippled. You broke some bones in your accident and they are healing. You will only be in this wheelchair for a very short time. Then you'll be able to walk again, to run again. So do not worry, do not be afraid, okay?"

Maggie said, "Okay," and she seemed fine afterward.

We know there will be moments like this as Maggie comes to terms with the accident. She is a very motivated and determined young lady. Our challenge with Maggie before her accident was never to get her to do more; it was to get her to rest. We used to have a regular discussion on the need for rest, especially when it came to her running. But she liked doing the work, and a day without exercise didn't feel right to her. We believe the mental part of her recovery will be harder than the physical part.

How long will it be until Maggie can walk on her own? At HCMC, we were told it could be two more months until she can bear weight on her legs. Until then, she will need us to push her wheelchair and to help her transfer from the bed to a wheelchair. She will need us to carry her, to do the running for her.

Yesterday, on the Fourth of July, there were two separate teams "Running for Maggie" in two different states. Steph and Hannah completed the Red White and Boom half-marathon in Minneapolis. Maggie's cousin Ellie along with her Aunt Lisa completed the Storm Lake, IA annual Ride/Run around Storm Lake, and they were riding and running for Maggie too. It is such a joy for us to have you running for Maggie! She wants to do it on her own, but she can't right now.

I've heard from several of you that you think of Maggie when you're out running, and that she has helped you finish a workout strong. When Maggie raced, she always had a great *kick*, the ability to finish strong. Keep running for Maggie for as long as she needs you to and keep finishing strong!

"Two are better than one, because they have a good return for their labor: If either of them falls down, one can help the other up. But pity anyone who falls and has no one to help them up. Also, if two lie down together, they will keep warm. But how can one keep warm alone? Though one may be overpowered two can defend themselves. A cord of three strands is not quickly broken" (Ecclesiastes 4:9–12).

All of the friends and family "Running for Maggie" gave us such a boost! The number of people praying for Maggie and spreading the word around the globe continued to grow. We knew that Maggie would be able to walk again, and the doctors told us she should be able to run again as well—probably not anywhere near the level she was at before the accident, but we were hopeful that she'd be able to run and ski with us as a family.

Maggie's overall health and mind were our primary concern, but we couldn't help but think of the things we did together in the past, and we hoped, prayed, and trusted that she'd be able to do them in the future.

July 4 was a special day for another reason. It was the first day that Maggie had any memory of the time since the accident. She'd had total amnesia for a full month! God shielded her from those memories, and she did not develop any PTSD from the accident.

CHAPTER THIRTY-TWO

Day 32—July 6, 2014

Wild had been told that Maggie's healing would not be in a straight line—that there would be days when it seemed like she didn't progress, or even went backward. We had not seen any of those days yet. Every day had shown continued progress, and Maggie's immediate healing moved forward.

Give me Your eyes
by Tad Weiss, July 6, 2014

It is Sunday—a day of rest and a day to worship our Lord, the Creator of all things. Thank You, God, for making us in your image and for sending Your Son, Jesus Christ, to earth to teach us how to live, and then to die on the cross and rise again, so that all who believe in Him can have eternal life with You here on earth and in heaven. Amen.

Yesterday was not as busy for Maggie, as she didn't have any therapy sessions. We do some of our own therapy, working on math problems, word games, and memory tests. Her answers show the depth of her knowledge, as she pulls out some answers that are truly impressive. There are many things she doesn't remember that she knew before the accident, but it seems that more and more of this knowledge and memory comes back each day.

Before the accident, Maggie had the discipline of journaling every day, and she asked to do this yesterday. She wrote the date, and then I took over the writing and she dictated what she wanted to journal. It will be fun to do this each day and measure her progress in a very tangible way.

Maggie wanted to keep things light yesterday, and we did. Matthew came by in the afternoon to hang out. He read a number of quotes from five- to ten-year-olds on marriage and relationships. We all thought they were funny, and a little too truthful in some cases.

Steve, Joann, and Leah Swenson came by with pizza for us at dinnertime. My brother, Matt, his wife, Jana, and Maggie's cousins, Andy and Ellie, came by for a visit. They have been such a great support for us throughout our journey.

One of the realities of this world that God has made clear to me over the past month is the amount of suffering there is all around us. And more importantly, how my eyes have been blind to this suffering. Of course, I've been there for loved ones and friends, but I've also not really engaged with the one that is suffering or their family. I haven't been there for them completely. Why is that? Am I afraid to really know the depth of their pain? Is it just easier if I send a card and then move on with my life? Am I too wrapped up in my own life that I don't have the time to support them fully? What am I afraid of?

On July 4, I went home from the hospital, and I had a wide-open afternoon.

Peter was off with friends enjoying the Independence Day activities, and Wendy was with Maggie at the hospital. I had to pay a few bills and do some odd jobs around the house, but other than that my afternoon was clear. I took a nap on the porch and then shopped for some music on iTunes. I wanted to pick up some worship music that has inspired me recently. One of the songs I bought was "Give Me Your Eyes"[14] by Brandon Heath, a song about opening one's eyes to all of the suffering around us.

The pain is out there. Come to the fourth floor of Bethesda Hospital, the traumatic brain injury floor, and you will see it. Maggie might be in the best shape of anyone on this floor. Go to any hospital and you will see it. But the pain is also out there in everyday life too; it is just usually more hidden. And that is where I know I can do a better job of supporting those in pain and suffering. The guy struggling in his marriage. The woman raising two kids on her own. The guy who lost his job. The girl suffering from depression or the guy fighting an alcohol addiction.

I received a text yesterday that included a devotional from Pastor Rick Warren on miracles. In the devotional, Pastor Rick uses the Bible story from Mark 8:22–25 to show what needs to be present for a miracle to happen:

They came to Bethsaida, and some people brought a blind man and begged Jesus to touch him. He took the blind man by the hand and led him outside the village. When he had spit on the man's eyes and put his hands on him, Jesus asked, "Do you see anything?" He looked up and said, "I see people; they look like trees walking around." Once more Jesus put his hands on the man's eyes. Then his eyes were opened, his sight was restored, and he saw everything clearly.

In this story, Jesus shows us the three conditions needed for a miracle:

1) Miracles happen when somebody cares. The blind man had friends who cared enough for him to bring him to Jesus. This is called intercession.

2) Miracles happen when we get close to Jesus. You can't be touched by Jesus unless you are close to Him. Healing comes from a relationship with Christ.

3) Miracles happen when we trust Jesus to lead us. If the blind man hadn't let Jesus lead him out of the village, he wouldn't have experienced the miracle.

To get something out of a Bible story, you have to first read it, and then ask how does this apply to me? In other words, how can I take this story and put it into action in my life?

Do you know someone that needs a miracle of healing? If so, the way to help them begin to experience the miracle in their life, to come to complete healing, is shown in the first condition. You must intercede not for your healing but for theirs. You must call them, send them a message, or go and visit them. You must intercede on their behalf. You have to care enough to take action, to realize that what the person needs more than anything is to know that you care and are there for them. You have to show them the way to Jesus. That is our job in this story.

Jesus does the work in the second and third conditions; that is His job. If you need a miracle in your life, you have to get close to Jesus first. Then you need to let Him lead you to the healing. If you need healing but don't know the way to Jesus, talk with a pastor or close friend who can show you the way.

Is there someone you know who needs the miracle of healing? If so, give that person a call or a visit. Tell them you are there to help them, just like you have done for us with Maggie. It makes me smile to think of a hundred phone calls or visits happening today that wouldn't have happened otherwise. Help make Maggie's accident, a bad event, become a truly blessed event. Spread the love of Jesus Christ around the world, and let Jesus do that healing thing as only He can do.

Karen Pagel, July 6, 2014

This is asking a lot, but if you have a moment, could you find a patient named Wade Johnson at Bethesda? He was paralyzed in an ATV accident about the same time as Maggie's accident. He could use some encouragement and you are just the people to do that. Thank you!

Jill Sievers, July 6, 2014

I am going to get in touch with my sixth-grade teacher, Mrs. Getchell (circa 1959). I heard she had a bad fall and have been meaning to do this—thanks for the heartfelt reminder about caring for others. Doing it with the heart of Maggie!

The fourth floor of Bethesda Hospital was eye-opening. We knew the degree of trauma Maggie had gone through, but it looked to us like she was in the best shape of anyone on the floor. This drove home how much God protected her from the impact of the bus and cushioned her landing on the pavement and how quickly she was healing.

There was an older patient in a room across the hall who swore like a drunken sailor, and he was loud. This upset Maggie, and frankly, us as well.

When you're in a condition where you can't control your thoughts or words, what is deep inside you comes out. Maggie was sweet and kind to everyone, even though she was in a diminished mental capacity. It was a great reminder to take care of your soul and your innermost thoughts. There may come a day when that spills out for all the world to see!

Maggie's eyes were a window into her healing. Back in Spain when she was fighting to open them, you could see in, but only a little. As the strain of opening her eyes went away, you could look into her eyes and see more of the real Maggie. The vacant, searching stare was replaced by the emotion, the sparkle, and the shine. We loved that the real Maggie was coming back, and we saw it more each day, just by looking into her eyes.

Fresh Air

by Tad Weiss, July 6, 2014

Maggie had a very nice Sunday. We went to church online and had breakfast, then went outside for the first time. The rain had cleared and there is a beautiful area in front of Bethesda Hospital with gardens and sculptures. Aside from a few medical transfers from the ambulance to the hospital or vice versa, this was the first time

Maggie had been outside since her accident, and she loved it!

The splendor of the gardens was beautiful, just two blocks from the State Capitol. I pushed Maggie's wheelchair along the path, and then her Uncle Matt and Aunt Jana and cousins Andy and Ellie came to visit and she took some laps with them. Auntie Kirki and Tom came by to visit too, and Matthew as well.

It was a nice morning and early afternoon, and then Wendy came and stayed with Maggie for the rest of the day. They read a book together and hung out, some great mother-daughter time alone. With the beginning of the work week, Maggie's therapy will kick in full steam tomorrow.

"Worship the Lord in the splendor of his holiness; tremble before him, all the earth" (Psalm 96:9).

CHAPTER THIRTY-THREE

Maggie was able to go outside again and greatly enjoyed the time spent outdoors in the gardens—a nice change of pace from more than a month indoors. She had a speech therapy and occupational therapy session. Her voice continued to get stronger, and her sense of humor was coming back.

She figured out that Matthew would do anything for her if she asked him for support. We pointed this out to her.

With a smile, she said, "Yes, I can use that for a very long time, can't I?"

Why?
by Tad Weiss, July 7, 2014

Do you ever ask God, "Why?" It can be a very hard question to answer. For Wendy and me, we feel God has given us profound clarity to answer the question as it relates to our situation.

Many things happen in life that don't seem to make sense. In the Bible, Jacob wrestled with God and wouldn't let Him go until He blessed him (Genesis 32:22). It is better to get the question out in the open and to wrestle with God; He wants us to do that. He will make us a new creation just as He did with Jacob. The old is gone and the new has come (2 Corinthians 5:17).

God, You created the world in six days. You sent Your Son to earth to die on the cross so our sins could be forgiven, and then You raised Him from the dead. Your power is infinite; You have no beginning and no end. You are the Alpha and the Omega. Why, God, with all this power at Your fingertips, did You not protect our daughter from this terrible accident? She loves You, God! Don't You love her? Don't You want only good things for her?

Why, God, did this happen? Why?!?!

God did not want this to happen to Maggie any more than

we did. We live in a fallen world where sin happens all the time. God gave us free will, and we all choose to sin at some point. The only one in all of history who didn't is Jesus. God's ways are greater than ours, and we simply don't have the capacity to understand every part of His plan. Could God have prevented this accident? He absolutely could have. If you can create the world, you certainly can grab a girl by the shoulders and keep her from leaving the curb. Well, why didn't He? That seems like a no-brainer.

We believe that sometimes God chooses to act, and sometimes He lets our human mistakes run their course. Wendy and I believe that God allowed this to happen because He knew that Maggie and her family would stay faithful to Him and handle it in His strength. He knew that we would be surrounded by an astounding support team that would lift us up, that would take over while we're asleep, that would cover us in prayer and Scripture twenty-four seven. He knew He would find the right people to give Maggie the perfect support team in Seville, and at home. He knew He could use a tragic accident to bring glory to Himself, and to change all of us so we will move closer to Him, wherever we are in life and our faith journey. God wants us to draw closer to Him and for His name to be glorified. He never said that He wants us to be happy all of the time; He wants us to be holy.

God refines us in our suffering, and He tells us why in Isaiah 48:10: "See, I have refined you, though not as silver, I have tested you in the furnace of affliction. For my own sake, for my own sake, I do this."

The world is about God and His glory, not all about our happiness here on earth. God can use suffering to allow us to help glorify His name. God turns things upside down if we let Him.

The greatest difficulties and hardships in life can turn into the greatest growth if we lean into God and let him refine us. Only through developing discipline, endurance, and patience can we find true reward. Through life's most difficult tests, we have the opportunity to grow to be more like Christ, which brings eternal glory to God. That simply can't happen when life is easy and times are good. God knows this, and that is why life works this way. We may not like it all the time, but God knows what is best for us in this life and in eternity.

Why did this happen in Seville?

We have always wanted Maggie to have an immersion experience to solidify her language skills. Spanish is one of the majors she is pursuing at St. Olaf College. She started running on the cross-country and track team this year, and she didn't want to take a full semester abroad and miss the cross-country or track season. So we ultimately decided that summer would be the best for the immersion experience, and she left for Seville, Spain, on May 25. That is why Maggie was in Spain.

The Spanish people are lovely. They are compassionate and caring. They are devastated that something like this happened to Maggie in their country, their city. They rallied around us and loved us so completely, in ways that just wouldn't have happened in other parts of the world.

The hospital Maggie was at is one of the best in all of Spain. She received some of the best care we could hope for. God had put in place the right doctors and caregivers to help save Maggie's life and to give her the chance for a full recovery.

In our time in Spain, we made many new friends: loving people that prayed with us, cared for us, and worked on our behalf. They served us in many ways, and they made Maggie's healing possible. Many of them drew closer to Jesus through the process too. We look forward to returning to Spain when Maggie is completely healed and celebrating with our brothers and sisters of Seville.

Why did it happen in this way?

God is accomplishing great things through Maggie's accident that He couldn't accomplish in any other way. If He could have accomplished all these things with less injury to Maggie, we believe He would have. If He could have accomplished all these miracles through an accident in Excelsior, Minnesota, where all of this would have been much easier to deal with, we believe He would have. If God could have accomplished all these things through someone else besides Maggie, we believe He would have. If God could have accomplished all of the great miracles that He has planned by Maggie getting injured in some other way, through getting hit by a car or a motorcycle, we believe He would have. But we know that God's ways are greater than ours, and that is why this happened in Spain, and that is why it had to be a bus.

"It had to be a bus." Wendy uttered these words over and over.

Something about a 20-ton bus traveling at 37 mph and hitting a beautiful young girl, throwing her twenty-five meters, with no protection, no identification, in a foreign country, where the hospital didn't even know who she was for four hours . . . and she lives! There is no other explanation than God's protection and mighty right hand.

It has been written many times over the past month: "It is a miracle that Maggie is alive." The God of the universe saved Maggie, and He is performing another miracle through her immediate healing. This can't be denied. God is alive, He saved my daughter, and He will also save you.

Why Maggie?

There have been some great posts describing Maggie. The word used most often is "sweet." Sweet Maggie. Yes, Maggie is very sweet, compassionate, and caring. She loves children and animals. She turns away from gossip. Maggie is very sweet.

The other words that are used to describe Maggie are tough, tenacious, determined, a fighter. Maggie ran a marathon at age seventeen. She runs cross-country and track. She was in spectacular shape, and she is disciplined beyond belief. As parents, we work to slow her down, not to get her to do more.

Our family loves to ski together at Jackson Hole, but part of what Maggie and I like is hiking at the resort. Most people only ride the lifts, but when you hike, you can get to special places. Skis on your back, climbing upward, breathing hard. It is difficult to do at 10,000 feet. Maggie loves it!

Maggie knows Jesus. If you are going to point others to Jesus, it helps to know Him. Maggie accepted Jesus as her Savior when she was six years old, in first grade. Maggie was ready, both physically and spiritually, for an assignment that she didn't know was coming. She was ready when God called her to action.

Why Wendy?

Wendy is a faithful servant of God. She is the children's supervisor for BSF in Chanhassen, a group of five hundred women that meet throughout the year to study God's Word. Two hundred children come to the BSF class and also learn about God's Word through the children's program. Wendy and many other faithful women take care of the children. The children are learning about God at a young age.

Wendy serves God in many other ways. Just like I try to get Maggie to slow down and take a day off from running, I also try and get Wendy to slow down. "You don't need to volunteer so much! People ask you because they know you are gifted and that you'll say yes! Stay at home more, take better care of yourself!!" I think she is the one who has it figured out, not me.

Wendy loves to garden. Gardeners like to get their hands dirty. Wendy is the one who fixes things around the house. Wendy is strong and resourceful. She is a servant, a mother, a caregiver.

Where does Wendy's strength come from? From God and God's Word. She is constantly in the Word. She starts the day with it, and I see her reading the Bible diligently throughout the day. God prepared her for this moment. When you're thrown into the fire, there isn't time to do a crash course on the Bible and God's teaching. You need to prepare in advance. She was prepared.

Why me?

I've written about the changes I've gone through over the past month. God knew I had plenty of things to work on. And He also knew that I wanted to work on them. I truly wanted to change; I just didn't know how. God showed me how to make those changes in a way I never could have imagined. I'm done asking questions. I want to honor and glorify God in whatever direction He chooses to lead me.

Why you?

Why are you reading this right now? One of our persistent prayers is that God will be glorified through Maggie's accident. We are hearing about it and seeing it happen, around the world. We are encouraged that the love of God is being spread through Maggie's suffering. It gives all her pain true meaning, for eternity.

So why are you reading this? What are you learning that can bring you closer to God, family, and friends? Write it down. Put it on your bathroom mirror. Don't forget it after a day, a week, or a month. It can be a small thing or a big thing. It can be one thing or many things. That is how a tragic event can be turned into a miraculous story of God's love.

I hope this post can help answer the question of "why" not only for Maggie's accident but also for the trials and tests that we all will face at some point in our lives. Many things in life don't seem to make sense. But the love and power of Jesus Christ can turn a terrible event into a thing of beauty. After all, that is what Jesus did for us when He died on the cross.

"As he went along, he saw a man blind from birth. His disciples asked him, 'Rabbi, who sinned, this man or his parents, that he was born blind?' 'Neither this man nor his parents sinned,' said Jesus, 'but this happened so that the works of God might be displayed in him'" (John 9:1–3).

Don Meyer, July 7, 2014

Thank you for this most practical and theological sound reflection. Profound, actually. It reminds me of Philip Yancey's recent outstanding book *The Question That Never Goes Away,*[15] which is, of course, the question, "Why?" If we can learn to trust God in the face of the most difficult "why," we are prepared to face anything. It seems as though you and your dear family are well prepared . . . for the glory of God. Our prayers remain with you and sweet Maggie.

Frank Mina, July 7, 2014

Beautiful words, Tad. Seeing Maggie recovering each day gives me an awesome feeling in my heart. Thinking back to when she was here in Spain makes me believe so much in God and how He made all this possible.

CHAPTER THIRTY-FOUR

Day 34—July 8, 2014

I received a message asking if I could drop in and visit Wade Johnson, a patient at Bethesda who had recently been in an ATV accident and was paralyzed from the waist down. I had to admit that my initial thought wasn't a positive one. We had our hands full taking care of Maggie, and I didn't need another thing on my plate. Couldn't someone else go visit him?

After letting my sinful reaction pass and thinking about it, and also rereading my post from just four days prior, I figured I should take my own advice. The next time the nurse came in to check on Maggie, I would run up and visit with Wade. I was so glad that I did.

I knocked on the door, and Wade and his wife were in the room. I explained why I was at Bethesda and why I was there to see them. We talked, and I prayed for Wade. They were glad that I stopped by, and I told them I'd be back the next time I had the opportunity. Wow, that wasn't so hard after all!

Maggie had a big day with multiple therapy sessions. Wendy and I tagged off, and she stayed with Maggie through the rest of the day and the night. Later that evening, we had our first real setback. Maggie maxed out and started speaking incoherently. She was agitated and confused, saying words that made no sense. Wendy was obviously concerned but was able to calm Maggie down and eventually get her to fall asleep.

She called me at home, and we prayed that this was just a short-term setback due to overstimulation. The doctors were right; this wasn't going to be a straight-line recovery.

CHAPTER THIRTY-FIVE

Day 35—July 9, 2014

Sleep cycles get thrown off in patients with traumatic brain injuries so that their nights become days. This had certainly been the case with Maggie in Spain. We thought that traveling back to the US had helped, and that the jet lag worked in her favor. She had been slowly getting back on a better sleep schedule and on this day had her first night that was close to normal, with only one period during the night of being awake.

Maggie had some occupational therapy, which at this point was mainly re-learning and practicing basic skills. She had breakfast and had a big appetite. She'd been on thicker liquids and was just starting to be able to drink water or other thin fluids.

Before her accident, she was a big coffee drinker, so she had gone thirty-four days without a cup of coffee! The coffee that came with breakfast was thickened, instant coffee. Not very good, according to Maggie, and I agreed. So after breakfast we set off for the café and a real cup of coffee . . . Starbucks dark roast, with a healthy dose of vanilla creamer. Now we were talking!

Maggie enjoyed her first cup of coffee out in the park, under beautiful sunshine on a nice, cool morning. It was great to see her start to regain many of the things that she loved in life.

Maggie had speech therapy later in the day. She wrote a few sentences, and her writing was improving each day. Maggie had always been a voracious reader and this skill was strong, but the writing was going to take some time. Her memory and recall were good on many things, but there was still a long way to go.

We talked about the accident with Maggie and showed her some pictures from her early days in ICU. This was upsetting to her, but she also recovered well. There would be a grieving process as she began to grasp what happened and what she'd be missing during her recovery. This had been easy for us; she was alive, and the length of time it would take for her to heal wasn't important. God was in charge of that detail, and we were leaving it to Him.

But that would be a tough one for Maggie to have patience around. So the process of understanding what had happened and coming to terms with it had begun.

We talked extensively with Maggie about all the good that came out of her accident. She was going through a lot of pain and suffering. But God was using this to draw her closer to Him—to draw all of us closer to Him—and for His glory. That was not an easy concept, but we prayed that Maggie would be able to embrace it during her toughest moments.

In for the Long Haul
by Tad Weiss, July 9, 2014

The combination of therapy sessions and visitors wore Maggie out, and last evening was a low point for us. It seemed like Maggie really regressed right before bedtime, and we think it was due to overstimulation. Her brain is processing a lot right now, and she's relearning some basic things that take quite a bit of her energy.

Up to this point, Maggie's progress has been very steady and we haven't really had a setback in thirty-four days, which is astonishing. Last night was the first setback. God probably felt we needed a reminder. There is no timetable on Maggie's recovery. He is in charge, and it will take as long as He knows it needs to take for her to recover completely. The doctors, therapists, and Wendy and I will do everything in our power to help her, but then we will trust in God on the timing. It will be a long process, and we are in for the long haul.

"For this reason, since the day we heard about you, we have not stopped praying for you. We continually ask God to fill you with the knowledge of his will through all the wisdom and understanding that the Spirit gives" (Colossians 1:9).

CHAPTER THIRTY-SIX

Day 36—July 10, 2014

We were thrilled to find out that Maggie's lead doctor at Bethesda would be Dr. Bob Sevenich. Bob and Wendy both went to Hill-Murray High School in St. Paul, and they became friends on a three-week high school trip to Germany in the summer of 1980. Bob went on to get his JD—juris doctorate—before becoming a doctor and earning his MD. We continued to be blown away by the talented, caring people that God orchestrated to care for Maggie!

Teamwork

by Tad Weiss, July 10, 2014

Yesterday morning in my post, I mentioned that Maggie had a temporary setback Tuesday night. We think she had just had too much stimulation, and she wasn't speaking coherently. Wendy climbed into bed with her, and I prayed from our house. It worked! Maggie slept very well; in fact, she has had two restful nights of sleep in a row. She awoke yesterday morning refreshed, and the confusion from the night before had passed.

Maggie's doctor came in first thing and told Wendy that Maggie's recovery was one of the best they had ever seen at Bethesda! Wow, did that change our spirits from the night before. God is going to keep reminding us until we get it: *I've got this for you. Do not worry, do not be afraid. Don't project into the future. You do your job and trust Me to do mine.*

It was a beautiful day in St. Paul on Wednesday, and Wendy walked and pushed Maggie around the State Capitol in her wheelchair. Maggie fed herself from the table for the first time, and she had good speech and occupational therapy sessions as well. She has started journaling again. What a difference from just four days ago! Last Saturday she struggled to write the date, and now she is writing complete sentences.

Her reading seems unaffected. We're reading a book on the national parks and although she's a little slower than normal, she gets all the words right. Wendy, Matthew, and Maggie hung out yesterday afternoon and had a calm and peaceful day. I arrived around dinnertime to take the baton. Maggie and I had a nice walk around the park. We finished the day with a couple of episodes of *The Office* and a little reading and journaling. All told, it was a fantastic day!

The concept of teamwork has been on full display for us over the past five weeks. The first responders and ambulance team were critical in saving Maggie's life the day of the accident. That is a job that requires grace and skill under pressure! The medical team in Spain was extraordinary.

Maggie's study program in Spain was through CIEE. Morgan was our main contact and was at most of our doctor meetings, but someone from CIEE was at every visit with Maggie and at every doctor visit for our time in Spain for twenty-three days.

Our group of visitors and prayer warriors on the ground in Spain were a powerful and faithful team.

The team at the AC Marriott provided the utmost in hospitality for us during our extended stay.

The air ambulance teams were the finest example of skill, sophistication, and teamwork. The pilots, doctors, and nurses were consummate professionals and teammates.

The doctors and medical staff at HCMC and Bethesda Hospital have covered Maggie in the finest medical care and attention since we landed in the States.

The team at Modus Advisors took care of my business for a full month. I didn't have the time or energy to even think about work, and I didn't for thirty days.

Our family has been a true team throughout this journey. Taking care of Peter and our house while we were in Spain, talking with us each day, and keeping Maggie and us in prayer. We have grown closer, and we are a stronger family—a stronger team—for the experience.

Wendy and I have been a team throughout. We literally were apart twice for a total of one hour in the first nineteen days of this journey. We prayed together, walked together, processed together, and cared for our daughter together. Our marriage is stronger for the experience.

The largest team of all is you! Each of you who has been supporting us through CaringBridge, through prayer, phone calls, visits, emails, and texts. Maggie has literally been covered in prayer twenty-four seven, around the world. And you haven't stopped since we've returned to Minnesota.

You are God's angel army.

The one common denominator with each of these teams is that they were hand-picked by God to help save our daughter and to make her whole again. Yes, God saved her and He is the author of her immediate healing. But God uses you and me to carry out His plans here on earth. Every member of each of these teams answered His call on behalf of our daughter, and we will forever thank you and praise God for His glorious plan!

Life will have its challenges; don't try to face them alone! Trust in God and rely on others to lift you up, to be your strength when you are weak. Do not be afraid to ask for help. God's angel army is out there ready to help you when you need it, just like you have been there for us. Life and faith are meant to be shared.

Team Maggie. It is a big team, and it needed to be! God is at the head; He is in charge. He uses us to fulfill His plans here on earth, to spread the love of Jesus Christ, and to glorify His name. Thank you for your obedience to Him and for playing your part in saving our daughter. God bless you all.

"Just as a body, though one, has many parts, but all its many parts form one body, so it is with Christ. For we were all baptized by one Spirit so as to form one body—whether Jews or Gentiles, slave or free—and we were all given the one Spirit to drink. Even so the body is not made up of one part but of many" (1 Corinthians 12:12–14).

Lisa, Mike, Brady, and Paige Sahr, July 10, 2014

You have given us all so much to pray about and consider— you are right, we are all a team! You have asked us to allow this journey to draw us all closer to God! As I try to lean into God's calling, it is very apparent to me that God is calling us all to be a prepared and willing member of His team.

I met with Kayla, the clinical social worker at Bethesda. We talked through the different rehab options for Maggie in the Twin Cities, what she qualified for, and what would be covered by insurance. Wendy and I expressed that we'd like to take Maggie home in one week and continue her rehabilitation from there, and Kayla was on board. She started organizing the care team, ordering the medical equipment we'd need at home, and setting up outpatient therapies.

We also received an email from St. Olaf, outlining the options for Maggie to return to school in the fall. That seemed unlikely, but her recovery had been astonishing and we were not ruling it out. If she could go back, it would be on a reduced schedule as she'd need to continue her various therapies through the fall.

But with God, all things are possible.

CHAPTER THIRTY-SEVEN

Day 37—July 11, 2014

Maggie started the day rested and with great energy after sleeping for six and a half hours straight.

Conform to the Image of Christ

by Tad Weiss, July 11, 2014

From the moment she woke up, she was asking which of her friends would be by to visit today. We've felt the need to cut back on visitors, but Maggie was asking and we thought some short visits would be good.

We sent off a few texts, and Laura, Kate, and Tatum (all roomies from St. Olaf) came to see her right after lunch.

They hung out in the room for a while and then went for a walk around the park. Thanks, ladies, for dropping what you were doing and coming to see Maggie!

Maggie had speech and occupational therapy. Wendy said she totally rocked her OT, and Peter, Matthew, and Wendy got to cheer her on. She beaded a bracelet in therapeutic recreation. Sonja came to visit, and Wendy, Sonja, Matthew, and Maggie enjoyed the evening in the garden. They wrapped up the day by reading some of your replies on CaringBridge before heading off to sleep.

Maggie is starting the grieving process of coming to grips with her accident. She wants to go to school in the fall, but it is too early to know what that could look like. She wants to get up and walk but is going to need to wait at least four more weeks. She has plenty of scars from the accident and surgery that she'll need to come to terms with. Wendy has started talking about the accident with her, and the words are hard to hear.

One of the things we tell Maggie is that although her accident was a very bad thing, and she has and will continue to endure pain and suffering from it, many marvelous things have happened because of her accident.

The greatest example of someone enduring pain for the glory of God is Jesus. He endured the ultimate in humiliation, pain, and suffering so we all could have eternal life. It isn't too much of a stretch to see how Maggie's accident mirrors this in a small way. I'm not saying the two events are equal, not even close. But Maggie is enduring the pain and suffering, and many others are learning about Jesus and drawing closer to God through her trials. Although she didn't choose this to happen, she is being conformed to the image of Christ through this tragic accident.

One of our callings on earth is to be conformed to the image of Christ. This is captured in 2 Corinthians 3:18:

"And we all, who with unveiled faces contemplate the Lord's glory, are being transformed into his image with ever-increasing glory, which comes from the Lord, who is the Spirit."

What does it mean to be conformed, or transformed, to the image of Christ? For starters, if you want to become like someone else, you have to know what you're aiming for. Through studying Scripture, we find that Jesus displayed these characteristics in his time on earth:

Love, joy, peace, patience, kindness, goodness, faithfulness, gentleness, self-control, forgiveness, humility, courage, friendship, gratitude, generosity, holiness, encouragement, wisdom, compassion, obedience, honesty, selflessness, and godliness.

To conform to the image of Christ, our objective should be to try to become better each day at practicing these attributes. Let me give two simple examples in my life:

Compassion: Through Maggie's accident, my eyes have been opened to the suffering in the world. Throughout each day, I'm trying to look for it instead of turning away, pretending it's not there. If I can do some small thing to comfort that person, I've allowed God to conform me to how Jesus would have acted in the same situation.

Patience: There's one easy place to practice patience, and that is on the highway. In the past, I've acted like I'm in the Daytona 500, jockeying for position, driving too fast, putting my self-interest ahead of others. Lately I've been slowing down, sitting in the same lane, and forgiving others for their mistakes. A simple thing, but the benefit to me is that I'm more at peace, and my outlook is closer to that of Jesus. It carries over when I get out of the car.

When we practice the little things daily, we are gradually conformed to the image of Christ. My encouragement for today is to pick one of His traits, preferably one you struggle with, and concentrate on improving in that area today. See if it doesn't bring greater peace, joy, and happiness to your life. If it does, pick another one tomorrow, and the day after.

> By understanding who Jesus is, and practicing His teaching in our daily lives, we all can be conformed to His image. Our individual lives will be better, the world will be a better place, and God will be honored and glorified!

My prayer life took a turn in the right direction the very first time Wendy and I visited Westwood Community Church in 2002, about twelve years before Maggie's accident. Westwood became our treasured church home. A man got up and gave his faith story, and he talked about how he used the time on his work commute to pray. That hit me, as I basically just killed time in the car by listening to the radio in the car. I decided to give it a try.

The first time I prayed while driving, I exhausted my prayer list in five minutes.

I continued the practice, and my prayers started getting longer, to ten or fifteen minutes. Pretty soon I was pulling into the office parking ramp in Eden Prairie, a twenty-minute drive from home, and I wasn't finished praying. Practice and steady repetition had paid off so that I expanded my time with God, prayed for others, and had a closer walk with Him.

I started to pray on my morning runs. Some days this would turn into an intense experience, especially when there was a beautiful sunrise. Talking to God and listening to His answers and guidance for my life, He would reward me with the most awe-inspiring vistas. That was God telling me that He liked to hear from me and encouraging me to continue. I found that I could run for an hour and pray the whole time, often finishing right when I veered into the driveway.

Prayer takes practice and consistency. God delights when we take the time to talk with Him, when we praise Him, offer up our prayers and petitions, and listen to His guidance. Prayer is powerful. Prayer works. We were so blessed to have people praying around the world for Maggie twenty-four seven.

God hears, and He answers!

CHAPTER THIRTY-EIGHT

Day 38—July 12, 2014

Maggie had a great night's sleep and went outside with Wendy for a walk around the park. She had quickly gotten back in the routine of wanting her morning coffee, and she liked to have it outside, just like on the porch at home.

A storm rolled in while they were outside, and they got stuck under the gazebo. They had to make a mad dash back into the hospital! I thought we might need to put "no more rain" on the prayer list.

Gramma and Grampa visited, as did Bonnie and Rachel. Matthew and Wendy hung out for the afternoon with Mags. She had occupational and speech therapy in the afternoon. Auntie Kirki and family came by in the evening for a visit, and then Maggie and I wrapped up the day watching TV, and she spent some time checking in with friends.

Praise and Prayer

by Tad Weiss, July 12, 2014

Maggie is becoming more aware of her scars from the accident and from her surgeries. She also had quite a bit of her hair cut off while in the ICU so they could treat her wounds, and she's becoming more aware of that as well. We've been told that she will come to grips with her physical injuries before she understands her cognitive limitations. Maggie needs to heal not only her body and her brain, but she also will need to work through the changes to her appearance caused by the accident. She seems to be handling it well, and we know that God will give her the strength to know that we all love her just the way she is.

Maggie continues to heal at a dazzling rate. She works hard in her therapy and is following all the doctors' orders. It is so much fun just to hang out with her. Wendy and I have been trading off spending time with Maggie in twenty-four-hour shifts. There isn't that much to do, and we greatly enjoy the extended time with her. We've really been convicted of how we try to jam so much into our days that we don't have time to just sit, relax, and be with someone we love. That has been a real blessing for us these past couple of weeks, and I hope that we can continue doing this when Maggie is out of the hospital. Being "stuck" in a hospital room forces you to just hang out, and it is great!

There will be a Praise and Prayer gathering for Maggie at Westwood Community Church tomorrow at 9:45 a.m. in the Woodside Room. Come early for the 8:30 a.m. worship service or stay after for the late service.

There can be no denying that God is hearing the passionate prayers and requests for Maggie and for us.

"Is anyone among you in trouble? Let them pray. Is anyone happy? Let them sing songs of praise. Is anyone among you sick? Let them call the elders of the church to pray over them and anoint them with oil in the name of the Lord. And the prayer offered in faith will make the sick person well; the Lord will raise them up. If they have sinned, they will be forgiven. Therefore, confess your sins to each other and pray for each other so that you may be healed. The prayer of a righteous person is powerful and effective" (James 5:13–16).

CHAPTER THIRTY-NINE

Day 39—July 13, 2014

I spent the night with Maggie, and we both woke up rested. She slept straight through from 10:00 p.m. until 6:00 a.m. and got eight hours of uninterrupted sleep! She had gotten into a regular sleep schedule, just taking a couple of short naps during the day and sleeping through the night. This was a huge answer to prayer. In addition to helping us all get our rest, it gave her energy to tackle the new day and work at her rehabilitation.

We enjoyed a slow day, and that was just fine. After breakfast, we had our coffee out in the park, and then Maggie took a shower to get ready for the day's activities. She had occupational therapy at 10:30 a.m., and then we took a quick nap.

Our good friends Gary, Kim, and Ashlyn arrived for a visit. Maggie and Ashlyn were Spanish "sisters," as Ashlyn was over in Spain for the last school year.

Maggie's godparents, Steve and Cheryl, came to visit, and our best man, Bret, paid Maggie and me a visit as well.

Megan—a sixteen-year-old who had just finished a shift volunteering at Gillette's Children's Hospital—rounded out the visitors, stopping by to see Maggie on her way home. She developed the gift of compassion at a very young age!

Matthew and Maggie hung out and watched *Pirates of the Caribbean*, while I got some work done. Then Wendy came at around 5:00 p.m. to take over for the rest of the weekend.

All in all, a very good day.

Spiritual Gifts

by Tad Weiss, July 12, 2014

I had previously met my friend Todd once before Maggie's accident. His wife and Wendy are good friends, and I met him once briefly at a store in Edina. I saw him in church occasionally. We would say "hi" when we crossed paths at church, and this probably happened a few times.

Todd sent me an email on June 9, four days after Maggie's accident. He mentioned that he was following us on CaringBridge, and then encouraged me to advocate strongly for Maggie and to strive to communicate effectively with our doctors. He finished the email with a prayer, and I responded to him later in the day that his prayers and encouragement were right on the mark for what we had faced that day.

The next day before our morning visit with Maggie, Todd prayed in an email that we would have a connection with her that day. June 10 was the first day that Maggie moved. Later that day, he emailed me, praying that we would have an abundance of peace so we could really rest and be refreshed for tomorrow, which was going to be a big day. We had a good night's rest, one of our first in Spain.

June 12 was the day of Maggie's pelvic surgery. Todd emailed me with advice that when we felt anxious or started projecting into the future, to let it be a trigger to thank God for what He was already doing and to make a "trust deposit." Wendy and I were at total peace during Maggie's surgery, a two-and-a-half-hour period of time spent in the waiting room with our Seville friends. It literally felt like thirty minutes had gone by, and we were hearing that the surgery was successful. We had been able to totally trust God throughout the entire operation.

Todd and I continued to email back and forth each day. On June 14, he encouraged me to view trust like a muscle that is developed. Each decision to trust, big or small, develops the muscle. And waiting is the place where the Lord does His deepest work. Trust while waiting, that was the encouragement for the day. Wendy and I talked about this in our time together at the hotel.

June 14 was the day that Wendy and I really grew in our trust and belief that God had the timing of Maggie's recovery all figured out, and that we could take that off our plate and give it to Him. We didn't need to worry about it and could concentrate on other things.

On June 15, Todd encouraged me to journal and capture all the exciting things that were going on around us. As he said, when you're in the eye of the storm and trusting Jesus, things will come at you so fast that you won't be able to remember it all. Great advice, and we renewed our efforts to capture all the miracles we were seeing.

Todd also felt that God was putting on his heart that we needed to be prepared to advocate for Maggie. He had no knowledge of this at the time, but we had our big "legal" meeting the next day. Wendy and I met with a room full of attorneys to discuss the issues surrounding the accident. They had prepared a preliminary investigation for us to review, and this was the first time we saw all the details of Maggie's accident. There were two issues in the report that we strongly disagreed with—one that we didn't believe was true and one that we knew not to be true. We voiced our beliefs, and we were heard. We had come into the meeting prepared to advocate for our daughter, and we did.

Over those first eight days, Todd had sent me many emails that showed he was locked into our situation and the emotions we were going through. With a couple of the emails, he relayed information to me that God had placed on his heart for situations that he had no way of knowing. My level of trust in his discernment was very high.

On June 17, Todd emailed me saying he couldn't get this idea out of his mind. He didn't know Maggie's condition or if this was a possibility, but he knew of a company called AngelMed Flight that did medical evacuations, and he gave me their website. God had put on his heart that there may be a benefit to Maggie being in the US sooner rather than later, and he outlined all the reasons why.

I remember sharing this with Wendy as we waited to see the doctor. The email was troubling to us. Maggie wouldn't be physically able to fly home for two more weeks, and we had come to trust our Spanish doctors. We would stay in Spain as long as we needed to, making sure Maggie was totally prepared to fly home. Todd had been right on the mark every time until now, but it seemed like his luck had run out.

We emailed him with more details about Maggie's condition and the situation and asked him to continue to pray. He said that maybe this was just a preparatory step for the future. It didn't drop my trust in Todd's judgment; nobody is right all the time, anyway.

We continued to share emails and they were a great encouragement to me. Todd's discernment continued to be very accurate, and I read all his emails with a high level of anticipation.

He sent another email, praying that we would have discernment on when to move Maggie from the hospital in Spain. On that day, June 25, I had an overwhelming sense that the time was right to move Maggie back to the States. We'd just heard from our doctor that we could be in Spain for two more weeks, and I sensed that everyone involved in the decision was moving in that direction. I knew it was wrong, and I knew it was time to push to get Maggie home as soon as possible. That afternoon, we made the calls that ended up getting the wheels in motion to fly Maggie home.

We were able to quickly get everyone on board, and this all came together in two days. How would this be done? Through a medical evacuation, using an air ambulance company just like AngelMed Flight, a portable ICU that would take her from her hospital room in Spain to a hospital room in the US. I had never heard of a service like this before Todd's email eight days earlier. That email had allowed me to research this service and to know it was possible. That is how we flew home on the first possible day Maggie could safely fly: June 28.

Spiritual gifts are endowments given by the Holy Spirit. They are described in various places in the New Testament. Some are "natural" abilities, like serving, teaching, giving, and mercy. Some are "miraculous," like healing, miracles, and prophecy. I by no means am an expert on this subject, but I believe that Todd had the gifts of wisdom and knowledge for me. By being closely connected to God through prayer and quiet time, he was able to receive and relay the encouragement and discernment I needed for that day's challenges. He did so with mystifying accuracy, and in some cases, on matters that he had no prior knowledge of. It was one of the coolest things I experienced in Spain.

Through dependency, faith, trust, and prayer, Todd walks very closely with God. He knew I was in a difficult situation, and it was one that he had experience with. He took the time each day to pray and be quiet, to seek the words that God wanted him to relay to me. I know that God provided him with this gift for me, but the important part is that Todd was prepared and willing to be used by God for this purpose.

Our God is an amazing God! He will use each one of us to serve His purposes if we let Him. God talks to all of us. For those that are connected to Him, He gives instruction that will help you live your life to its fullest and serve others. He still communicates with everyone else, but when we're not connected to Him all He can do is yell to get our attention. I thank God that Todd was faithful and allowed God to use him to serve me at my time of greatest need.

"To one there is given through the Spirit a message of wisdom, to another a message of knowledge by means of the same Spirit, to another faith by the same Spirit, to another gifts of healing by that one Spirit, to another miraculous powers, to another prophecy, to another distinguishing between spirits, to another speaking in different kinds of tongues, and to still another the interpretation of tongues" (1 Corinthians 12:8–10).

Kim Houtz, July 13, 2014

I think, through you and Todd, He's telling me to do a better job reaching out to people rather than just thinking about them. Difficult situations I've been through prepare me to provide support or insight to others in their time of need. What a blessing Todd has been! It reminds me that you never know what God has in store for you, and I need to be willing to give of myself to whomever God places on my path.

CHAPTER FORTY

Day 40—July 14, 2014

Maggie continued to sleep well, which was a big answer to prayer and helped us all. Wendy spent the night with her and was encouraged that she slept from 10:00 p.m. to 6:00 a.m., then fell back asleep until 7:30 a.m.

Day 40
by Tad Weiss, July 14, 2014

Maggie had breakfast and coffee, and with no therapy scheduled for today, she had an open calendar for visitors. Wendy's brother, Jeff, and our niece, Elliot, arrived with their new puppy, Quinn! He was quite the hit at Bethesda, and he made a lot of new friends on the fourth floor of the hospital.

Maggie also had a nice visit from Kelsey, Moriah, and Coach Gelle from the St. Olaf Cross-Country/Track team. Being able to run again is the most frequent thing that Maggie asks about. It was a good day on the east side of town.

Over here on the west side, we had a great Praise and Prayer Gathering at Westwood. Around seventy people came together to give thanks and praise for the astounding healing God is doing in Maggie! After a time of giving praise, we offered our ongoing prayers and petitions to the Lord. Today is day forty in Maggie's journey. In some ways it has been a very long time, but in other ways it has gone very quickly. The number forty pops up quite frequently in the Bible too, and it usually relates to a period of testing or a journey of some type:

- Israel ate manna for forty years (Exodus 16:35).
- Moses was with God on the mountain, forty days and nights (Exodus 24:18).
- Moses and the people of Israel wandered in the wilderness for forty years (Deuteronomy 34:7).

- Jesus fasted forty days and nights (Matthew 4:2).
- Jesus was tempted forty days and nights (Luke 4:2).
- Jesus remained on earth forty days after resurrection (Acts 1:3).

One of the most famous "forties" is the story of Noah and the flood. God saw the wickedness of the people of that time, and He decided to wipe the earth clean. But Noah was a righteous man. God provided a way for Noah and his family to survive the forty days and nights of rain He was ready to unleash on the earth. By building an ark, Noah and his family, along with pairs of living creatures, were saved from the devastation.

In this story, God sends forth two kinds of judgment. The first is the wrath of God, poured out on the ungodly. Anyone who wasn't in the ark perished during the flood. The second judgment is used by God to awaken his people, to bring them to a closer "walk" with Him. This judgment saved Noah and his family. God provided the means for them to be saved from the devastation that the rest of the earth deserved.

On Saturday at the hospital, Matthew and Maggie were watching a movie while a dear friend of mine came to see us. He and I broke away to talk. Deep, spiritual stuff—hard questions. One of his deepest questions was: How could a loving God allow all of the pain and suffering that occurs in the world? If God is so good, why doesn't He just eliminate the suffering? We know He can do it, so why doesn't He?

I know I won't come up with a complete answer to the question, but I do believe that part of it hinges on our understanding of God. God sent Jesus to teach us how to live and to die on the cross to forgive the sins of the world. The two greatest commandments are to love the Lord your God with all your heart, soul, and mind and to love your neighbor as yourself. Jesus embodied perfect, unconditional love in His time on earth. Jesus is love. That part of God is easy to understand.

The part that's harder to understand is the wrath of God. We don't like to think about this, and many of us choose to pretend it doesn't exist. But God's wrath is a part of who He is too. His wrath is clearly explained in the Bible. God gives us every opportunity to come to, follow, honor, and live our lives for Him. But there will come a time when God's patience ends, either at the end of our life here on earth or when He ultimately judges the world.

My encouragement for today is to take time to learn about God. Learn about all His characteristics and attributes, not just the ones that sound good to you. They are all written in the Bible. Spend time with a friend who can teach you about God. When we learn who God is and commit our lives to walking with Jesus, God fills us with his Holy Spirit and blesses us with eternal life, here on earth and forever with Him in heaven.

It's been forty days since Maggie's accident, and in many ways this seems like a very long time. Eternity is a lot longer than forty days. Commit your life to Jesus, and the God of all grace and mercy will bless you in unimaginable ways, forever and ever. Amen.

"The Lord then said to Noah, 'Go into the ark, you and your whole family, because I have found you righteous in this generation. Take with you seven pairs of every kind of clean animal, a male and its mate, and one pair of every kind of unclean animal, a male and its mate, and also seven pairs of every kind of bird, male and female, to keep their various kinds alive throughout the earth. Seven days from now I will send rain on the earth for forty days and forty nights, and I will wipe from the face of the earth every living creature I have made.' And Noah did all that the Lord commanded him" (Genesis 7:1–5).

Maggie loved animals, especially dogs. Wendy and I had owned three black labs throughout our marriage: Sadie, Josie, and Carly.

Back on day twenty-two, I talked about the chocolate lab that we kept seeing on our morning walk to the hospital and how I viewed that as a sign from God that Maggie would need a "therapy" puppy to help her recovery. It didn't dawn on me that we were going to the hospital at the same time every morning, and this owner and his puppy just happened to be on the same schedule! All I could say in my defense is that it isn't always easy to determine what comes from God and what's just normal, everyday life.

Our last dog, Carly, had died earlier that year, and we'd decided to wait to get another dog. My good friend Rob Holt had recently bought a new breed of dog called a Dakota sport retriever. The breed is a mix of golden retriever and cocker spaniel. The dogs look like a mini-golden retriever, which seemed perfect to me. Smaller in size and easier to handle, but still a good-sized water dog.

Maggie and I started looking on their website at the puppies that were available, but we didn't break the news to Wendy yet.

CHAPTER FORTY-ONE

Day 41—July 15, 2014

Things were progressing beyond what we could even hope. For example, it was impressive how far Maggie's writing had come in nine days. When she first started, she could barely write the date. She was now writing full sentences, and her handwriting was almost back to normal.

Take it Slowly
by Tad Weiss, July 15, 2014

Wendy did double duty staying overnight with Maggie both Saturday and Sunday night, so I hadn't seen Maggie for almost two full days. You literally can see the change in her when you walk in the room every day, but this was magnified over two days. She is more confident, her speech is stronger, her motor skills are improving, and her memory is coming back.

Aunt Jana came to spend the day, which allowed Wendy to go home and work on a few things. Our family has been an extraordinary support, and I know we will all be closer from the experience. Jana's brother Mark, sister Lisa, and her daughter Paige came by to visit too. Paige and Maggie got to speak a little Spanish together while the older folks looked on.

A couple of my longtime friends/clients came by to visit— Tom Evans and Pam Holm. Pam brought a beautiful jar filled with individual Scripture notes, and I know Maggie will enjoy pulling one out each day and reading God's message for her for that day.

Maggie and I went out for dinner at the Bethesda Hospital café, a first for us. Maggie's friend Sonja from St. Olaf came by to visit in the evening and they talked and looked at puppies online.

We have some great news to share: Maggie is on track to be discharged from Bethesda this Thursday, and the plan is that we will take her home that day! She has a doctor's appointment with the HCMC doctors in the morning, and if everything continues to improve, we'll keep driving west to our home in Victoria!! Once we're based out of our house, we'll drive Maggie in for therapy a few days a week, most likely to Courage Center in Golden Valley. Being at home will be great for Maggie and for our family.

On Sunday, I stopped at Lifetime Fitness for a much-needed workout. I ran into my friend Paul. He asked about Maggie, and we spent a few minutes talking on our walk to the weight room.

Paul is in the kind of physical shape that most of us only dream of. His dedication and commitment are on a different level. So we were both going to lift weights, but what I do and what he does in the weight room are two totally different things. In any event, we both were heading in that direction.

As we settled in, I told Paul that this would be my first weight workout in six weeks!

He laughed and gave me some good advice, saying, "Take it slowly!"

If I had been inclined to really get after it (which I wasn't!) and had tried to do a workout that I would have been up for two months ago, the results would not have been pretty. The next morning the soreness would have been unbearable. You just can't start lifting weights again after a six-week break without incurring a lot of discomfort. His advice was spot on; take it slowly, and ease your way back in. If I take my time, and increase the intensity over a few weeks, I'll get back to where I want to be and won't get discouraged along the way.

Maggie talks a lot about wanting to run again. She wants to jump out of bed and go for a five-mile run. She's going to need to take it slowly too. She won't be able to bear weight on her legs for another month, and then I'm guessing it will be a long process of learning to walk again with assistance—walking on her own and then some very slow jogging. She will need to take it slowly and rebuild the muscles and endurance she had before the accident.

If you are new to this "faith thing," I think the same advice makes sense. God wants us to walk with Him all our lives. Just like with a successful fitness program, you need to get started and build up over time. The objective isn't necessarily to see how fast you can get to some destination. No one ever completely "gets there" anyway. We all are a work in progress, and faith is a journey. There are highs and lows, times of great improvement, and times where we feel we're stagnating or going backward. The important point is to be in the game and to take the necessary steps to grow closer to God consistently throughout your life.

Up until last February, I served on the Board of Directors at Feed My Starving Children. It was a fabulous experience, and FMSC is a prodigious organization. At one point, I was in a meeting with Mark Crea—the CEO—and Matt Muraski—the VP of International Programs. I expressed that I thought it would be great if FMSC could be recognized as the thought leader in the field of eliminating childhood starvation.

Mark and Matt both listened intently but then shared their viewpoint that they wanted FMSC to be known as the action leader in the field. They stated that there are plenty of people and organizations that do a lot of great thinking but not as many that are committed to doing the work that truly makes a difference. Yes, you need to think and plan wisely, but they wanted FMSC to be known for feeding God's starving children, not just thinking about it.

Many of you have told me that God has been tugging at your heart since Maggie's accident. You're feeling that God wants you to draw nearer to Him. You may be very new to a faith in Jesus or a very mature Christian. If you are feeling God prompting and thinking about it, take the next step. Move your thoughts to action to experience all that God has in store for you.

How exactly do you do that? Here are a few suggestions to help you get started if you are relatively new to faith:

1) Go to church. God uses the church to build up his people and to serve the world. At a church service, you will find inspiring music, biblical teaching, and community. There are many churches, and you will find the one that fits you best. Give it a try and see if it doesn't jump start your faith journey.

2) Read the Bible. There are many great Bible studies you can join, or you can jump into the Word on your own. Start with Genesis, the Psalms, Proverbs, and the Gospels: Matthew, Mark, Luke, and John. Read every day for ten to fifteen minutes and see how God will speak to you.

3) Find a friend or a group who can help you on your faith walk. You can't do this faith thing on your own. There are people waiting to help you, so don't be afraid to ask.

4) Pray. God wants you to come to Him in prayer. When you pray, first honor God for who He is, and give thanks for the blessings in your life. Then come to Him with your prayer requests. He delights in having that conversation with you.

What if you've already committed your life to Christ but need to reinvigorate your walk with the Lord? Here are a few suggestions:

1) Go to church. Get involved through worship and service.
2) Join a small group. Wendy and I joined a group this spring and it has been a great way to study God's instruction for our lives and to get to know friends in a deeper, more meaningful way.
3) Find an accountability partner. When I was over in Spain, I found a partner that I hadn't even considered previously. I'm looking forward to having other men to share my struggles and triumphs with, and to being there for them.
4) Join a Bible study. I've studied the Word on my own and in a group. You need to do both, but a structured Bible study will produce the most learning and the greatest growth.
5) Serve others. At the appropriate time, tell them about Jesus. We are all called to do this, but too often we consider faith a private matter. Seek out opportunities to listen to others and share how walking with Jesus has changed your life.

If God is prompting you to make a dramatic change in your life, follow His call. For most of us, we need to start adopting the practices and building the discipline that will allow us to walk with God consistently throughout our lives. You don't have to do it all today, but you do have to start. Thoughts are great; action is better. If you're feeling that tug on your heart, that is God calling you. Honor Him today by answering the call.

"Therefore, since we are surrounded by such a great cloud of witnesses, let us throw off everything that hinders and the sin that so easily entangles. And let us run with perseverance the race marked out for us, fixing our eyes on Jesus, the pioneer and perfecter of faith. For the joy set before him he endured the cross, scorning its shame, and sat down at the right hand of the throne of God" (Hebrews 12:1–2).

CHAPTER FORTY-TWO

Maggie and I went down to the café for coffee and breakfast and then got ready for the day. Wendy came to be with Maggie at around 10:00 a.m. so I could head off to work. Maggie had a big day with speech therapy at 10:30 a.m. and 1:30 p.m., occupational therapy at 2:30 p.m., and recreational therapy at 3:00 p.m.

Maggie practiced using the computer for memory and mind games, which was something she could continue at home. She finished her bracelet in recreational therapy. Roommate Laura, St. Olaf profs Jeane and Gwen, and Wendy's college friend Leslie stopped by. Matthew came by to spend the afternoon, and all together it was a big day.

Maggie kept doing a great job in her recovery. We were all very excited to continue the journey at home, and we were on track to make the move the following day.

Peter and Matthew
by Tad Weiss, July 16, 2014

From the beginning of Maggie's return to consciousness, there were two guys she always asked about: Peter and Matthew.

Peter is Maggie's "little brother." They have always had a special relationship, and they like to hang out and tease each other a fair amount. Like most siblings they are different in many ways, but they are a great complement to each other too. Each has traits that the other admires and it is fun to see them interact.

In many ways, Peter had the toughest job of anyone in our immediate family. His sister was in a terrible accident, and Mom and Dad took off with only a phone call to him. He had to hold down the house while we were gone for twenty-four days, and we still haven't been home that much. He asked all the hard questions—the ones no one wanted to ask, but the ones that obviously were on his mind. He stood firm during our journey and was always there for Maggie. I am happy for him with Maggie's recovery. He is getting his sister back.

Matthew and Maggie met each other less than two years ago. They were friends their freshman year at St. Olaf and only started "officially" dating at the end of last year. We had met Matthew several times through the school year. He came to Maggie's track meets, or we would see him when we visited the campus.

We've gotten to know Matthew quite a bit better over the past six weeks. We talked on the phone nightly while we were in Spain.

Since we returned on June 28, Matthew has been to the hospital to see Maggie every day except one. I told him I thought he should stay home one day and take some time for himself. Maggie would not be recovering this quickly or completely without Matthew, and we are so thankful for him.

Over two thousand years ago, Peter and Matthew were two of the twelve disciples, and two of Jesus's closest friends. They witnessed awe-inspiring events, some of which only a few people saw. Peter was an example of the forgiven sinner, passionately declaring Jesus as the Son of God but then also denying him three times before his crucifixion. Jesus declared Peter to be "the rock" that His church would be built upon.

Matthew was a tax collector driven by greed until Jesus chose him as a disciple. He displayed one of the most radically changed lives in response to an invitation from Jesus. He was an accurate recordkeeper and great observer, and those traits served him well when he wrote the Gospel of Matthew.

Peter and Matthew, you are displaying many of the great characteristics of the disciples whose names you share. Thank you for bringing so much joy, fun, and love into Maggie's life.

"And I tell you that you are Peter, and on this rock, I will build my church, and the gates of Hades will not overcome it" (Matthew 16:18).

"As Jesus went on from there, he saw a man named Matthew sitting at the tax collector's booth. 'Follow me,' he told him, and Matthew got up and followed him" (Matthew 9:9).

Donna Bredemus, July 15, 2014

Although I don't know Maggie personally, I have been praying and reflecting over her situation. Our daughter worked at Bethesda. There's some great work going on there, as you know. I only wish you could have spent time in our hometown of St. Paul under better circumstances! Take care and trust that all will be well.

CHAPTER FORTY-THREE

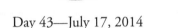

Day 43—July 17, 2014

Moving day! We could not have been more excited. Wendy had taken all of the flowers and gifts home and had been preparing the house for Maggie's arrival. It would be a glorious celebration, and I looked forward to sharing it with our friends.

The Power to Endure

by Tad Weiss, July 17, 2014

Maggie had a busy day on Wednesday. Gramma and Grampa came to visit, as did Barb and Kate Roy. Maggie had speech therapy, occupational therapy, and then a test to measure her progress. We've been in contact with Courage Center and are getting her outpatient rehabilitation therapy scheduled for next week.

Maggie has been so well taken care of at both hospitals we've been at in Minneapolis and St. Paul. But I'm not going to kid you, we are ready to go home! It will be so nice to spread out, to eat on our own schedule, and to sleep in our own beds. The first seventeen days of our journey, Wendy and I hardly left each other's side. For the last twenty-six days, we have been like two ships passing in the night.

I've been amazed at how when we're trusting in God, He gives us the strength we need for the task at hand. When we moved over to Bethesda in St. Paul, we didn't think much about how long we would be here.

We initially thought the next move for Maggie would be as an inpatient at a long-term rehabilitation facility. When we got the word that we could go home in a few days, it was impossible to hold back the anticipation. So here I am, typing in the hospital room with only a few hours to go, excited beyond belief to take Maggie home, and feeling like I couldn't last another day in the hospital.

I was doing some reading last night on God's power. As with many things, the way God defines power is different than the way the world defines power. Jesus's teaching in Matthew 20 is that whoever wants to become great among you must be your servant, and whoever wants to be first must be your slave, just as Jesus came to serve. That hardly lines up with worldly thinking on power and greatness.

Paul also prayed for a different kind of power, as shown in Colossians 1:9: "May you be strengthened with all power, according to his glorious might, for all endurance and patience with joy."

Paul isn't praying for the power to accomplish everything he wants immediately. Instead, he's praying for the strength to endure patiently and to be joyful in the process. The Bible is filled with stories of God demanding patience from His people. God knows that patience is good for us and that our greatest growth will come when we are dependent on Him, trusting in Him, and waiting. It is a hard thing to do, but God will give us the ability to do the things we simply can't do on our own power, if we simply put our trust and faith in Him.

Our strength comes from God and from the people He uses to complete His work on earth. That is where you come in. We have been surrounded by your love and support for these past six weeks. As someone said early on in this journey, Maggie is everyone's daughter. You have taken her in and given us the strength we wouldn't have had on our own. Our journey isn't over, but it feels great to be taking a large step toward a full and complete recovery for Maggie in the comfort of our own home.

"First, I thank my God through Jesus Christ for all of you, because your faith is being reported all over the world" (Romans 1:8).

Laura and Dirk Nelson, July 17, 2014

Home sweet home. There's no place like home. Home is where the heart is. No matter how you say it, there's no better place! I trust the move has gone well today and you are all enjoying the comforts of home together. Sonja said she noticed such a significant improvement in Maggie in the five days between her visits. I can imagine how much more healing will happen in her own home. Blessings!

CHAPTER FORTY-FOUR

Day 44—July 18, 2014

Maggie and I had been looking at puppies online and we had found the one. "Coty" was a cute little guy with black and gray coloring—a *blue merle* coat pattern with the cutest face. We had talked it over with Wendy, and she wasn't thrilled with the idea.

"We're going to take our daughter home in a wheelchair after what we've just been through, and you want to get a puppy?"

Coty's breeder lived in South Dakota but was in the process of selling his farm and moving to Tennessee. If we wanted to get the little guy, we had to act fast.

After leaving Bethesda Hospital, we drove to HCMC for a visit with Dr. Templeman, Maggie's orthopedic surgeon. Maggie, Wendy, and I were sitting in the waiting room. I sat in the corner on my laptop, with my credit card out, making the down payment on Coty and thinking, *This better work out, or I'm going to be in the doghouse in more ways than one!*

A Glorious Homecoming

by Tad Weiss, July 18, 2014

Good morning from Victoria, Minnesota! It brings me great happiness to type those words.

We had a busy first half to the day yesterday. Maggie and I had breakfast, showered, got dressed, and packed up the room. We met with the doctor and nurses one last time, received our discharge papers, and they turned us loose.

Wendy met us at HCMC, where Maggie had X-rays and a doctor visit. Dr. Templeman was pleased with the healing of her elbow and her pelvis. She will go back for another checkup in three weeks, and if she continues to heal with no setbacks, it is possible that she can begin walking then!

The doctor visit went a little longer than expected so we had Matthew meet us at Maggie's favorite restaurant, Christo's in Minnetonka. What a blessing to enjoy one of our favorite things—having a good meal together in a comfortable place.

After that, we traveled to our home to settle in. Neighbors Bill, Lance, and Barb had done some nice decorating of the road and house. A big shout-out to Shaw Stewart Lumber Company and Aulik Design Group for donating and constructing a wheelchair ramp for Maggie!

It is hard to adequately describe our feelings about being home. Happiness, joy, excitement, relief, familiarity. We mainly just sat around all afternoon; Maggie took a nap, the guys watched a little golf on TV, and we started the process of settling back in at home.

When Maggie woke up, she opened a few of the hundreds of cards she has waiting for her. Maggie, Matthew, and Wendy worked on dinner, cooking Maggie's favorite dish of *Bott Boi*, or "pot pie" as we call it. The smells and sights and sounds of home; there is nothing like it and we are so overjoyed to be here.

This has to be the happiest homecoming I can remember. Maggie was away for almost two months. Wendy and I were out of the country for three-and-a-half weeks, followed by two-and-a-half weeks of sleeping every other night in the hospital room, and we haven't really seen each other in a long time. It truly is one of the greatest feelings.

As great as this homecoming is for us, the Bible tells us about one that is far greater. The joy we've experienced today is one of the happiest feelings you can have on earth, but it will not hold a candle to the great homecoming available to us all in heaven.

In his book *Heaven*,[16] Randy Alcorn says:

If you're a child of God, you do not just "go around once" on earth. You don't get just one earthly life. You get another one far better and without end. You'll inhabit the new earth! You'll live with the God you cherish and the people you love as an undying person on an undying earth.

The world we live in has a way of seducing us into thinking the good things of this earth are the end goal; they are what we should be striving for. They aren't. God wants us to strive to be holy, to give our lives to Jesus, and to serve others. When we do this, we find what our hearts truly desire and what God desperately wants for every one of us. We find true peace, satisfaction, and joy—not the temporary happiness of the world.

God's Word is true, and all of life's answers can be found in the Bible. In John 14:1–6, Jesus teaches:

"Do not let your hearts be troubled. You believe in God;

believe also in me. My Father's house has many rooms; if that were not so, would I have told you that I am going there to prepare a place for you? And if I go and prepare a place for you, I will come back and take you to be with me that you also may be where I am. You know the way to the place where I am going."

Thomas said to him, "Lord, we don't know where you are going, so how can we know the way?"

Jesus answered, "I am the way and the truth and the life. No one comes to the Father except through me."

There is so much truth in this passage. It is relatively easy to believe in God. But do you also believe in Jesus? He has prepared a room for you in heaven, and He will come back for you. Thomas, also known as "doubting Thomas," asks Jesus how to get there. We all ask that question at some point in life. Jesus provides the answer. He is the Way—the only way to heaven. Get to know Jesus and commit your life to Him. He will show you the way to heaven and will have a room waiting for you. That will be the most glorious, greatest homecoming that you will ever experience!

Our posts will probably become a little less frequent over the coming weeks. All those things that we do in "normal" life take time, and we are looking forward to that normalcy. We will continue to share how we are seeing God's hand in Maggie's healing and the details of her "immediate" healing. It just won't be every day.

Many of you have told us to just ask if there is anything you can do to help. Wendy and I will take you up on this! We've talked a lot about God and Jesus on this site, and we want to offer the same to you. If Wendy or I can help you in your faith walk, please let us know. We don't have all the answers, but we usually have an idea on where and how to get them!

Carmel Willett, July 18, 2014

Over these past forty-four days Maggie has come to my mind daily. When she does, I pray for her. She was in my first second-grade class thirteen years ago! I am often in tears as I read your posts! I have learned and grown so much in my faith through these past forty-four days. I know that God is the Great Physician and can indeed heal immediately! He has taught me that I should not doubt His power in the most awful situations! He is totally awesome!

25 Meters to God

Todd Mills, July 18, 2014

What an incredible testament to God's faithfulness and healing power. You have inspired our family to fight the good fight and praise Jesus for this miracle He has done. We are very excited for your family!

PART THREE

MOVING FORWARD

CHAPTER FORTY-FIVE

Maggie loved being back in our house and took joy in all the simple things—coffee on the porch, looking at the lake, a favorite meal, sitting in the living room, talking with friends. Time with family and friends in a comfortable setting was exactly what Maggie needed at that point in her recovery.

Home Sweet Home

by Tad Weiss, Jul 21, 2014

On Friday morning, Wendy took Maggie in for her first visit to Courage Center. They put Maggie through an aptitude test that covers five main areas. She scored extremely well or "normal" in three of the five areas: attention, executive function, and visual and spatial skills. There are two areas that she needs to focus on: language and memory. Short-term memory is tough at times, and she also can't pull up the words that she wants as easily as in the past.

It has been extraordinary to see Maggie improve in all these areas on a daily basis. We know that God is in charge of her healing, and we will continue to be patient and trust in His timing. Maggie does not seem to be anxious about how fast things are coming back to her, and that is an answer to prayer as well.

Maggie and Wendy also went in for a routine blood draw. Maggie will need regular checkups over the next few weeks. Wendy has received a crash course in nursing over the past few months and she continues to do a stupendous job taking care of Maggie.

Being at home has been everything that we had hoped. Proverbs 24:3–4 states it well: "By wisdom a house is built, and by understanding it is established; by knowledge the rooms are filled with all precious and pleasant riches."

Joshua 24:15 is a favorite verse of ours: "And if it is evil in your eyes to serve the Lord, choose this day whom you will serve, whether the gods your fathers served in the region beyond the river, or the gods of the Amorites in whose land you dwell. But as for me and my house, we will serve the Lord."

The last part of this verse hangs on a sign as you enter our house. Oftentimes, that is the only part of the verse that's quoted. The entire verse gives the whole story though.

Joshua is instructing the Israelites to follow the one true God, and to not be led astray into worshipping false gods. This same warning holds true for us today. There are many temptations in the world—many false gods that draw our attention away from the Creator. Take time today to worship Him. Spend time with God in prayer, in worship, and in fellowship. Time set aside today for the Lord will help properly establish your priorities and will set you up for a great week that honors and glorifies Him.

We went to the early service on Sunday morning at Westwood. It was important for us all to be together at worship and to get our day focused on God.

Maggie had several visitors throughout the day, and she worked on some brain games in between the visits. We fired up the grill for dinner and ate outside and then watched a movie to end the day.

On Monday, it was back to work for me, and Maggie and Wendy had another doctor visit and a trip to Courage Center. Maggie would be going there three times a week for speech and occupational therapy, with homework to help in her healing. She was told that she could start doing some upper body exercise, so they planned to go out and have Maggie push herself around in the wheelchair.

Maggie asked about the upcoming cross-country season, and we had to break the news to her that she wouldn't be able to run with the team that fall. She had a good cry; it was really the first time she let it all out. We viewed this as a good sign that her brain was healing enough that she could start grasping the big picture of the accident.

At the same time, it was hard to see. She would need to come to terms with her limitations and how her life would be different until she could be made whole again.

Get After It

by Tad Weiss, July 22, 2014

Maggie received a very cool gift basket from Carrie Tollefson and all the campers at Carrie's training camp last week. Carrie is from Minnesota, and after a record-breaking high school career, she won five NCAA championships individually and was a member of the 1999 NCAA Cross-Country Championships team at Villanova and went on to compete in the Olympics. She had all the campers at her running camp send Maggie notes, and they have been inspirational to read.

The theme of Carrie's training camp, and life in general, is "Get After It." Maggie can't wait to get after her physical rehabilitation, and we know she's going to excel at it, just as she has in all areas of her recovery.

This week, I realized I can apply that principle to my faith life.

Have you ever attended church and just gone through the motions? I know that there have been times for me where I've been checking the box and not really participating. This Sunday wasn't one of those times. For starters, I had a deep feeling of gratitude that we could just be there, together, as a family. The second song was "Beautiful Things," with the words that God "makes all things new." God has made me new through Maggie's accident, and he is also making her new in His image.

Next in the service was a dedication, where a young child and his parents were blessed and prayed for by the congregation as the parents committed to raising their child according to God's ways. Parents need a supporting community to come alongside them to help in raising their child. Wendy and I have seen this in how you've supported and encouraged Maggie and us.

The worship was followed by the sermon and the Bible story of Matthew being called to follow Jesus. Once Matthew said yes to this call, he ate with Jesus at his house, and many tax collectors and sinners ate with them. The Pharisees asked why Jesus would associate with sinners, which was unheard of for them.

On hearing this, Jesus said, "It is not the healthy who need a doctor but the sick. But go and learn what this means: 'I desire mercy not sacrifice.' For I have not come to call the righteous, but sinners."

There is a common misconception that churches are filled with people who have this faith thing all figured out. That simply isn't true. We're all striving to draw closer to God and to live our lives for Him. Church is a safe place to help us in this process. When we submit to God, seeking forgiveness and the power of the Holy Spirit, He will speak to us very clearly and in new ways. God talks to us when we come to Him in prayer, fellowship, and worship.

The next time you go to church or talk to God, enter the time with openness and expectation, and God will speak to you.

My encouragement for you today is to *get after it!* Just as Carrie does in her running camp, as Maggie is doing in her rehabilitation, and as I was able to do at church on Sunday. God wants us to live our lives for Him and to live life to its fullest! We hope that you experience all that God has in store for you on this day.

"Whatever your hand finds to do, do it with all your might" (Ecclesiastes 9:10).

CHAPTER FORTY-SIX

July 23, 2014, was a special day—Maggie's twentieth birthday! It was hard to believe that our little girl was no longer a teenager.

Maggie and Wendy made a trip to the Eden Prairie Mall yesterday and did a little shopping. Maggie had received clearance to start exercising her upper body, so she practiced moving the wheelchair around the mall on her own.

We started the celebration a little early. Matthew, Peter, Wendy, and I joined Maggie the night before her birthday for dinner and birthday cake.

Then on her birthday, we took Maggie out for a boat ride. The hard part was getting her down to the boat, but Wendy figured out that with a little momentum we could get the wheelchair through the grass. The ride down to the dock was as exciting for Maggie as the boat ride! She liked being out on the water and getting a little sun too.

Happy Birthday Maggie!

by Tad Weiss, July 23, 2014

Wendy and I are excited to see what God has in store for Maggie in the third decade of her life. We certainly didn't plan for it to start in this way. We know that He saved her life, and that helps us keep everything else in perspective.

How many times have you gone through a difficult event, then looked back on it and realized that what seemed like something bad turned out for the best? Maggie's accident was high up on the list of bad things that can happen, and we believe God will use it to bless her in extraordinary ways in the future.

Thank you all for lifting Maggie and us up in your prayers on this special day. We hope that you also can celebrate the gift of family and friends.

"'For I know the plans I have for you,' declares the Lord, 'plans to prosper you and not to harm you, plans to give you hope and a future. Then you will call on me and come and pray to me, and I will listen to you'" (Jeremiah 29:11–12).

Kathy Christensen, July 23, 2014

Happy birthday, Maggie! And happy day to you Tad and Wendy as you recall the day you became her parents and all the joys you have experienced with her and her brother since then. This parenting thing is something wonderful . . . and scary sometimes. Thanks be to God for carrying us all in His loving arms!

Peter and I traveled to Las Vegas for an AAU basketball tournament. It was nice to take a break and to spend time with him, but Vegas is a different world. I went for a run at six o'clock one morning, and it was already a hundred degrees.

The trip was a great break for me, though, hanging out with other dads and watching some quality basketball. Wendy had her hands full taking care of Maggie by herself, but we both felt the need to spend more time with Peter and to make up for the past seven weeks.

I remember a phone call with Pete after just a few days in Spain. He had a lot of freedom with Mom and Dad being 4,300 miles away. I told him that he had to stay solid, strong, and out of trouble while we were away. We didn't have the bandwidth to overcome any more adversity. He got the message and displayed a level of maturity beyond his years. He was forced to grow up fast, and he did. Peter's maturing was another "good thing" that resulted from the accident.

Steady Progress

by Tad Weiss, July 27, 2014

Maggie is very locked into conversation, and she is tracking things very well. The healing of her brain is steady, and every day shows a little improvement. She is cracking a lot of jokes too, so everyone is on their toes around here.

Over the weekend, Maggie went through many of the cards that have been received in Spain and here in the States—at least a hundred with more to go. I know she'll cherish your messages and posts on CaringBridge in the days ahead as well.

"Be joyful in hope, patient in affliction, faithful in prayer" (Romans 12:12).

Our lead attorney at RZS, Diana Sanchez, contacted me by email on several issues. They wanted to have a phone conversation with Maggie in September, but I didn't know what purpose that would fulfill. Maggie had no memory of her time in the hospital in Seville, let alone of the accident.

Diana also needed us to obtain a power of attorney so she could represent Maggie in court in Seville. The document needed to be written in Spanish and translated to English, and then we needed to obtain an *apostille*—some form of notary for documents in Europe.

No one could understand what needed to go into the document, let alone where we would go to obtain an apostille. Nothing could bring us down from the mountaintop faster than dealing with the legal system, let alone in a foreign country! I wanted to find an attorney to take this off my plate, but no one would touch this, and I didn't blame them.

On top of all that, the whole country of Spain would go on vacation in two days for the month of August.

CHAPTER FORTY-SEVEN

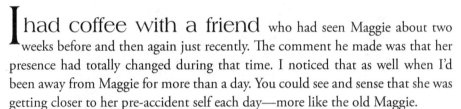

I had coffee with a friend who had seen Maggie about two weeks before and then again just recently. The comment he made was that her presence had totally changed during that time. I noticed that as well when I'd been away from Maggie for more than a day. You could see and sense that she was getting closer to her pre-accident self each day—more like the old Maggie.

How long would it take until we got there? That was one of those questions we weren't supposed to ask. It would take as long as it took. And while we patiently waited for God to completely heal Maggie, doing all we could to help the process along, we did our best to trust in Him and enjoy each day.

The Better Way
by Tad Weiss, August 3, 2014

Maggie has had several great days since we last wrote. She had speech therapy at Courage Kenny on Thursday, lunch at Macaroni Grill with Wendy, and visits from several people. Ashlyn and Mary came by, and Wendy was able to go out and run a few errands. On Friday Maggie had a doctor visit, and Jeane from St. Olaf came by, as did Ashlyn, Donna, Anne, and Rachel. We had a big family get together on Saturday to celebrate all the birthdays that have happened in the last month and to enjoy the beautiful weather on the lake.

Back on day thirteen, I felt God prompting me to get Maggie a puppy. I'm trying to be obedient to Him as best I can, even if it may seem crazy to get a dog right now. Well, the big news around our house is that on Friday, Peter and I drove to South Dakota to pick up our new puppy!

Our puppy is 50 percent golden, 25 percent English cocker, and 25 percent American cocker. They call the breed a Dakota sport retriever. The breed fit the bill of what we were looking for—a little smaller than the black labs we've always had, but still a water dog with some spunk.

His name is Corbet, but we call him Corby. Corbet is a nod to one of the best ski runs in North America, Corbet's Couloir in Jackson Hole. But all Weiss dog names have to end in the long "e" sound: Sadie, Josie, and Carly. So that is where Corby comes from. He'll only be about twenty-five to thirty pounds, so he'll be a great therapy dog for Maggie when he's worn out enough to sit still!

We lost our black lab, Carly, back in February. She was a marvelous dog, and there was a big hole in our lives when we had to put her down. We decided to not get another dog for a while, even though Wendy and I have had a black lab for the last twenty-five years. Life was just easier without a dog. You don't have to take them outside to go to the bathroom or clean up after them. You don't have to take them to the vet or hurry home to let the dog out. You don't need to worry about them wandering off.

The upside of having a dog, as many of you know, is the fabulous joy they bring to your lives. Dogs are the perfect example of unconditional love. They never seem to have a bad day, and they are always thrilled to see you when you get home. Puppies are a lot of work, but the cuteness and curiosity, combined with a little clumsiness, makes for a lot of entertainment while you work through all the naughtiness that comes in the package. Yes, life is easier without a dog, but at least for us, it is more complete *with* one.

Last year around this time, Wendy asked me if I wanted to volunteer at church with her, mentoring a small group of high school students. It was a two-hour commitment once a week on Wednesday nights that would last throughout the school year. I declined. I didn't think I'd have the energy or desire after a full day at work. I didn't know if I was equipped for the job. I wanted to have the time to myself. Life would be easier if I said no, and it was. But I don't think I made the right decision. It was an opportunity to help a group of young men during a tricky time of life, and I'm sure I would have grown in my faith too. I took the easy route for selfish reasons, and it was the wrong decision.

Today's church sermon was about spreading the gospel. Why is it so hard to tell people what it means to have a personal relationship with Jesus? Our relationship with Him is supposed to be the closest and most important relationship in our lives, yet it is hard to talk about. We may think faith and religion are supposed to be private. We may be afraid that people will think we're "Jesus freaks." We may be afraid that we'll be shunned for our beliefs, not invited to certain events, or cast out from the "in" crowd. If you believe that you need to know Jesus to go to heaven, and you truly care for someone, don't you owe it to them and yourself to share the good news?

Once again, the easy way is to be quiet and keep it to yourself. The harder path, however, is the way, the truth, and the life.

Jesus could have taken the easy way, but for our sake He chose not to. In Matthew 26:52–53, when He's about to be arrested, He tells Peter, "Put your sword back in its place, for all who draw the sword will die by the sword. Do you think I cannot call on my Father, and He will at once put at my disposal more than twelve legions of angels?"

Jesus could have vanquished His foes and taken the easy way out. But He chose to be obedient to His Father's will, knowing that His actions would lead to the most painful death on the cross for Him, but eternal life for us.

As we all make choices and decisions throughout our daily lives, my prayer is that we will all seek God's will to help us make the right choice. It may not always be the easier way, but when we are in His will, the rewards always outweigh the sacrifices.

"Because of the service by which you have proved yourselves, others will praise God for the obedience that accompanies your confession of the Gospel of Christ, and for your generosity in sharing with them and with everyone else" (2 Corinthians 9:13).

Megan W., August 3, 2014

Your new puppy is darling!! I'm struck by how much healthier Maggie looks each time you post new pictures! What a miracle she is. Praying for good news this week as she visits the doctor. I'm sure you're all anxious for her to be able to start walking again.

CHAPTER FORTY-EIGHT

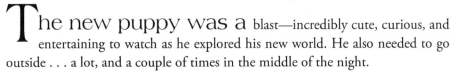

The new puppy was a blast—incredibly cute, curious, and entertaining to watch as he explored his new world. He also needed to go outside . . . a lot, and a couple of times in the middle of the night.

I took that duty, since I was the one who'd gotten him. Corby and I slept out on the screened porch so we didn't wake everyone up on our middle-of-the-night trips to the bathroom. I was spending my nights in the "doghouse" with a little furry creature, but it was still better than trying to sleep in a hospital room in a reclining chair!

Praise You in This Storm
by Tad Weiss, Aug 5, 2014

Peter and I were driving to South Dakota last Friday to pick up our new puppy. It was a four-and-a-half-hour drive straight west on Highway 12 to Aberdeen, South Dakota. Since we left early, Peter crashed in the front seat, and I drove for a few hours and listened to my music collection on iTunes. One of the songs I have in my collection is "Praise You in This Storm"[17] by Casting Crowns. It was the top worship song of 2006, and I've always liked the song, but I never understood the words until a couple of months ago. How do you praise God during the storms of life? Before Maggie's accident, that made no sense to me. I could certainly praise God for the good things in life or when my prayers were answered "Yes." But I'm really supposed to praise Him when things are going the wrong direction? I'm supposed to praise Him when the answers to my prayers are "No" or "Wait"? I'm supposed to praise Him when my daughter gets hit by a bus? Really?!?

Through Maggie's accident, I'm starting to gain a better understanding of who God is. My willingness in the past to praise God was situational; if I got what I wanted, I'd praise

Him. If I didn't get what I wanted, I assumed that God either knew what was best for me or that He simply had other things He was working on that were a higher priority. But I certainly didn't praise Him when things weren't going well. That was beyond my ability to grasp.

What I've learned in the last couple of months is that God doesn't promise us happiness or a pain-free life. In fact, He tells us the opposite in John 16:33: "I have told you these things, so that in me you may have peace. In this world you will have trouble. But take heart! I have overcome the world."

God created a pain-free earth, but because He gave humans free choice, sin entered the world. We chose sin, so we live in a fallen world. God could still say "Yes" to all our prayer requests, but He chooses not to. Does that make God mean? No, it is the exact opposite. God knows better than we do what is good for us, even though we may not see it that way. The number-one commandment is to love the Lord our God with all our heart, soul, and might. Could we really do that if we always had everything we wanted? Would we feel the need to depend on God for anything if we always had everything?

If you have children, do you want them to be happy? Of course, you do! Do you give them everything they ask for? Of course not! Why not, if you want them to be happy?

The answer is easy. If we give our kids everything they desire, when they aren't fully developed and able to make the best decisions on their own, they'll grow up to be spoiled brats. They won't appreciate anything. God knows the same thing holds true for us. If God answered "Yes" to every prayer request we made, not only would the world fall into chaos, but it also would have no meaning or purpose.

That is where I've finally come to understand this song. God both gives and takes away. We may see the reason why God allows certain "bad" things to happen, and this has been very clear to me with Maggie's accident through all the unforgettable good that has come as a result.

But certain events will happen that may never make sense to us. That is when we need to trust that God is sovereign, that He will walk beside us through life's most difficult moments, and that He can bring good out of even our darkest moments.

Learning to praise God *at all times* is a tough one. Our God is the God of mercy and love, who will walk beside us through all of life. We just need to open our eyes and realize He is there. We need to learn about God to fully appreciate the depth of this love. When we do, the natural reaction becomes one where we always praise God, in both good and bad. That is a great place to be, and one I hope to work toward every day.

Maggie continued to improve daily and had started reading on her own. It had always been one of her favorite things to do, and it was heartwarming to see her return to this.

Maggie did surprisingly well in her speech therapy. She was able to retain things in her short-term memory, even though she was intentionally distracted and working against the clock. Wendy often said that Maggie's twenty-year-old brain did better at these exercises than Wendy's (almost!) fifty-year-old brain did!

We were also noticing that even though Maggie still needed to nap during the day, she was not completely wiped out after therapy anymore. This was a huge improvement in only a few weeks, and we praised God for her "immediate" healing!

Back on Our Feet

by Tad Weiss, Aug 7, 2014

Wendy took Maggie down to HCMC this morning and I met them down there. She had her elbow and pelvis X-rayed, and then we met with the doctor. Maggie was given clearance to begin weight-bearing activities, which includes walking! Here is a picture of her standing in the doctor's office.

We are thrilled, relieved, excited—you name it!

Big things seem to happen on Thursdays for us, and it was exactly nine weeks ago that Maggie's accident occurred. For her to be able to walk, and for her brain injury to have healed so well over this time, is nothing short of a miracle. God's awesome healing powers, combined with excellent medical care and all the prayers and support Maggie has received, has combined to make this possible.

We talked and prayed about today's doctor visit. We were hopeful and prayed fervently that we would receive this answer to prayer, and we did. Thank You, God! We also discussed what it would mean if the answer to prayer was "Wait" instead of "Yes." It is easy to say that we trust in God's timing for Maggie's healing, but how we back it up really gives the answer as to if we totally trust Him. It could have been a huge setback if we didn't at least consider the possibility that the answer might not be "Yes." I'm very happy we didn't have to go there, but I think we could have handled it too. There will be tough moments and setbacks in Maggie's recovery, along with the great moments. For today, we're going to fully celebrate the great moment and keep working on our trust in Him to help us in the future.

"Jesus left there and went along the Sea of Galilee. Then he went up on a mountainside and sat down. Great crowds came to him, bringing the lame, the blind, the crippled, the mute and many others, and laid them at his feet; and he healed them. The people were amazed when they saw the mute speaking, the crippled made well, the lame walking and the blind seeing. And they praised the God of Israel" (Matthew 15:29–31).

Kimberly Wolf, August 8, 2014

This is wonderful news! God is healing Maggie before our very eyes. "Go, *walk* through the length and breadth of the land, for I am giving it to you" (Genesis 13:17).

In our meeting with Dr. Templeman, we asked if Maggie could also start swimming—something she did occasionally before the accident. He didn't like the idea at first, but when I explained it would be in a shallow pool with me right beside her, he agreed.

We gathered our things together to go over to the Lifetime Fitness pool in Chanhassen. As we were getting ready, Maggie said she needed her watch to time her laps. I explained that we weren't going to swim laps but were just going to see if she could swim at all. Yes, her brain was healing, but she still didn't fully comprehend her limitations.

The swim was a success. Maggie swam eight lengths with a lot of rest in between. She just wanted to move, and we couldn't blame her after nine weeks of confinement.

CHAPTER FORTY-NINE

W e made it to August 13—day seventy—and the completion of ten full weeks since our journey began. Time flies even during times like this.

Can't Hold Her Back!

by Tad Weiss, August 13, 2014

The last I wrote was almost a week ago, when Maggie received clearance to begin weight-bearing activities. She started walking last Thursday, and it has gotten easier for her each day. Although she's still a little shaky, she can walk without assistance.

Today at Courage Kenny, she was able to up the speed a little, and it has been great for her to start to regain her independence.

Yesterday was Maggie's first day with two therapy sessions: speech and occupational. Speech therapy consists of working on organizational skills, such as using a planner and making lists of the things she needs to get done. She also plays card games and does other brain activities to help her memory and her thinking skills.

Maggie also received clearance to swim, which she's been doing every day since last Thursday. She started out at five minutes and has worked her way up to thirty minutes of laps! When she asks us if she's improving, we need to remind her that 99 percent of the population can't swim for thirty minutes continuously. Yes Maggie, you are improving every day by leaps and bounds!

In medical news, Maggie is now off all medications. She was able to discontinue the oral blood thinner earlier this week. We're sending the hospital bed back tomorrow, as Maggie can now negotiate her way downstairs. We'll hang on to the wheelchair for a while, but it hasn't been used for six days now.

We go to St. Olaf on Friday to discuss Maggie's options for the fall. It is a little tricky as we must make some decisions soon and we don't know what she'll be up for in three weeks, let alone three months. We're trying to be conservative and not rush things, but at the same time we know it will be good for her to be with her friends.

Corby is turning out to be a great therapy dog, as Wendy is going to need some therapy until he gets out of the puppy stage! He's a lot of fun, sleeps through the night better than me, and is a sweet little guy. He cuddles best at 5:00 a.m. or when he's on the boat, but besides that he's either going full speed or he's crashed.

"May the Lord direct your hearts into God's love and Christ's perseverance" (2 Thessalonians 3:5).

The Watt Family, August 13, 2014

My heart was full of joy last Sunday! I was able to get a hug and have a moment with the Weiss family. Seeing the tender hugs and Wendy's sweet touch on Maggie's shoulder through-out our church service, Peter driving to the front of church to pick up his family, and Tad leading his precious daughter to the car . . . truly I was blessed as I peeked into part of their day, a glimpse of heaven and God's design at work.

We were having a real struggle with the court case and legal system in Spain. I wrote to the law firm representing us to try to make sense out of it. They told me to go to Chicago, a four-hundred-mile drive, to see the Spanish consulate to interpret the document they were asking me to sign.

We were also concerned with two findings from the private investigator our law firm had hired. The first was the unsupported conclusion that Maggie "burst into the service road while her traffic light was still in red, and green for the bus." This was based on "testimony of witnesses," yet the investigator didn't speak directly with any of these witnesses.

The second was that Maggie was probably wearing headphones. I'm not an attorney, but this seemed like simple stuff to me. Why would they speculate and assume events and circumstances that worked against us?

The bus company was paying all our medical bills in Spain, and that seemed like an admission of guilt to me. The legal system in Spain continued to baffle us.

We received word from Navigators that they would reimburse us for one of our plane tickets and $5,000 of expenses in Spain. That covered most of our out-of-pocket expenses. The big one of course was the air ambulance from Seville to Minneapolis, easily exceeding $100,000, and Maggie's emergency medical repatriation was also being covered.

It was a blessing to not have any significant financial worries around this so we could focus all our attention on Maggie and her healing.

CHAPTER FIFTY

We went to St. Olaf to meet with Tim Schroer, the dean of students. Maggie was excited to be back on campus, and we could tell that the school was getting ramped up for the new year.

We still didn't know what the fall would look like, but she would stay registered, and we'd cut back her schedule as needed. A big part of this would be determined by her therapy schedule, and we'd figure that out over the next two weeks. We were grateful for how flexible St. Olaf was.

After that, Maggie and Wendy went to IKEA for a little shopping and then picked up Maggie's rings that were being repaired. When she first arrived at the ER in Spain, they cut off her three rings (they also cut through all her clothes and took the rest of her jewelry off). The rings were in rough shape, but we were able to get them looking good as new. We were thankful for small things that made life seem more normal.

Wendy was off at BSF training on Saturday, and Maggie and I went for a swim at the gym. Then we had a nice afternoon on the boat with Peter and Corby. Maggie slept in her bed downstairs for the first time; just another marker as we move things back to normal.

The improvement in her cognitive abilities brought the ability for Maggie to better understand what had happened to her, and that raised a lot of the big picture questions that Wendy and I had wrestled with two months before.

25 Meters

by Tad Weiss, Aug 17, 2014

Maggie and I swam laps this morning. I started thinking about the length of the pool, which is 25 meters. It dawned on me that 25 meters is the same distance that Maggie was thrown by the impact of the bus.

There are two totally different ways to view Maggie's accident. The normal human reaction is to say, "Why me?" Only by faith and trust in God and His power can Maggie say "thank You" for what has happened. "Thank You, God, for saving my life and for the immediate healing You are performing in me and for using me to draw others closer to You. That is our greatest calling and purpose here on earth, so thank You, God, for choosing me for this assignment. Although I can't always see or understand Your plan for my life, I'm going to trust and have faith that You know what is best for me and that You will always protect me."

We all face decisions and choices in life. Some are big, life-changing decisions, and some are routine and ordinary. In the simplest form, we can choose to let Jesus guide our decisions or not. As we enter this new week, let Him guide your decisions and allow you to experience the true life that He wants for each one of us.

"But let all who take refuge in you be glad; let them ever sing for joy. Spread your protection over them, that those who love your name may rejoice in you" (Psalm 5:11).

Mary Cisar, August 18, 2014

As the mother of a swimmer, I can completely visualize 25 meters, but not being thrown that far by a bus. With thanks for small and *large* miracles, like you, Maggie.

Beth and Todd Smits, August 17, 2014

Tad, I read this post several times and had to really process your point about thinking differently about asking "why," and instead saying "thank You." I have a feeling I will spend the rest of my life wrestling with that concept. And then I start praying that Maggie will quickly get to the point where she is wrestling with it as well, because it's the crux of having faith!

CHAPTER FIFTY-ONE

Maggie and Wendy went to see her orthopedic surgeon. It had been two weeks since she began walking.

The X-rays looked good again, and she was given clearance to ride a stationary bike, use an elliptical machine, and to do light weights and core exercises. This would provide some nice variety to her swimming, which Maggie had been doing almost every day for the last two weeks. She would see Dr. Templeman again in six weeks, and he predicted that she should be able to begin running at that time!

We also met with a new physical medical and rehabilitation (PM&R) doctor. She had seen some of Maggie's records (with a promise to read everything—a daunting task). At the beginning of the visit, I gave a five-minute summary of what Maggie has been through and where she was in her recovery.

When I told the doctor that we thought the best thing was for Maggie to go back to school in some capacity in two weeks, she gave me a blank look.

Then she shook her head. "No way."

She then proceeded to give Maggie a thorough evaluation. By the end, she had changed her mind and agreed that Maggie's recovery was well ahead of schedule. She felt that Maggie could go back to college on a limited schedule while continuing her therapy sessions.

We were all excited with this news and began working on the logistics of scheduling therapy in Golden Valley and Northfield around Maggie's class schedule. It would be a busy start to the fall, but we would figure it out!

As the summer wound down, Maggie had a lot of friends heading back to college and there were several last visits. Maggie joined some of her teammates at cross-country team camp, then went to the State Fair with the team on Friday—her first overnight away from Mom and Dad.

Even though Maggie wouldn't be able to run that fall, she was excited to still be a part of the team and to contribute in different ways.

Strength in Weakness

by Tad Weiss, Aug 24, 2014

Last weekend it became clear to Wendy and me that Maggie's physical and cognitive healing was on a great track, but she wasn't ready emotionally and spiritually to go back to school and be away from us. We knew that it was the right time to start having some of those deeper discussions. If she is going to go back to school, she needs to be equipped to work through the challenges she will face.

The first breakthrough Maggie had was after reading last week's post. Her initial reaction was, "I'm lucky to be alive."

While that is true, it isn't the whole story. After processing for a day, Maggie had a great discussion with Wendy. Maggie was able to move very quickly from, "Why did this bad thing happen to me?" to "Why did you save me, God, and what am I supposed to do with my new life?"

We're not naive enough to think she fully grasps this yet, but it is a great start. One of our most fervent prayers is that Maggie will eventually view her accident as a gift from God that He will use for His glory in spectacular ways, if she will join Him.

The other breakthrough came later in the week. Maggie has had a few thoughts that she can't stop. Nothing bad, but also not positive thoughts to have continuously. We talked about her latest thought, and she said that she can't stop obsessing about it no matter how hard she tries. That is where the breakthrough occurred. The truth is that she can't get rid of the habit or thought in her own strength. But if she can turn the thought over to Jesus, He will carry the burden for her, and it will go away. Once again, this wasn't an instant cure and she will need to work on it, but Maggie is able to understand the power of God and how He can take the burden from her and fill her mind with pure thoughts that glorify Him.

The concept that Maggie is relearning and putting into practice is "strength in weakness." Throughout the Gospels, Jesus teaches that if we lean on His strength and depend on Him fully, that he will carry our burdens and allow us to accomplish things that we can't do on our own.

Do you have an impure thought, a habit, or vice that you have tried to fix on your own, but you can't? I know that over the years I've had many of them. I know how I want to think and act and how God wants me to think and act, but I can't change my behavior.

The apostle Paul states it very succinctly in Romans 7:15: "I do not understand what I do. For what I want to do, I do not do, but what I hate, I do." The problem lies in trying to fix the problem in our own strength.

Instead, if we can admit our weakness and rely on God's strength, the problem or the sin can be fixed. That is the essence of how we are strongest when we are weak. The admission of our weakness can take us to a place of total dependence on God, and His strength and love, which is infinite, can be ours.

The date of Maggie's accident, June 5, 2014, was a new beginning for me. It was the first time I fully understood that I do not control my own destiny no matter how hard I try. That day took me to a place of total dependence on God, and it is an exciting place to be! In her recovery, Maggie is learning that she cannot do this on her own. She also needs to depend totally on God, to submit her life to His will and His ways.

The world teaches that the biggest, the strongest, the most talented and most wealthy are the best. Jesus teaches the opposite—that we are strongest when we are weak. If the world's ways aren't giving you the peace and joy you desire, try His ways instead. All things, including what the world calls impossible, are possible through Him.

"But he said to me, 'My grace is sufficient for you, for my power is made perfect in weakness.' Therefore, I will boast all the more gladly about my weaknesses, so that Christ's power may rest on me. That is why, for Christ's sake, I delight in weaknesses, in insults, in hardships, in persecutions, in difficulties. For when I am weak, then I am strong" (2 Corinthians 12:9–10).

CHAPTER FIFTY-TWO

Maggie had another swallow test that she passed, allowing her to go off thickened liquids. Passing the test was a huge victory for Maggie to feel more normal. We were so thankful that her airway had healed completely, although her vocal cords were damaged to the point where she no longer had the ability to sing, shout, or project.

We thanked God that He already had done the work in Maggie's heart so that there was no bitterness regarding her inability to sing or speak onstage. God had first removed her desire to perform in theatre after high school. Although she was admitted to St. Olaf as a vocal performance major, God had also changed her aspirations early in her freshman year to concentrate her studies in areas other than vocal performance.

God had moved Maggie to leave choir at the end of her freshman year, even though St. Olaf was well known for their extraordinary choral programs. She retained an appreciation for theatre and music but pursued athletics, as she did everything, with her whole heart. We stood in awe of how God had again shown us His loving care of our daughter in every detail.

Up to this point, we had very little resistance from the insurance companies. The bus company covered all of Maggie's medical bills in Spain, and Frontier-MEDEX and Navigators paid our travel back home and some of our incidental costs. Now that we were back in the States, our health insurance company, PreferredOne, got involved. They felt that the bus company should also be paying for Maggie's medical bills at home.

After numerous calls, I was able to get PreferredOne to agree to pay the claims. They, in turn, would seek reimbursement from the bus company.

The costs were dramatically different too. We were told that Maggie's medical bills in Spain were ridiculously low, even though she spent seventeen days in the ICU and seven more in the hospital. I guess that was one advantage of socialized medicine. Her hospital and rehabilitation costs in the US would exceed the costs in Spain many times over.

PreferredOne requested a copy of the police report, which had been finalized. The two police officers who worked on the case helped us get a copy of the report. It was eighty pages long and written in Spanish.

Our attorneys said they'd use the police report to put together their final report, and they'd show it to us before it was filed with the court. The law firm was working the case on a contingency basis, but there were other costs that we needed to cover, such as the private investigator.

I tried to get a handle on how strong our case was and what compensation we were seeking. We were being asked to move forward without knowing if it made sense financially. I was not getting answers from the law firm working the case, RZS.

I brought Carlos Lopez back into the loop, the attorney that Zurich sent to help us. He was able to get RZS to draft the power of attorney in a two-column format, Spanish and English, for Maggie to sign in front of a notary, and then the apostille's signature. He also got the police report translated into English and had RZS cover the private investigator bill, which they'd get reimbursed for with a favorable settlement. He also requested a summary of potential outcomes so we could determine if this was worth the time and effort. We wanted to get some compensation for Maggie, but we also had enough on our plate dealing with her recovery and reengaging in life.

We subsequently received the police report in English. The report placed joint responsibility but more on the bus driver than Maggie. They did remove the part about her wearing headphones, and it was noted that the bus driver initially tested positive for a foreign substance in his system. The bus company wanted to have a good relationship with us for public relations purposes, so that helped.

Navigators and PreferredOne placed a lien on any settlement. RZS told us Maggie needed to travel to Spain to be reevaluated and to testify. The legal end of things was turning into a big mess.

Message from Maggie

by Maggie Weiss, September 10, 2014

Hello all! To add variety to your daily routine, this is Maggie typing instead of Dad (aka Tad). So, hello to you all from Maggie!

I'd like to take this opportunity to thank you all for your prayers and support. Especially to all the people who have helped my parents out, because I know this was a stressful time for them.

In other news, I'm back at St. Olaf. I plan to come home about twice a week, which I really enjoy. I don't have class on Tuesdays and Thursdays, so Mom takes me to Courage Kenny for speech and occupational therapy on those days and I spend the rest of the day at home and sleep overnight. I'm taking 2.5 credits now (the .5 credit is a gym class), and it's been going well.

Gym is going really well! We had a 1.5-mile time trial today, and since I can't run, the professor (Coach Koz) let me work on the cardio machines upstairs! He's so accommodating for my injuries. I'm not sure how well I'm comprehending Spanish and poli-sci because we haven't been evaluated yet, but I think I'm getting things. My roommate, Laura, quizzes me whenever I finish both classes, and I really appreciate that.

Speaking of being appreciative of people, my friends have been so helpful since I've been back at school. Laura and I live in a pod with seven other girls. They're honestly like a family away from home, and I know they're helping me heal as much as therapy is.

I may not be able to run this semester (or at least compete), but my coach is letting me help in other ways! Although I do wish I could run, at least I can be with the girls and support them as they compete. That's enough for now. Also, there's a 5K for me this Saturday, and I'm looking forward to seeing many of you at the fun run! This whole accident was a bummer, but one good thing that's come out of it is, I've seen how much people and God love me.

I'm going to enjoy the rest of my night and probably do a little homework. It was nice to be able to write to you all! Thank you for praying for me. Love, Maggie

Candace Wisely, September 11, 2014

I remember early on thinking won't it be great the day Maggie writes in this journal! Or more honestly, I thought, I wonder if some day Maggie will be able to write the journal post. You were hurt so badly, and many of us were praying many times a day, "Lord protect and heal her brain, heal her body. We look to You Lord for this miracle!" And here it is, you, thinking clearly, on your feet again, back at school . . . by God's grace. We treasure seeing His name being made great in your life!

Maritheresa Frain, September 11, 2014

We have not met but I worked for the State Department and CIEE in Seville. I was with your parents and you at the ICU during those first very difficult moments. You and your family have been an inspiration to me and my family. I have your photo—which your mom sent with a thank you note, as if she had nothing else to do in her life. I look at you to help me put life's trials and tribulations into perspective and to remember the power of faith. I only wish your time in Seville had been less traumatic. I hope you return someday soon. *Te mando muchos abrazos desde Portland, Maine. Besos a tus papas.*

25 Meters to God

5K Fun Run for Maggie

by Tad Weiss, September 14, 2014

We had a truly joyous celebration yesterday at the 5K Fun Run! The day was spectacular. Sign-up and T-shirt distribution started at around 8:30 a.m. It was great to see so many of Maggie's friends from college and many supporters who came down from the Cities.

We started the run at a little after 10:00. There were some running standouts participating: Olympian Carrie Tollefson, the St. Olaf Women's Cross-Country team, and the Division III national champion Men's Cross-Country team. On the back end were about thirty of us that walked the course with Maggie. After the women's team got their workout in, they looped back and walked the final mile with Maggie.

The run was on the St. Olaf 5K competition course, a beautiful track that loops through the woods and meadows on the north end of St. Olaf. Maggie walked the entire course, and even gave a finishing kick with about twenty yards of easy jogging at the end!

We first heard that St. Olaf would be sponsoring the 5K for Maggie in the second week of our journey. Aside from being incredibly touched, I remember thinking how great it would be if Maggie would heal so fast that I would be able to push her in a wheelchair for the event. For Maggie to be able to walk the whole 3.1 miles was beyond what we could even hope for three months ago. The same goes for the healing of her brain. A month in, Wendy asked me if I thought there was any chance Mags could go back to school in the fall. We thank God for the healing He is performing in our daughter, and we thank all of you for your love, prayers, and support.

CHAPTER FIFTY-THREE

Wendy was doing the bulk of the driving. She went down to Northfield on Tuesday mornings, took Maggie to Courage Kenny in Minneapolis, then brought her to our house in Victoria for the night. She drove her down for her classes on Wednesdays, then repeated the process on Thursdays and Fridays. It was a couple of hours of driving each day, and we were fortunate that Wendy could fit it into her schedule.

Take Every Thought Captive to Christ!

by Wendy Weiss, September 21, 2014

Tad's birthday was yesterday. We went to St. Olaf for the cross-country teams' invitational. Maggie feels part of her team, as coaches Chris and Gelle have her helping with various tasks.

We go back to her orthopedic surgeon for another X-ray on October 2 to determine whether she can run . . . tough to wait, but Maggie is busy working on other things in the meantime.

Classes seem to be going well for her. She has yet to be formally assessed, but she is managing her time, reading well, and still getting therapies in on off days.

Maggie is sleeping well, but this week in therapy, she was told she needs to be aiming for about nine hours per night to truly rest her brain and allow it to continue to heal. At this point, we are so grateful for all the healing that has taken place in Maggie's body, but when she is tired, we especially see the brain injury rear its ugly head. Her frontal lobe injuries manifest themselves in recurring thoughts that are troubling and hard for Maggie to shake. She reviewed some self-talk techniques this week in therapy to help with these thoughts, but ultimately we know that it is God who can really help her with this.

We love the children's devotional book *Thoughts to Make Your Heart Sing*[18] by Sally Lloyd-Jones, which my friend Patti gave Maggie this summer. The illustrations are beautiful, as are the inspirational thoughts—not just for children, but for all of us. One is titled "No Birds' Nests!" The devotion is based on the old proverb, "You can't help it if birds come and land on your head. But you don't have to let them build nests in your hair!" Love it! We all have those thoughts that pop into our heads; even Jesus was told lies by Satan. We do, however, have a choice regarding what to do with those thoughts, and so does Maggie! She does not have to listen to awful thoughts. She can send them away!

"We take captive every thought to make it obedient to Christ" (2 Corinthians 10:5).

Maggie liked being with her friends and being on campus, but she also couldn't stay up late and attend any of the social activities. She started wanting to come home on the weekends.

As much as we wanted her life to return to normal, it was becoming clear that would take more time. Many people, medical professionals included, told us we should keep Maggie home for the fall semester. She wanted to be at school with her friends and living a normal life. We believed there was a mental component to her healing that would be helped by her being on campus.

The schoolwork was hard, but she was doing it with the support provided by the school. Maggie was one of twenty students receiving some type of academic accommodation, and four of those had brain injuries. We really didn't know how much injury of this nature existed.

The lighter course load allowed us to get her to her therapy sessions, continuing her mental and physical healing. The emotional piece was the tricky part. Maggie looked healed on the outside, but she was changed. If we broke her healing down into physical, mental, spiritual, and emotional, the emotional piece may have been the hardest.

Confirmation That We Are Doing the Right Thing

by Wendy Weiss, September 28, 2014

Hi all, Wendy here again, on Sunday night after one of the most beautiful weeks I can remember. Such a lovely fall we are having here in Minnesota. Isn't our Creator awe-inspiring with all the beautiful colors in His palette?

Maggie came home yesterday after the Griak Invitational in the Cities (cross-country). She hung out at home yesterday and went to church with us this morning. As Tad and I talked over the week on the way home, I can summarize it as being a difficult but good week.

At the beginning of the week, we were wondering if we should bring Maggie home and have her withdraw from college for now. I won't go into all the details of the many conversations we had with Maggie and her therapists. Suffice to say, we made great strides in understanding that *now* is the time for Maggie to be integrating back into college life, while she is in therapy (so they can coach her through any rough spots) and that Maggie would benefit from a little more time at home. So the goal will be to get her home maybe one or two more nights a week. She seemed so good tonight when we brought her back to school.

We will continue with twice-a-week therapies for at least this week, but still hoping we can scale back soon. We do, however, feel confirmed that we are on the right track, that Maggie should be at school—and that she should still be spending time at home. A tough balance to be sure, but it is comforting to know we are doing the right thing. It was confirmed by her joy, smiles, and behavior this week.

Maggie has a big week ahead. We are hoping for the green light that it is time to *run* again!

"For the joy of the Lord is our strength!" (Nehemiah 8:10).

CHAPTER FIFTY-FOUR

We'd been looking forward to this for a long time. Wendy took Maggie to HCMC for her checkup. After watching her walk and hop and checking her balance, Dr. Templeman gave her clearance to begin running. He also told her that he has never allowed a patient with her type of traumatic pelvic injury to run this soon.

Her surgery in Spain was clearly a success, and Maggie's healing continued at an encouraging pace.

Until the Whole World Hears
by Tad Weiss, October 2, 2014

It rained all day in Minneapolis but after being unable to run for four months, a little rain wasn't going to stop Maggie.

I came home early from work, and we went out together this afternoon. Maggie was told to stop running if she felt any pain, which she didn't. There certainly is some soreness, and some muscles need to be strengthened, but she completed the run and wanted to keep going (which her father overruled). We took a video to commemorate the occasion.[19]

We can't tell you how thrilled we are for Maggie! This is a huge hurdle to overcome, not just physically, but mentally. Maggie will feel more complete being able to do something she loves again. Her pelvis is healing quickly and perfectly. God performed a miracle in saving her life, and He continues to perform a miracle in the speed of her recovery. We give all thanks, glory, and honor to God for healing our daughter.

After seeing how far Maggie has come in such a short period of time, there is no denying the miraculous healing powers of Jesus. In addition to thanking and praising God, we owe so much thanks to all of you! Your prayers and support have truly lifted us and sustained us, and we wouldn't be here today without you. Please join us in singing praise to God, until the whole world hears!

Sarie and Paul Anderson, October 2, 2014

From a fellow runner, this is absolutely AMAZING!!! So very happy for Maggie!!! I am confident she will be running for Jesus the rest of her life!

Carey Owen, October 3, 2014

I'm bawling like a baby as I read this post and watch the video. Glory to God. I'm really at a loss for words. To see where God has brought Maggie from June to now. Just wow!

Ryan and Jane Wenning, October 3, 2014

Awesome video. It is so obvious how much God loves you and how He knew you would be a tremendous witness for Him. All praises to God, you are an incredible young woman (not to mention *you rock*)!

CHAPTER FIFTY-FIVE

After having been given the clearance to run over two weeks before, Maggie was challenged not to overdo it. She wanted so badly to train again, but she was experiencing overuse injuries (especially her knees) when she tried to do too much. So she continued to have her patience honed, as she worked on stretching, balance, and strength.

Physically she was doing remarkably well, but she needed to give it time. She continued to receive physical therapy four times per week. Maggie's hope was to be able to compete in the indoor track season that winter.

Academically she received assessments in the classes she was taking. So far, so good. It appeared she would at least pass those classes, and that was a major victory.

Maggie felt frustration with certain cognitive skills. Word retrieval was difficult at times. Organization of thought was a challenge.

She continued to do two sessions each of both occupational therapy and speech-language pathology at Courage Kenny. They worked with her on planning, organizing, strategizing, and expressing cohesive thoughts, in addition to focus (especially with distractions), memory, and other brain activities that most people took for granted. The plan was to continue with the full schedule for the remainder of the semester, then take a break over Christmas and possibly during the January term, when she would likely take one class at St. Olaf.

Maggie's biggest challenges involved the day-to-day social interactions with professors, other students, and friends. She appeared so normal from the outside that it was a surprise to many who didn't know her well to learn that she was struggling.

She continued to battle persistent thoughts about germs, sickness, disease, and death. We thanked God for the healing within Maggie's brain and waited for the perseverations to abate.

We continued to bring her home three times per week—for Tuesday and Thursday therapies in Minneapolis, as well as at least one night on the weekend.

We prayed that as the brain injury healed, Maggie's confidence to spend more time with her friends would increase.

As for the family, we persevered right along with Maggie. We were very familiar with the drive to Northfield, as the therapy schedule had increased. There was not much margin for anything extra, but we were reminded often that Maggie's life was preserved and that she would heal. We were grateful that she was with us and that she continued to improve.

The Dot and the Line

by Tad Weiss, October 19, 2014

The weeks have been busy, but we've also been enjoying the beautiful fall weather here in Minnesota. I hope that this weather holds out for a few more weeks, as it helps to shorten up the winter.

Last Wednesday morning I awoke to some very sad news. Our good friends Marc and Anne lost their nineteen-year-old son, Gunnar, in a tragic skateboarding accident. Gunnar was a great young man who had battled alcohol and drug addiction. He had been clean and sober for fourteen months and was turning his life around.

The funeral was on Saturday, and I had the honor of reading Gunnar's eulogy, beautifully written by his father. Gunnar loved his family and friends and was loved by many. He had a fantastic personality, and as Anne said, "Maybe Gunnar was so over the top, so entertaining, so funny and sometimes so naughty because he needed to squeeze a lifetime of memories into nineteen short years."

This tragic death at a young age hit us hard. First, Marc and Anne have been close friends for over thirty years, and their children are just a couple years ahead of ours. Second, Gunnar died due to a fall and head trauma. On the surface, Maggie's accident was more severe than Gunnar's, yet Maggie lived and is recovering, and Gunnar died almost immediately.

During the memorial service, the pastor talked about what we know and what we don't. One thing I certainly don't know is why Maggie's life was spared and Gunnar's wasn't. I can speculate and try to come up with reasons that make sense, but the fact is we don't always know why certain things happen or don't happen. I just have to trust that God's ways are higher than mine, and when I see Him face to face in heaven, I believe He will explain life's mysteries to me. I firmly believe that God can bring good out of tragic circumstances, but also that God is sovereign and His plan and purpose for our lives are simply beyond what my finite mind can comprehend.

Although there are many things I don't understand regarding Gunnar's and Maggie's accidents, there are many things I do believe and understand. One is that God loves Gunnar, Maggie, and all of us equally, so much so, that He gave His one and only Son for the forgiveness of our sins so that all of us have the opportunity to live eternally with Him in heaven. We are all saddened by the loss of Gunnar here on earth, but he has brought his laughter and joyful personality to heaven now, where he will no longer struggle with addiction, pain, or hardship. I will choose to praise God that Gunnar is with Jesus in heaven and that Gunnar touched so many lives in his nineteen years here on earth. I also will choose to praise God that He saved Maggie's life and that we still have the opportunity to work through our struggles and difficulties as her recovery continues.

Many years ago, I heard a speaker talk about *the "Dot and the Line."* It looks like this:

o-->

The dot is the small circle at the beginning. It represents our time here on earth. For some of us, like Gunnar, it is too short, and for others it can last a long time, but around a hundred years is generally the maximum, if you have great health and great luck.

The line is everything after the dot, and it really isn't a line. The term in geometry is a *ray,* meaning the line goes on forever. You'll notice that the line is a lot longer than the dot, and in fact, it doesn't end. Eternity doesn't end; it goes on forever and is infinite.

None of us knows how long our dot will be, and it can be taken away in a heartbeat. The dot does a good job of keeping us busy and distracted. Make sure to take time this week to talk with God, to figure out how you can live your life for the line instead of the dot. Enjoy the benefits of a life lived for God both today and for eternity.

"But our citizenship is in heaven. And we eagerly await a Savior from there, the Lord Jesus Christ" (Philippians 3:20).

Carole Miller, October 20, 2014

I am Marc's mom and I met you many years ago. I want to join Marc and Anne in thanking you for the beautiful way you shared Gunnar's eulogy. Your post about the "Dot and the Line" is a new thought for me and it is one I find myself reflecting on throughout the day. To know that Gunnar is with our caring and loving God in heaven has brought me a sense of peace. My prayers will continue for your brave Maggie.

Marc Miller, October 20, 2014

Tad, your delivery of Gunnar's eulogy was so passionate and heartfelt . . . I think it reached everyone at the church on Saturday. Thanks for addressing some of the questions surrounding Gunnar's sudden death in your most recent post. As you can imagine, we have been wrestling with these and others. I agree wholeheartedly with your thoughts on "Why" and I have decided not to deliberate it. I think that deliberating over the question assumes that I could somehow understand God's infinite wisdom . . . I can't, and I am not going to pretend that I can.

CHAPTER FIFTY-SIX

Wendy and Maggie were able to figure out Maggie's class schedule for the spring. It looked like Maggie would take three academic classes. She was working her way back to full-time-student status but would still need time for therapy and rest. The good news was that she was on schedule to graduate in the spring of 2016, thanks to all of the AP classes she took in high school.

The other good news was that Maggie was spending a full weekend down at St. Olaf, which she hadn't done in a while. We viewed this as a sign that she was gaining confidence and trusting herself more.

I loved to run with Maggie. It helped the time go by quickly, and we had great conversations. We were out for a run one beautiful fall afternoon, and she told me she was in two group Bible studies and was also praying and studying the Bible on her own. She expressed that she wanted to feel closer to God and to gain a better perspective and understanding of her accident, but it just wasn't happening.

She wondered what was wrong, and what did she need to do to draw closer to Him? Why weren't the answers clear to her?

Ready Yourselves

by Tad Weiss, October 26, 2014

The title of this post comes from the song "Until the Whole World Hears"[20] by Casting Crowns. We've all heard words of advice, such as, "Get ready," "Be prepared," "Get your house in order," and many others. But I really like, "Ready yourselves." It just begs the question, ready for what? There's something important coming that I need to be ready for. But what is it?

Life is full of difficulty, hardships, and challenges. Jesus Himself tells us life will be this way in John 16:33: "I have told you these things, so that in Me you may have peace. In this world you will have trouble. But take heart! I have overcome the world." We need to ready ourselves for the challenges we will face in life. This verse not only tells us what to expect, but also provides the way out. Through Jesus, we will find peace, and He will help us overcome life's challenges and difficulties.

The first part of the answer is knowing where to turn for help in our daily lives: toward Jesus. Where exactly can we find that help? Through Scripture, prayer, and Bible studies. Through going to church, hanging out with others who can help us in our faith walk, listening to inspirational Christian music, and many other ways. The more time we spend readying ourselves, filling our hearts and minds with God—His will and His ways—the more He will reveal the answers to life's difficult questions to us.

But there's a bigger and more important issue at play here. Jesus will return to judge the living and the dead. When will He return? Only God knows. It could be tomorrow or it could be another two thousand years or more. The point isn't to speculate or try to determine when Jesus will return, but to be ready when He does.

So how do we get ready for Jesus's return? By admitting we are sinners in need of a Savior, by believing that God sent Jesus down to earth as our Savior and that Jesus died on the cross and rose again, and by committing our lives to Him.

Maggie's advisor reminded her that life is not a sprint, but a marathon. In life's marathon, we don't have to go it alone. God provides us with the signs to find our way. God provided us with Jesus to guide us. He isn't called the Way because it is a cool nickname. Jesus is the Way to follow for a full and complete walk with God through all of life's circumstances. And Jesus is the Way to heaven and to eternal life with God. Let Him lead you on the journey this week and always.

"So get yourselves ready, prepare your minds to act, control yourselves, and look forward in hope as you focus on the grace that comes when Jesus the Anointed returns and is completely revealed to you" (1 Peter 1:13).

Joy!

by Wendy Weiss, November 19, 2014

How can we describe the range of emotions we've felt over these last months? Despite our circumstances, we've experienced indescribable *joy!*

Sure, there was fear and anxiety. And there continues to be, at times, uncertainty and frustration, but as we approach the six-month anniversary of Maggie's accident (December 5), we are overjoyed at her progress.

Physically, Maggie is able to do just about everything she could before her accident—not as fast as she would like (hence, the frustration). Her physical therapist calls her the "dream client," because Maggie does exactly what Kim tells her. With her friend Rachel's help, Maggie does PT three times a week on her own, working on balance, coordination, hip strengthening, and stretching. Balance and coordination are improved as the brain continues to heal, but also by forcing the brain to work hard.

Maggie is running every two to three days. She actually ran in a race, and because Kim told her to, allowed herself to come in *last place*—that was a tough one for our Mags! Kim will now see Maggie just once a month through February.

Because Kim knows Maggie will continue to do her own PT, we will no longer have weekly appointments. Maggie is planning to compete in the indoor track season, as she will be staying on the St. Olaf campus for the interim term.

Maggie was blessed to be allowed into *exactly* the class she hoped to take—an environmental ethics class with a writing component. She's registered to be a full-time student again for second semester, with three academic classes, which will start in February. Maggie is doing quite well academically! She will finish her 2.5 classes this semester—far from failing! This is so much more than we had hoped for when we started the academic year.

One of the reasons she was so overjoyed to get into the interim class was that she could work on her writing, as she continues to struggle a bit in the areas of thought organization, word retrieval, and clear expression of concepts. Taking a writing class will be great therapy.

Maggie's cognitive therapy continues at an exhausting pace—two occupational therapy sessions and two speech pathology sessions each week. However, she will be done with OT at the end of December—joy! She will take a six-week break from speech therapies from the middle of December through January. She will resume speech therapies in February, but we hope just once a week, and only to ease her back into full-time student status.

Last week, Maggie saw her PM&R doctor, who was happy with her progress. It was heartwarming to see the pleasure on Dr. Roehr's face, as she interacted with Maggie. She told Maggie, in very carefully worded language, that if she met her on the street, there would be nothing about her that did not seem like a regular college student. Indeed . . . we have been noticing these same small changes in Maggie's affect. She's more engaged, and she smiles her beautiful, genuine smile again.

Other incremental changes include more emotion. Dr. Roehr commented on how "flat" Maggie was when she first met her. This had its benefits, in a way, because it meant that in the early months of her recovery, Maggie just rolled with things. We see more of the pre-accident Maggie emerging, which basically means she's returning to a more dramatic and emotional self. Since Maggie inherited this from me, her mother, I can tell you it's not always easy to deal with the highs and lows, but the fact that this is really Maggie is encouraging!

Maggie herself identified this just last week when she was having a hard day. "Mom, you know what? I think I am really starting to feel emotions again . . ."

All I can say is, *Praise God*, because it is further evidence of her brain healing immediately and completely.

There are other little things too, like her starting to wear contact lenses again. She perseverates less; her thoughts are more positive. She is not as obsessed about germs. She is leaning on God, continuing in her disciplines of reading the Bible daily and journaling. She's embracing the concept of sanctification, knowing that God continues to refine her through this trial and grow her in Christ's image. It's so encouraging, as God prompts me to see each of these small victories as another step in the right direction.

Maggie will take a big four-hour neuro-psych exam next Wednesday, November 26. The results from this exam should give us a clear picture of where Maggie is in her recovery from the traumatic brain injury.

May you experience *joy* in the everyday and in the extraordinary today and as we celebrate with family and friends for Thanksgiving next week!

"Consider it pure joy, my brothers and sisters, whenever you face trials of many kinds, because you know that the testing of your faith produces perseverance. Let perseverance finish its work so that you may be mature and complete, not lacking anything" (James 1:2–4).

Vicki, Andy, and Lindsey, Nov 20, 2014

Love that girl! The *joy* is contagious! Thanking God for this astounding recovery!

CHAPTER FIFTY-SEVEN

Six months ago, Maggie was fighting for her life in the ICU of a hospital in Seville, Spain, and Wendy and I were somewhere over the Atlantic on our way to be with her.

How much had changed in all of us in just half a year.

Six Months Ago Today . . .

by Tad Weiss, Dec 5, 2014

We're often asked if the time has passed slowly or quickly. The answer is, very quickly.

The twenty-four days we spent in Spain absolutely flew by. The three weeks Maggie spent at hospitals in the US, and then the time spent recovering at home, seem like a distant memory. It feels like we were just figuring out if she could function at college and take a limited class load, and now we're ten days away from the semester being over. So while there are parts of the journey that have dragged on, we feel very blessed that the time has gone by quickly.

Maggie had her four-hour neuro-psych exam last week, and we'll get the results in a couple of weeks. The psychologist told me how Maggie almost tries too hard to answer things that she can't quite figure out yet. The desire to heal is certainly there, but time is a part of the process too.

Wendy and I remember a conversation with Dr. Flores in Seville about ten days after the accident. Maggie had gotten through the pelvic surgery. She was starting to regain consciousness, and the doctor was confident that she would eventually heal completely. We told him we'd be back to visit with Maggie so he could see in person her full recovery. He said that would be great, but to wait at least until Christmastime because the majority of Maggie's recovery wouldn't happen until the end of the year.

His prediction has proven to be very accurate. What seemed far off in June has gone by quickly, and we thank God every day for the miracle of healing that has taken place. While we celebrate Maggie's healing over the last six months, we also wait for her complete healing. We will continue to do everything we can to help the process along, and we know the day will come. We don't know when, but we know that God will reveal that to us at the right time.

We had a joyful Thanksgiving and we hope you did too. We are now in the season of Advent, a time of expectant waiting for the arrival of Jesus. We wait with the assurance that Jesus will come again, the second coming. We don't know when that day will be, but it will come. God will reveal that to us at the right time. Our prayer is that we all will do everything we can to be ready for Jesus's return, both during this Advent season and in the years ahead.

"She will give birth to a son, and you are to give him the name Jesus, because he will save his people from their sins" (Matthew 1:21).

As much as we liked sharing the positive news on Maggie's recovery, she was really struggling in her relationships and her ability to be a normal college student. She couldn't stay up late, finding that she needed to go to bed at around nine o'clock. That was basically when social activities got started on the college campus.

Maggie looked healed on the outside, but she had a lot of doubts and concerns. She suffered a panic attack at school, and we had to get to St. Olaf as quickly as possible while her friends tried to settle her. Life moved on, but Maggie didn't have the ability, confidence, or desire to reengage in the college social scene. That meant more time spent at home and questions on what spring of 2015 would look like for her.

As much as we rejoiced in Maggie's healing, her period of testing, and ours, wasn't over yet.

A Time of Testing

by Tad Weiss, December 15, 2014

We hope you are enjoying this season of Advent, a time of anticipation as we wait for Christmas Day and the coming of Jesus. It feels like spring here in Minnesota, but do not fear, winter will return soon!

Maggie is doing well as she completes her finals for the fall semester. Two of her classes are complete, and she is studying hard for the last one. She's stressed out, but what student isn't during finals?

The Bible is filled with stories of God's people going through times of testing, and some handled it better than others. God gave Abraham the promise that the Redeemer would come through his family, and that his descendants would one day be a great nation. Abraham and his wife, Sarah, were past child-bearing age when God gave them Isaac. God told Abraham to take Isaac to a mountain and sacrifice him to the Lord. God never intended for Abraham to kill Isaac; it was a test to see the depth of Abraham's faith, and he passed the test.

Mary, the mother of Jesus, certainly had her faith put to the test. The angel Gabriel told her she would give birth to the Savior.

Mary asked, "How will this be?" She knew that she couldn't have conceived a child, since she was a virgin. Along with the impossibility of this happening, she also faced the fear that she would be rejected by society and by Joseph, the man she was betrothed to marry.

The angel told Mary that nothing is impossible with God, and she responded humbly, "I am the Lord's servant. May it be as you have said."

The story of Job in the Old Testament is one of the best when it comes to someone being put to the test. Job was a good and prosperous family man who worshipped the Lord. Satan told God that the only reason Job worshipped the Lord was because of his wealth and success, and God let Satan put Job to the test. All that Job had was taken away from him—his property, health, and children. But Job would not turn his back on God, no matter how difficult his situation became. God eventually rewarded Job's faithfulness and restored his health, property, and family.

What's the common theme that allowed Abraham, Mary, and Job to thrive during their time of testing? Faith in God's promises. John Piper calls it "future grace"—total trust that God is sovereign and He will do all that He has promised when we face trials or tests in the future.

During our time in Spain, Wendy and I took great comfort in the Bible verses that many of you shared with us on Car-ingBridge. These verses detail God's promises to His people, outlining how God would help us get through our test. Here are just a few of the verses that spoke to us:

Isaiah 41:13: "For I am the Lord, your God, who takes hold of your right hand and says to you, 'Do not fear, I will help you.'"

Philippians 4:13: "I can do all things through Christ who strengthens me."

Proverbs 3:5: "Trust in the Lord with all your heart and lean not on your own understanding."

It is human nature to want life to go smoothly, but the Bible tells us we will have suffering and be tested. You may be going through a period of testing; we certainly are in our household. But our hope and assurance are that God's promises and provision of future grace will carry us through the test. Hold onto those promises; that is faith. You also can emerge from the test victoriously, just as Abraham, Mary, and Job did. In the process you will grow closer to God, and He will be pleased.

"Blessed is the one who perseveres under trial because, having stood the test, that person will receive the crown of life that the Lord has promised to those who love him" (James 1:12).

CHAPTER FIFTY-EIGHT

Maggie finished the fall semester very successfully! St. Olaf provided a lot of assistance through academic accommodations, and we were thankful. Finals were challenging, and we could see the cumulative effect of intense studying wearing Maggie down, but she made it through.

Happy New Year!

by Tad Weiss, January 2, 2015

Happy New Year! As remarkable as 2014 was, we are ready to see what 2015 has in store.

Maggie came home mid-December. It took about a week for her to wind down. The last two weeks she's been seeing friends, working out, and just hanging around the house with Corby and us.

We received the results of Maggie's neuropsychology exam. This was a four-hour test designed to measure the healing of her brain by taking her through a series of tests, exercises, and brain games. We received a lot of information about her brain injuries—more than we had in the past. God has truly miraculously healed Maggie!

The results were very good, but there is more healing to come. Maggie is very strong in intellectual functioning and verbal memory. She functions quite effectively daily and takes good care of herself and the things she needs to complete each day, but she tires easily and becomes less effective as the day wears on. We will take January off from therapy, then reevaluate what she needs.

Maggie had a six-month checkup with Dr. Templeman, her orthopedist. Because she's running again, he feels she is six months ahead of schedule in her physical healing. We give thanks to God for all the mental and physical healing that has taken place for Maggie in 2014!

We've also been focusing on Maggie's spiritual healing. Fortunately, God provides a lot of guidance. We believe that spiritual healing is where Maggie has made the biggest strides recently, and that will allow the mental and physical healing to be completed too.

On Christmas Eve, Maggie, Peter, Wendy, and I did a devotion centered on praising God for all things. It is easy to praise God for the good things, but can you also praise Him for the seemingly bad things too? We believe that the answer can and should be *yes!* Since God is sovereign and wants all good things for us (Romans 8:28), nothing is out of His control or ability to work for His purposes and glory.

To see Maggie praising God for all things, including the fact that she was hit by a bus, brought great joy to our hearts. Not just saying the words, but *believing* them. Trusting God and all His promises, including the promise that He will take a tragic event and turn it for good, just as He did with Joseph in the Old Testament (Genesis 50:20). God's promises are as true today as they were four thousand years ago, and they are ours to have if we simply know them and claim them. Maggie is claiming those promises, and you can too for whatever trials or challenges you are facing.

We'd like to suggest a New Year's resolution. Find one new way to explore and experience God and all His promises. It could be going to church regularly, starting each day reading the Bible for fifteen minutes, praying regularly, joining a small group, or one of hundreds of other practices. Commit to the new practice, give it time to work, and experience the blessings God will provide as you honor Him!

The healing that Maggie needs the most—that we all need—is spiritual healing. God provides this when we seek Him and ask for it through the power of Jesus Christ.

"Ask and it will be given to you; seek and you will find; knock and the door will be opened to you. For everyone who asks receives; the one who seeks finds; and to the one who knocks, the door will be opened" (Matthew 7:7–8).

Jan Carlson, January 2, 2015

This is the best New Year's devotional I have read. It gives all praise to our Lord!

Jim Thomsen, January 2, 2015

Beautiful words to begin the New Year, Tad! I will take you up on your "one new way challenge."

Maggie had been scheduled to travel to Ghana in January with a group of students from St. Olaf. Her accident led us to cancel, as she was in no way ready to travel to that part of the world. Because the Ebola virus was spreading in West Africa, the school had to cancel the trip for all the students, which helped Maggie feel less of a loss.

The social challenges Maggie faced became more apparent during the interim term. This four-week period was a quiet time on campus, with one course and a lot of free time to relax, read, exercise, and hang out with friends. We could tell that Maggie wasn't thriving in her relationships.

She had attended a large high school with over seven hundred and fifty students in her class. The size of the school required she find a smaller social group, which she found in her great group of choir and theatre friends.

Before the accident, Maggie had found a new social status at St. Olaf and was one of the more outgoing and popular kids. She enjoyed being liked and admired by others. At the time, we hadn't noticed a big change in her persona, but in hindsight, we had seen her moving in a more worldly direction.

As hard as it was to see her struggle, we appreciated what the Lord was doing to draw her closer to Him.

CHAPTER FIFTY-NINE

Maggie completed her interim course, Environmental Ethics. We wanted her to take this class, as it had a heavy writing component—an area in which Maggie had experienced challenges since her accident. The class was considered a philosophy course, so there was also a lot of deep thinking. Maggie did extremely well, which was another sign to us that her brain continued to heal at an impressive pace.

Back in September, Maggie had to write a one-page paper before the start of one of her fall courses. Writing had always been a strength for her, and she was thinking of going into journalism. The paper she wrote was probably at about an eighth-grade level. The paper she wrote for her philosophy course was very close to her abilities right before the accident—an astonishing turnaround in four months.

New Challenges
by Tad Weiss, February 8, 2015

Maggie will take three courses this spring semester, which starts tomorrow: two regular classroom courses and an internship. She has been training with the track team, although she doesn't have plans to compete. She'll also resume her role as the arts and entertainment editor for the school newspaper, the *Manitou Messenger.*

Part of her challenge is that she looks so normal, as if she's not dealing with any of the effects of the accident. She has a hard time getting the rest she needs, and she has anxiety in many situations. She has times when she gets frustrated, as she can't do many of the things she used to be able to do.

We see the improvement and have no doubt that she will regain most, if not all, of her pre-accident abilities. Not only that, but she will have new talents and perspectives as a result of what she's been through. We look forward to seeing how she will use her accident to help others and to honor and glorify God!

One measure of Maggie's continued progress is that she only came home once during the month of January—quite a change from the fall, where she was home every two to three days. She also traveled to Florida last week with four of her roommates: Caitlin, Laura, Tatum, and Rachel. This is the first time she's traveled since she went to Spain.

Peter, Wendy, and I are all taking on new challenges as well. Peter is finishing up high school basketball season and we're hoping for a strong finish to a great year. He is narrowing down his college choices and has a few more months to decide.

Wendy has been carving out time to take care of herself, getting back into a workout routine that she didn't have time for last year. Our new puppy provides great motivation. He's a small guy who needs lots of exercise!

As for me, I'm going to give a talk on our experience in Spain to a men's breakfast group this coming Saturday. When we returned from Spain, God put it on my heart to figure out how to use our journey to help others and honor Him. I met a pastor/coach by the name of Leary Gates, who has helped me with this. Leary arranged the speaking engagement, and I'm excited to tell our story.

Part of my message is that this really isn't Maggie's, Wendy's, or my story; it is God's story that we get to participate in. God performs miracles today just as He did in the Old Testament, and he uses ordinary people to tell His story, just as He did thousands of years ago.

"I always thank my God for you because of his grace given you in Christ Jesus" (1 Corinthians 1:4).

Maggie and Matthew broke up. We had seen it coming, and it was hard on Maggie.

Her friendships seemed to be changing too; some were deepening and some weren't. She simply couldn't join in on the social activities that were a big part of college.

Life moved on, and Maggie couldn't or didn't want to participate. She looked normal on the outside, but inside she had been changed. Unseen injuries, like a brain injury, are harder to support than visible injuries.

I understood. During my senior year in college, I had a friend who had been in a serious car accident and suffered a traumatic brain injury, just like Maggie. At the time, I talked with this friend frequently, but we simply never discussed her brain injury. This was probably a function of my not knowing what to say, not caring enough to ask, and being too self-absorbed to really engage with her. I had other priorities, and they didn't involve finding out how I could help her. I was twenty-one at the time and not equipped to be there for my friend.

We've been able to see God through Maggie's accident in many ways, but this one was hard on all of us. Maggie had been through a lot but was now feeling rejected and having to deal with new feelings of inadequacy. We knew that God loved Maggie, and He wanted what was best for her, but that didn't match up with what we felt or wanted.

We talked about faith in God and His plan and that His ways and thoughts are higher than ours. Many of Maggie's friends played an important role in her healing in the early months after her accident, and we gave thanks for all that they did for her. They literally stopped their lives to be there for her, and she wouldn't have healed as quickly without them. We'll forever be grateful for the role they played in Maggie's healing.

People move in and out of our lives at different times and for different reasons. We just had to keep the faith, be patient, and allow His plan to play out. It felt like God was stripping away all of Maggie's past, and it was a painful process, but we also trusted that the pain we were going through had a greater purpose.

CHAPTER SIXTY

Maggie suffered two panic attacks within a couple of weeks.

From a practical standpoint, the first attack helped Maggie assess her stressors and decide that she had gone back to too many responsibilities for the second semester. She decided to step down from the editorial position on the school newspaper, and that helped immensely. Additionally, she took a break from track. She continued to work out on her own and planned to rejoin the team for the spring season.

The second panic attack happened on a Sunday. Because she and her roommates knew what was happening, she was able to get it under control more quickly.

Until We Perfectly Reflect His Image . . .

by Wendy Weiss—March 5, 2015

Today, we mark the nine-month anniversary of Maggie's accident.

We see great things coming from Maggie's difficult circumstances. She's realizing, as we all must at some point, that she cannot do everything in her own strength. She is learning to trust God for the little and big problems in her life. It isn't easy for a capable, self-reliant young woman who has experienced success in most areas of her life (pre-accident) to relinquish control. We are proud of how much Maggie is growing in her faith and trust in God.

We love what God is doing in Maggie's spiritual life! She has been attending a new church in Northfield with friends who love Jesus. She also attends chapel at St. Olaf and has a great relationship with Pastor Matt. She just finished her fourth week of classes. The professors she has this semester are three of her favorites. They are so supportive, and she loves being in class with them. We have also made a connection with a wonderful Christian counselor.

Thanks for sharing this journey with us! It is not lost on me that babies are made in nine months, and I feel like Maggie has just been reborn in a sense; God is doing a "new thing" in her (Isaiah 43:18–19)! Enjoy this Lenten season, as we prepare to celebrate Jesus's victory over sin and death! God is able to do a "new thing" in all of us! To God be the glory for what He continues to do in and through Maggie as she heals.

"I will refine them like silver and test them like gold. They will call on my name and I will answer them; I will say, 'They are my people,' and they will say, 'The Lord is our God'" (Zechariah 13:9).

CHAPTER SIXTY-ONE

Maggie had been running most days of the week, although she had some occasional hip pain. She was practicing with the track team at St. Olaf and planned to race in the spring season. She had some reservations about this, as she was afraid she'd be nowhere near her times from the previous year in the 1,500-meter distance. In one race the year before her accident, she broke the five-minute mark, which was an exceptional performance.

I told her there was only one way to find out where she was. So one Saturday morning, we headed to the track. With her old man running with her, she came in with a time of 5:46! Not too bad, and a lot better than she expected. We tried not to focus on the times and to just appreciate her ability to run and be a part of the team.

Every step toward getting back to her normal life was a step in the right direction!

Meditating on the Word

by Tad Weiss, April 5, 2015

Today is not only Easter Sunday, but the ten-month anniversary of Maggie's accident. It is truly a miracle that she has recovered so much in such a short amount of time.

We just returned from a spring break family trip to Mexico. Maggie loves speaking Spanish, and she enjoyed conversing with the Mexicans. We wouldn't be surprised if her eventual career choice or volunteer work will utilize her Spanish-speaking skills.

The biggest breakthrough of the past month came from an unusual place—an accident report that we received from an investigative firm in Spain. The report was quite extensive—eighty pages, in Spanish—and included an animated video re-creating the accident.

We weren't sure if we should show it to Maggie, but it ended up being the right thing to do. By seeing the re-creation of the accident, she was able to clearly see that she's alive due to God's protection. God saved her life, and it makes sense that He saved her for a purpose. She may have said that she believed that before, but now she believes it fully in her heart.

We are happy to report that she hasn't had any more panic attacks and that she is learning ways to cope with the range of emotions she is feeling. A special thank you to all of Wendy's Jesus-loving friends who wrote cards to Maggie this month. It is great for her to hear your words of encouragement and to know that there are so many people praying for her.

I just finished the book *Celebration of Discipline* [21] by Richard Foster, which has been around for over thirty-seven years. In it, Foster outlines twelve spiritual disciplines that can help us all deepen our faith and our walk with Christ.

The first discipline is meditation. Foster states that Christian meditation is the ability to hear God's voice and obey His Word. He provides several ways that a beginner in this discipline can get started. One way is to take one Bible verse and study it daily for a week. That sounds like a lot of study on one short verse, but I've been trying a lot of new things lately, so I thought I'd give it a go.

Romans 8:28 is one of my favorite verses: "And we know that in all things God works for the good of those who love Him, who have been called according to His purpose." This is one of God's greatest promises. I spent a week, roughly ten minutes a day, breaking it down: first thinking on each word, then on the word combinations and phrases, and finally putting it all together. Here are some of the main thoughts that started to stand out over the course of the week:

And we know . . .

When you "know" something, there is no doubt. There's something coming that I can know and about which I can be certain.

That in all things . . .

Not a few things, or most things, but *all* things and *all* circumstances, the good and the bad. That's a pretty big statement and a pretty big promise!

God works . . .

God worked for six days to create the world, and He's still working today. His power is infinite and is available to us all!

For the good . . .

God not only works, but He works for our good and our benefit here on earth, as well as in heaven for eternity.

Of those who love Him . . .

This is who gets the promise, for whom God will work for their good in all things.

Who have been called according to His purpose . . .

To love God, you also must have been called by Him to help fulfill His purpose in and for the world.

Isn't that a mind-blowing promise? That the Creator of the universe can and will bring good out of any situation or circumstance, if you love and follow Him!

Can you see how, if you really own this verse and trust in God so completely to bring good out of any situation, that nothing can get you down for long? Instead of blaming ourselves, God, or others for the circumstances, we can look for the lessons or opportunities that God is providing to help others, grow in our faith, and let God lead us in the direction He wants us to go.

Wendy and I are excited because we feel that Maggie is starting to own this verse. Her accident was traumatic, and the recovery has been difficult and still continues. She has asked the hard questions of God. The answers aren't always apparent or immediate, and that is where faith, trust, and patience come into play.

Maggie is starting to see the good that God will bring into her life through the accident. She is learning that following His will may require her to go in new directions, but His ways are the best and the rewards will last forever.

The greatest proof of Romans 8:28 is in the crucifixion and resurrection of Jesus Christ. Jesus died the most painful and horrific death, taking my sins and yours to the cross, so that we could have the greatest "good" of all time—eternal life here on earth and in heaven with God. All we have to do is love Him back and to live our lives for Him.

"But Christ has indeed been raised from the dead, the first-fruits of those who have fallen asleep" (1 Corinthians 15:20).

CHAPTER SIXTY-TWO

We were starting to get some glorious spring weather. The grass was greening up, the flowers were about to come out, and we had many months of warmer weather to look forward to.

Maggie hoped to race on the St. Olaf track team that spring, and the first meet was at Hamline in St. Paul. Her event was the 1,500-meter distance, which is just plain hard. She knew she wasn't going to be as good as before the accident, so she had to find a different reason to run than striving to beat her times from the previous year.

The reasons not to run were evident to Maggie. We knew where those thoughts came from, and they were not from God! What did we believe God was saying to her?

Maggie, I reached down and performed a miracle to save your life. I did that for a reason . . . because I knew you would point others to Me with your life. It doesn't matter what your time in the race is, and it doesn't matter where you finish. What does matter is that you go to the starting line, that you run the race to the best of your ability, that you point others to Me, and that you bring glory and honor to Me by running. I saved and healed you. You are ready to race; you are ready to fight. Be strong and courageous!

The hardest part for her would be getting to the starting line. She would need to trust in God and be strong and courageous.

Maggie did go to the starting line, and she ran a great race! She was placed in the fourth heat and ran a 5:27.85, only about twenty seconds off her time from her first race last year . . . unbelievable! We could not be prouder of her, and you could tell the joy and sat-

isfaction Maggie felt. She had conquered the demons, trusted in God, and run the race. She was strong and courageous, and she pointed people to God by doing the best she possibly could on that day.

The spring semester continued to be hard for Maggie on the social front. She was only spending two to three nights a week on campus and chose to spend most nights at home with us.

As we talked about her upcoming senior year, Maggie expressed the desire to go back to Spain. As crazy as that sounded, we were beginning to feel it might be the best thing for her. She didn't want to be on campus, and she had a powerful desire to have the full experience of Spain that was cut short the previous year.

We contacted Morgan at CIEE and Antonio and M'awy, her host parents. Everyone was on board for Maggie to return to Seville in the fall, to attend the same school and stay with the same host family. God had gotten us this far, and if He wanted this for Maggie, we were not going to stand in the way.

An Update from Maggie
by Maggie Weiss, May 5, 2015

Hi everyone! This is Maggie bringing you the eleven-month update! As great as Dad and Mom have been in writing these updates, I thought you all would like to hear from me.

We're nearing the one-year anniversary, if you can believe that! While it has been a difficult year, it has also been a good year—a year in which I've seen God and God's blessings.

To begin with, God saved my life. I don't remember anything from June 5, but from what I've heard and read, I know the accident was scary. I consider it a blessing that I don't remember. However, after seeing the investigator's report, I have a clear understanding that I was saved by God. There are so many small factors that ended up saving me. I can't even begin to describe how grateful I am to God for aligning all these things to carry me through the accident.

I've seen a lot of blessings as the year has gone by. The love and support from so many people have touched me deeply. I've been able to stay on schedule to graduate from St. Olaf in the spring of 2016. I went back to running on the track team much more quickly than anyone predicted. While I get nervous before each race, I feel it will all be okay. Before the gun goes off, I remind myself to be grateful to God that I can run this race. I don't have to worry about where I'll finish. God saved me, and it's a miracle that I can even run.

I've also had a change in what I want to do with my life. While I wanted to pursue journalism before I went to Spain, I now am more interested in pursuing some form of social work. I have an internship this summer at TreeHouse,[22] a Christian organization that assists at-risk youth, and I couldn't be more excited! I'm not sure what God will end up doing with this newfound passion, but I know He can use my experience from the accident to help others. God put this desire in my heart, and I'm excited to pursue it.

This brings me to some news. I'll be spending the fall semester studying abroad in Seville, Spain! I am so excited to go back and to experience what I only got a small taste of last year. Not only will this be good for my Spanish, but it will be redemptive on many fronts. I plan to meet the police officers assigned to my case, the doctors who cared for me, and all the people who visited me and my parents at the hospital. While I can't say that it doesn't make me nervous, I trust that God will protect me. I choose not to live in fear, but in the knowledge that God has worked and will continue to work this accident out for my good.

"For the Spirit God gave us does not make us timid, but gives us power, love and self-discipline" (2 Timothy 1:7).

Juan Carlos and Ana, May 5, 2015

Maggie, it is so wonderful to hear that you will return to Seville. We will be happy to meet with you again, and we pray that our Lord will continue empowering your faith. You are a living testimony of God's mercy for all of us. Blessings in Christ!!

Maggie had to relearn to drive for her internship at TreeHouse. We decided that I would be the driver's ed teacher.

For those who have taught their kids how to drive, the first few sessions can be a little nerve-racking, and that was the case with Maggie's second go-round. She struggled primarily with spatial awareness—knowing where her vehicle was in the lane and relative to other cars.

The highway system in Minneapolis was busy, and no one slowed down to make the process any easier. With God's help, we got to the point where Wendy and I were comfortable sending her out on her own, but safety on the highways was added to our prayer list!

CHAPTER SIXTY-THREE

We reached the one-year mark of when our life was turned upside down and would never be the same.

Yes, the year had many difficult moments filled with trials and adversity. It had been a year of challenge and change for Maggie, as she struggled to do the things that used to come so easily for her.

In the midst of the trial, however, God delivered on all His promises. As a family, we learned what it meant to truly trust God in all things.

We thanked God for Maggie's perspective. The day before the one-year anniversary, Maggie said to Wendy, "Looking back over the last year, I wouldn't change a thing."

God sometimes takes things out of our lives that we don't want to give up, but He knows what is best for us. When we replace what He's removed with the things that are from Him and of Him, our lives are changed for the better. Maggie had come to understand this, and we couldn't have been happier for her.

What a Year it Has Been!
by Tad Weiss Jun 5, 2015

I'm symbolically hitting the "send" button on this post at 8:00 a.m., June 5, 2015—exactly one year ago to the minute of when I received the phone call from Spain informing me of Maggie's accident. So much has happened in the past year, and we continue to move forward.

Our son Peter graduated from high school last night. *Congratulations, Peter!!!*

I've been working on a slideshow for his grad party. As I look through the pictures of his life, one question runs through my mind; where did the time go? Eighteen years have gone by in the blink of an eye.

Time goes fast on this earth for a reason. God designed it that way to help us realize that we shouldn't be living for the things of this world. We should be living for Him and for eternity. My encouragement for you today is to reflect on this and to realize that God has a plan for us after this life is over.

"Trust in the Lord with all your heart and lean not on your own understanding; in all your ways submit to him, and he will make your paths straight" (Proverbs 3:5–6).

Karla and Craig Johnson, June 15, 2015

It was nice to see Maggie and Wendy energetically bounce down to Marshall Heitkamp's grad party yesterday. I have followed her journey and my faith has deepened just witnessing yours. Maggie is as lovely as ever and it is nice to see how beautifully God restores and replaces! Wow . . . back to Spain. Enjoy and I will be praying!

CHAPTER SIXTY-FOUR

Maggie finished the spring semester and track season and was home for the summer. It was great to go for runs with her and just spend time on the porch talking. She started her internship at TreeHouse mentoring nine kids, as well as performing other duties.

She would be going back to Spain in late August. Wendy and I planned to travel with her to get her settled in. We were already excited for this trip and to see our friends there. Since Maggie had no memory of that time, she'd be "meeting" most of the people for the first time.

Peter would head off to Iowa State University around the same time. One chapter of our lives was ending and a new one beginning. We were all excited to see what God had in store for us!

Month 13: The Latest News

by Wendy Weiss, July 6, 2015

Yesterday marked the thirteen-month anniversary of Maggie's accident. One year ago, Maggie was recovering at Bethesda Hospital in St. Paul on the brain trauma floor, just regaining her memory and beginning her rehabilitation. This year, on July 4, 2015, Maggie and Tad ran an inspiring half-marathon in Minneapolis—the Red, White, and Boom! We praise God for Maggie's continued ability to return to the things she did before the accident.

Maggie and Tad had a chance to tell our story for KARE11, the local news channel. Before they went to meet with the reporter, we prayed that they would say the right things to give the glory to God.

Afterward, they felt the interview had been fine, but neither felt like the story would have much of a faith component based on the questions they were asked and their replies.

KARE11 asked us to send some pictures, so we did. A couple were of Tad and me reading from the Bible to Maggie in the ICU, and those were two of the pictures they chose! It was very cool that God answered our prayers even when we felt like we'd missed an opportunity.

God has been giving Maggie a lot of opportunities to tell her story lately. Besides the KARE11 news story, she was also featured one evening during our church's Vacation Bible School, appropriately named, "Everest: Conquering Challenges with God's Mighty Power!" Maggie was living proof to the seven hundred-plus children—who had prayed for her last year during VBS—that prayer works, and God still performs miracles.

Maggie just finished volunteering for the month of June in the classrooms at Hope Academy, whose mission is "to foster hope in God within the inner-city neighborhoods of Minneapolis by providing youth with a remarkable Christ-centered education." This week, she will begin tutoring through the St. Louis Park School District. Busy? Yes, but firmly in the center of God's will and loving the direction her life is going. God has been so good to show us opportunities for her to learn, engage, and minister to others, as she continues to heal and look forward to studying in Spain this coming fall semester.

"In that day you will say: 'Give praise to the Lord, proclaim His name; make known among the nations what He has done, and proclaim that His name is exalted'" (Isaiah 12:4).

One of the things that made Maggie feel normal was her ability to exercise. The first exercise she was given permission to do was swimming. This allowed her to exercise daily without subjecting her body to the pounding of running.

Back in 2000, Maggie was five and Peter was three. We were at a neighbor's house, and the kids were playing with some toys on the floor. As we got ready to leave, I bent over to pick up the toys and immediately threw out my back. I wasn't in great shape at the time and my new injury put me in a funk, both physically and mentally.

A couple of months later, I was recovering and watching the 2000 Olympics. The triathlon event was new, and I was mesmerized. Simon Whitfield from Canada won the event, and I was hooked. Nearing forty, I needed to get back into shape, and I found my motivation.

I had some friends who'd competed in triathlons, so I asked them how to get started.

The triathlon consists of three events: swimming, biking, and running. I joined a group and started swimming three times a week. The next year, I competed in four triathlons.

When people find out that I compete in triathlons, many ask if I've done an IRONMAN triathlon.[23] That would be like asking someone who likes to climb mountains if they've ever climbed Mt. Everest. As I got more into triathlons, started hanging around triathletes, and frequently got asked about the full-distance triathlon, my desire to complete one took hold.

The full-distance triathlon is a 2.4-mile swim, followed by a 112-mile bike ride, with a 26.2-mile marathon run to finish. It can take anywhere from eight to seventeen hours to complete.

I trained through the winter, spring, and summer of 2002 for my first full-distance race in September, the inaugural IRONMAN Wisconsin in Madison. I had a great race, completing the event in eleven hours and fifty-seven minutes. It was one of the best experiences of my life, but it also was a huge time commitment, and we were a busy family. I competed in a few more triathlons the following year but then hung up my swim goggles, bike helmet, and running shoes at the end of 2003.

A year after the accident, I asked Wendy what she thought about Maggie competing in a triathlon. She was gaining so much confidence and a sense of purpose by rebuilding her body, and she already was a good swimmer and runner. All we had to do was get her a bike. Wendy agreed.

Riding a road bike wasn't difficult, but Maggie's sense of balance and spatial awareness had been compromised by the accident. But the girl was fast! Her cardio system, light weight, and strong legs translated into the ability to really motor on a bike.

Maggie registered to compete in the Lifetime Fitness Olympic-distance triathlon in Maple Grove, Minnesota, and I pulled together my old gear to do the race with her. We entered with no expectations. Our goals were to complete the race and stay healthy.

The "fourth" discipline in triathlon consists of the two transitions—changing from swimming to biking and then biking to running. Maggie's transition times were awfully slow, but we hadn't practiced them, and getting the best time possible wasn't our focus. Even with her slow transitions, she ended up winning the Female Age 20–24 Division. She beamed with pride as she received her trophy at the awards ceremony!

Through the sport of triathlon, we had stumbled into a way for Maggie to gain confidence and to know that she wasn't damaged goods.

CHAPTER SIXTY-FIVE

Maggie had a great summer, filled with her internship, time with family and friends, working out, and doing a couple of races before getting ready to go back to Spain.

Back to Spain!

by Tad Weiss, August 27, 2015

People often ask where I think Maggie is in her recovery. When it comes to physical healing, I would have to say she's 100 percent! She ran a half-marathon on July 4 and completed her first triathlon last Saturday. She won the 20–24 Age Division and finished fifteenth out of 106 women in the Lifetime Fitness Triathlon in Maple Grove.

When she was younger, she swam competitively. She loves to run. She's new to biking, but seems to have the knack for that too. I think she has found her new sport and it will be fun to see her compete in more triathlons in the future.

The big news is we are heading back to Seville, Spain, this weekend! Mags is going to study there for the fall semester, completing the journey that was cut short last summer. She'll be staying with the same host family as last year and taking a full course load.

We are excited to introduce her to all the great new friends we met last summer, and we truly believe this will be a redemptive experience for her. Yes, there is a leap of faith involved in doing this. But God protected her and saved her last year, and He won't stop watching over her. It will be a challenge, but it feels right, and we believe this will be an incredible experience.

I continue to be amazed at how God puts the right people in our path at the right time with the message we need to hear. At church last Sunday, the sermon was on love and fear, from 1 John 4:17–18. There is negative fear and positive fear. The antidote to most of our fears is to fear God. Fearing God means to hold Him in awe. When you think of who God is, there is no reason to fear anything else.

We have seen the power of God and the love of Jesus Christ up close over the past year. One of the blessings of going through a trial like we have is that you come to understand that nothing that happens in this world can separate you from the love of Christ. When we understand that, the fears of this world drift away. And that is a great way to live!

"By this is love perfected with us, so that we may have confidence for the Day of Judgment, because as he is so also are we in this world. There is no fear in love, but perfect love casts out fear. For fear has to do with punishment, and whoever fears has not been perfected in love" (1 John 4:17–18).

Danise McMillen, August 27, 2015

We asked God to heal Maggie, and He replied, "Watch Me . . ."

CHAPTER SIXTY-SIX

Wendy and I returned from Spain on September 7, very tired from a long day of travel. It would take a couple of days to get back on Minnesota time, and we were grateful for the Labor Day holiday to help us adjust.

I was eager to update our CaringBridge friends and family.

She is Ready

by Tad Weiss, September 7, 2015

Maggie, Wendy, and I left for Spain on August 27. We stopped in Barcelona and spent a couple of days seeing the city. Barcelona is absolutely stunning!

On our first full day there, we rode the city tour bus—an open-air double-decker. It is a great way to see the sights and learn the history of Barcelona while taking in the sunshine. Last Sunday, we took the high-speed train from Barcelona to Seville. Train travel is much more relaxing than flying.

On Monday morning, Maggie and I went for a run, covering the same route as her fateful run last year. Yes, there is some anxiety about running again in the city, as there should be. We found a safer place to cross the *Torneo* and had a nice run along the river.

Maggie moved in with her host family, M'awy, Antonio, and their six-year-old daughter, Olga. The reunion was beautiful to see. It is a joy to witness the reaction of people seeing Maggie again, perfectly healed. We are so pleased that Maggie can stay with this loving family again.

Later that day, we walked to CIEE and met with many of the staff who supported us so greatly last year. The initial visits were a little strange for Maggie; Wendy and I know the staff and they know Maggie, but Maggie has no memory of all the time we spent together. She will create new memories with the CIEE team, and it is a great comfort to us, knowing that they will be teaching and watching over Maggie for the next few months.

We met with many other friends throughout the week. Frank—an American and a runner living in Spain—who heard about Maggie and came to support us. Carlos, an attorney provided for us by our friends at Zurich Insurance. Sofia, the manager at the AC Marriott where we lived last summer. We met with two members of a local running club, Jose and Carlos, who reached out to Maggie when they heard she was coming back to Spain. They will be available to provide running partners and races Maggie can go to if she wants. The city of Seville is welcoming Maggie back, thrilled that she is returning to their beautiful city and we could not be more thankful for all the support.

On Saturday, our last full day in Seville, we took the metro train to Montequinto to see our friends Carey and Sharon Owen. They are the missionaries from Seville who we met on our second day in Spain last summer. One of the projects they are working on is establishing a new Christian school in Seville, and we were able to meet with them and see the progress. Approximately twenty of us met and had a time of worship together.

The leader of the school and our worship time is Juan Jose, and the first song he sang was "How Great is our God"[24] by Chris Tomlin, in Spanish. It is hard to describe the feeling that immediately came over Wendy and me. Our Christian brothers and sisters, who prayed so powerfully for Maggie last summer, singing a song we love, in a language we don't know. It was a powerful picture of the love of Jesus that binds us together across borders and accomplishes great things for His glory.

Sunday morning was our time to say goodbye. It was hard, but as Wendy and I settled into the taxi, Maggie waved one last time. We could see the confidence in her smile. The peace that passes all understanding was upon us all.

Maggie is ready for the next three months. She is not alone. She is supported by the people of Seville, by family and friends, and by the faithful around the world praying for her. And most of all, Jesus will be walking with her, all day, every day. She is ready; thank You, God!

"Have I not commanded you? Be strong and courageous. Do not be afraid; do not be discouraged, for the Lord your God will be with you wherever you go" (Joshua 1:9).

CHAPTER SIXTY-SEVEN

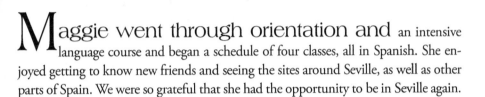

Maggie went through orientation and an intensive language course and began a schedule of four classes, all in Spanish. She enjoyed getting to know new friends and seeing the sites around Seville, as well as other parts of Spain. We were so grateful that she had the opportunity to be in Seville again.

Month 16: Settling In!
by Wendy Weiss, Oct 12, 2015

We have completed another month in Maggie's healing and transition to living in Spain. Things are so, so good, and I want to thank you for all of your prayers!

Maggie has settled into a routine, and let me tell you, Maggie likes routine. In her own words, she has "really started feeling at home . . . calmer and more at peace."

She continues to run by the Guadalquivir River. The surgeons who repaired her pelvis did an incredible job because she has no pain, even on long runs! She has received a volunteer assignment at a local school and is looking forward to that also becoming part of her routine.

One huge blessing to me is how often Maggie tells me that she loves reading her newly purchased Spanish Bible; God is speaking to her in that language! God saved and healed Maggie, and now He's redeeming her experience in Spain.

"He is before all things, and in him all things hold together" (Colossians 1:17).

Maggie's experience in Spain was all we could have hoped for. She was able to complete and thoroughly enjoy the experience that had been cut short a year and a half before. It felt like we had come full circle, yet her story continued.

She still wasn't excited to go back to campus life at St. Olaf, and we were thankful that she and her good friend Amelia could go to Nicaragua together for the month of January. It was a great comfort to us that she had another strong woman to support and encourage her.

Maggie also received word that she qualified for the USA National Triathlon event in Omaha the next summer, based on her time at the Lifetime Fitness triathlon. Maggie was getting ready for the upcoming track season but was really excited to see what she could do with triathlon.

Back in the USA, Again!
by Wendy Weiss, February 2, 2016

As we approach the twenty-month anniversary of Maggie's accident, we realize we have not updated this site since October, when Maggie was still in Spain. Since then, she has successfully completed her semester in Seville, and a month-long internship in Nicaragua. Now, we are very happy to have her home!

Maggie's time in Spain was very redemptive. She accomplished what she set out to do: study abroad, become immersed in language and culture, improve her Spanish, make new friends, deepen existing relationships, train for and run a couple of races, and travel extensively throughout Spain. We praise God for her health and safety through it all!

I joined Maggie in Seville in mid-December. We traveled for a week in Germany, visiting family friends and several Christmas markets in Frankfurt and Nuremberg.

Maggie came home to Minnesota for Christmas before departing with her good friend Amelia for Nicaragua.

As interns at *Finca Esperanza Verde*, Maggie and Amelia experienced an intensive Nicaraguan immersion! Maggie was blessed by living in a gorgeous mountain landscape and getting to know the beautiful people. Escaping Minnesota in January wasn't all bad either!

On February 8, Maggie will begin her final semester at St. Olaf; praise God she will graduate with her class in May! She has already completed the requirements for graduation in her Latin American studies major and will finish her Spanish major and media studies concentration, as well as run track.

We continue to meet people every month who know our family through Maggie's story and CaringBridge. We are blown away by the impact Maggie's story has had.

"Do not be anxious about anything, but in every situation, by prayer and petition, with thanksgiving, present your requests to God. And the peace of God, which transcends all understanding, will guard your hearts and your minds in Christ Jesus" (Philippians 4:6–7).

Maggie returned to campus for her final semester. The social challenges remained, and Maggie was ready to move on from her college years. The track season was a bright spot for her, and she was remarkably close to meeting her times from before the accident.

St. Olaf hosted a triathlon, and Maggie won the women's division. The kids in the St. Olaf Triathlon Club asked her where she'd been for the last few years!

This was a small triathlon, but each moment of success was another boost of confidence and another step in her healing.

CHAPTER SIXTY-EIGHT

In early May of 2016, we received a notice that Maggie needed to take a medical exam in Seville as the final step to complete the legal proceedings that arose from her accident. We scheduled the exam for the week after her graduation from college and decided to tie in a family vacation along the way.

But before we could take our trip, we had a graduation to celebrate.

Two-Year Anniversary
by Tad Weiss, June 7, 2016

Maggie graduated from St. Olaf College on Sunday, May 29, finishing cum laude with a Bachelor of Arts degree, double major in Spanish and Latin American studies, having received distinction in the latter. She was disappointed that she was .01 from finishing magna cum laude, but considering the challenges of overcoming traumatic brain injuries in two areas of her brain, we think she did pretty well!

The ceremony was an adventure. It was outside on a beautiful day, until some unexpected rain rolled in. Still, it was beautiful to see Maggie graduate along with all her classmates.

We left the graduation, drove home, grabbed our bags, and headed to the airport for a 10:00 p.m. flight to Amsterdam. We arrived in Seville the next day and checked in to the same hotel Wendy and I stayed in two years ago. Maggie's medical exam took place the following morning—two hours with doctors and attorneys detailing the physical and emotional trauma she's dealt with over the past two years.

We've spent the past two years trying to take a positive approach to everything, but this was a time to be brutally honest about the difficulties Maggie has faced. We were glad to get our "business" completed and move on to the enjoyable part of the trip.

We visited the hospital, toured the Maria Luisa Park, and

met Maggie's high school friend Hannah for tapas. The next morning, we rented a car to drive to Granada in southern Spain. Three blocks out of the car rental lot we were rear-ended—just a scratch, and *not* my fault!

With three navigators reading the GPS and shouting instructions, I did my best Mario Andretti impersonation to get us out of Seville. Once we left the city, the two-and-a-half-hour drive was pleasant, and we arrived in Granada without further incident. Peter congratulated me for making it to our destination with only one accident!

Granada is a beautiful city in the foothills of the Sierra Nevada mountains. It's home to a palace called the Alhambra, the most visited tourist destination in the world. We spent a day in Granada, then drove to Malaga, a beach city on the coast of the Mediterranean. The drive in the country is easy, but the cities are a whole different ballgame! The streets are tight, the traffic is intense, and scooters and motorcycles are free to drive wherever they please. We were very close to our hotel but couldn't pull off the last couple of blocks to reach our destination. After multiple attempts, Peter came up with the brilliant idea of paying a taxi driver to take Wendy and Maggie to the hotel, and we followed behind in our car. The plan worked, and I couldn't have been happier to turn over the keys to the valet!

The next day, we rented bikes to ride along the coastline, before driving back to Seville for the last three days. Back in the city proper we ditched the car and spent two full days seeing all of the sites. We went to the cathedral and climbed to the top of the *Giralda*, visited the *Alcazar, Triana*, and various neighborhoods, dining outside and immersing ourselves in the city. Maggie knows the city very well, having spent three-and-a-half months there this past fall. It was great to have her be our tour guide and interpreter and to see and experience all that Seville has to offer.

Our last full day in Seville was Sunday, June 5, two years to the day since Maggie's accident. We recalled the first anniversary, a year ago, when we noted the specific times throughout the day—when the accident occurred, when I received the phone call, when we saw Maggie for the first time, and so on. This year, we noted 7:35 a.m., the time of the accident, and that was about it. We were within a half mile of the accident site, but we chose not to go there.

Time heals most wounds, and we had a beautiful day together as a family, thankful to God for all the healing that has taken place over the last two years and looking forward to an exciting future.

Speaking of the future, Maggie has accepted a position with Erik's Bike Shops and will start learning the cycling industry when we return. She was exploring career options that would utilize her Spanish but decided she wanted to pursue a career in fitness. Maggie and I were on a bike ride a couple of months ago and she said that she feels most alive when she's on her bike, and we encouraged her to pursue this passion. She's going to live at home for a while, work, and train for several triathlons over the summer.

I've often wondered when Maggie's accident would "be over," and I think the best answer is that it won't. We've been changed; some changes have been difficult and gut-wrenching, and many have been beautiful. We won't ever return to exactly how life was before Maggie's accident, and we shouldn't desire that. Instead, I hope that because of the accident and the healing we experienced in and through it that we are better equipped to serve the Lord and to help others and that we'll have the faith and commitment to go where we are called to go.

"'For I know the plans I have for you,' declares the Lord, 'plans to prosper you and not to harm you, plans to give you a hope and a future'" (Jeremiah 29:11).

Having qualified for the USA Nationals triathlon championship in August, Maggie started training hard in the summer of 2016. We signed up for several races to help her get ready.

She finished second at the Lake Minnetonka Triathlon, a "sprint" that took an hour and a half to complete. Her breakout race was at the Lifetime Fitness Olympic-distance race in Minneapolis. She came in fourth in a strong field with a time of two hours and nineteen minutes. She was improving in all areas, including that fourth discipline, the transitions, which allowed her to compete with the best athletes in the state.

Nationals were in August in Omaha, Nebraska. Omaha in the dead of summer is hot and humid. There were over two thousand athletes from around the country competing in the different age groups, in five-year increments, for the men's and women's divisions.

Maggie's group, the 20–24 women's division, had fifty-five women from around the country competing. Each had qualified at a local race, and many of the best amateur women in the country were there. The heat took its toll on everyone, including Maggie, but with a strong bike ride and a solid run, she finished thirteenth in her age group. The top fifteen were invited to compete in the World Championships the following year, and Maggie accepted her invitation.

Maggie finished the triathlon season with a half-distance event in Minnesota, with each part of the race exactly half of the full distance triathalon—a 1.2-mile swim, followed by a 56-mile bike ride, and a 13.1-mile run.

The day was warm and windy, with twenty-mile-per-hour winds. Lake Waconia is a big body of water and there were white caps on the waves. They should have called off the swim portion of the event, but they didn't. Maggie made it through and had a solid race, finishing in five hours, fifteen minutes for a second-place finish among the women. She had hoped to break the five-hour mark—the gold standard for the half-distance—but conditions didn't allow it. That wrapped up a great triathlon season.

Maggie had found a sport that she loved and was exceptional at. It was an answer to prayer and confirmation that with God's help she could do anything she set her mind to.

CHAPTER SIXTY-NINE

Maggie worked at the bike shop through the summer and then decided to focus on triathlon training full time. We hired a professional coach that fall, and Maggie trained through the winter while living at our house. We didn't have any illusions that Maggie would be a professional triathlete, but we also wanted to see how far she could take this. We were excited that the sport was helping her with both her mental and physical recovery.

Three-Year Anniversary
by Wendy Weiss, June 5, 2017

Just like last year, this anniversary passed by without much fanfare. The three of us (Peter is back from a semester in Canberra, Australia, but is living in Ames this summer) went to dinner in downtown Excelsior, got ice cream at Lick's, and walked around the Excelsior Commons near the lake. Such a beautiful summer evening!

Physically, Maggie is 100 percent healed, stronger and "better than ever." I put that last part in quotes because that is literally what the Lord spoke to me one day while I was praying about Maggie's healing—that Maggie would be "better than ever!" She experiences no pain and is in the best shape of her life.

She really rocked the triathlon circuit last summer with eye-popping results in area races and then at Nationals in Omaha. For the past year, Maggie has been training full time for this summer's triathlon season and the Worlds competition this fall.

Although her training prevented her from working full time this past year, she was able to complete a long-term substitute teaching position at Chapel Hill Academy (the elementary school she and Peter attended kindergarten through eighth grade). She taught Spanish for the lower grades, and enjoyed connecting with former teachers and staff. But now . . . school's out for summer!

To borrow a concept from Eugene Peterson, Maggie is experiencing the sanctification that comes from "a long obedience in the same direction," which means that as we continue to practice patience in our daily living and obedience to God's commands, we continue to grow in Christ-likeness. Maggie has a lot of good things hardwired into her. She loves structure and organization and has an astounding ability to "get after it." Maggie perseveres through thick and thin. But she has also taken this opportunity to grow closer to God. Sometimes she is just like other young adults, but at other times, she is very different, having been matured beyond her years through the accident, rehabilitation, and healing process.

"May God Himself, the God of peace, sanctify you through and through" (1 Thessalonians 5:23).

I had many people tell me I should write a book. I'd been looking for the ending—the natural point when the story reached a fitting conclusion. I thought I had it on June 5, 2017.

Maggie was signed up for an Olympic-distance triathlon in Buffalo, Minnesota. Most of the best athletes in the state were signed up for the race, and it was a loaded field. This was one of the few local events that had prize money: $400 to the winner. Since it was the first race of the year, we didn't have grand expectations, but Maggie was excited to race after training hard through the winter.

The day started out warm, windy, and humid, with temperatures in the 70s, and they would rise to the upper 80s. It was the first hot day of the year, and Maggie and all the other competitors had trained primarily in cooler temperatures. We went through our pre-race routine; Maggie needed to be reassured on just about everything, from pacing to transitions. It was a function of Maggie's thoroughness but also of her brain injury.

Maggie came out of the water in sixth place with a solid swim. The bike segment was turning out to be her strength, and she made up ground on the leaders, passing all but one. She rolled into transition with the leader, a woman who had won dozens of races throughout her career. She was a stronger runner than Maggie, but we were excited that she was having a solid race.

Being a spectator at a triathlon was not logistically easy. We usually watched the swim start and then hung out near the transition area to see and encourage Maggie as she went from swim to bike and then bike to run. Then we had the agonizing wait for her to finish the run.

For some reason, I told Wendy I was going to drive out to the run course. I hopped in the car and drove to the two-mile mark of the 6.2-mile run. I'd see Maggie at mile two and then at mile four as she headed to the finish line.

When I got to mile two, the leader was struggling due to the heat. Maggie wasn't far behind, and I encouraged her to keep plugging away. She was in second place, and the leader was faltering. When Maggie came back around, she was in the lead! There were only two miles to go, and Maggie had a chance to win the race!

Could this be the ending for the book? It would be the perfect ending . . . on the three-year anniversary of Maggie's accident, she competed in one of the top races in the state and came away with the victory!

I jumped in the car and moved another mile down the road. What I saw made my heart sink. Maggie was still leading but clearly succumbing to the heat just as the leader had. And then Maggie went down. A couple of athletes stopped to help her, and I ran to her. We made her sit until the ambulance came.

Maggie had pushed too hard and hadn't taken in enough fluids. I drove back to get Wendy, and we rushed to the hospital where Maggie was hooked up to IVs to replenish her fluids. Instead of a victory ceremony and the winner's trophy, we spent the afternoon in a hospital, just like three years ago.

I realized that Maggie's story, and the book, weren't finished quite yet.

CHAPTER SEVENTY

Maggie reconnected with some friends from her Chapel Hill days who went to Bethel University in St. Paul. We enjoyed getting to know them, with large groups of young adults coming over to our house occasionally for cookouts and boating.

She wanted to meet the right guy but that hadn't happened yet. We had many conversations about this and about God's plan for her life. She had to practice trust and patience, like Wendy and I had a few years before! We fully believed that God was preparing the right guy for her, but the time wasn't yet.

Rotterdam Triathlon

by Tad Weiss, September 22, 2017

Maggie competed in the ITU World Age Group Triathlon Championships in Rotterdam last Sunday!

There were fifty women from around the world in her division, with four from the US. Maggie had a fantastic race, finishing in just under two hours, nineteen minutes. She took seventeenth place in the female 20–24 age group.

After the race, we traveled to southern Germany to visit friends, then to Munich, and we'll finish our trip in Frankfurt before flying home. We deeply appreciate all of your prayers, support, and encouragement!

Finishing the triathlon season was a relief for Maggie. She had a great season, but she was ready for a break. Working with a coach had provided structure to her training, but Maggie responded best to me. I didn't have the knowledge of a full-time professional coach, but I knew my daughter and what made her tick. We agreed that it was time for Maggie to start working again and to pursue triathlon as a hobby, rather than as a full-time career.

In early October, Maggie surprised me by asking what I thought about her joining my financial planning company, Modus Advisors. My first reaction was surprise. Maggie was a Spanish and Latin American studies major, and she had no finance background. I told her I'd think about it, but in the meantime, I gave her two books to read on the profession. If she read those books and wasn't bored to tears, we could talk more.

Maggie read the books and wanted to give it a shot. I told her she could join our team of four, but she had a lot to learn and would be starting on the ground floor. I also told her that if we were going to work together, it was time for her to move out of our house. I love Maggie dearly, but I knew that seeing each other twenty-four seven would not be the best idea.

The lawsuit from the accident had been settled earlier that summer. I really had no idea of the process and how they came to a final number. I thought back to the first time we met with Carlos. He told us that what might be a million-dollar settlement in the US would be, in his words, "Maybe enough for Maggie to make a down payment on a house."

And that was what she used it for—the down payment on a townhouse in Chanhassen, Minnesota, less than ten minutes from our house. She started working with me at Modus in October and moved to her new home in December, finding a couple of roommates to help her cover the mortgage.

Maggie enjoyed working at Modus, but she had a lot to learn. She signed up to take a series of classes through Boston University that would prepare her to sit for the Certified Financial Planner® exam and continued exercising at the gym to stay in shape.

She went on a few dates but nothing clicked. The message from God was the same: *Wait and trust.* I prayed that she would meet the "right guy" and that the "wrong guys" would be blinded and wouldn't take an interest in her.

Maggie wanted to continue racing in the summer of 2018, and I decided to join her. It was hard for me to go to triathlons and watch. If I'm going to be there anyway, I might as well join in the fun. I started training with Maggie through the winter, and we had a blast. We swam together in the mornings and did indoor spinning classes at the gym, followed by runs on the treadmill.

To assist in Maggie's training, we had her take a metabolic assessment test, a scientific method to determine heart rate zones to help guide effort level during various workouts. The test also provided a score for volume of oxygen, known as VO2. The score represents the maximum amount of oxygen the body is capable of using at any one time, and the higher the better for an endurance athlete. A score over 37.0 is categorized as "great," and a score above 41.0 is considered "optimal."

Maggie's score was 70.9! To put that in perspective, the highest recorded VO2 for a woman at that time was marathon runner Joan Benoit at 78.6. There are other factors that also determine speed, but God had blessed Maggie with a big aerobic capacity that she had finetuned through her training.

We signed up for an Olympic-distance event in Madison, Wisconsin, in mid-May and then a half-distance triathlon in early June, also in Madison.

At the Olympic-distance event, Maggie won the women's overall race but took a hard fall toward the end. The run portion was mainly on a cross-country course that was grass versus pavement, and she went down coming around a corner. She was able to get up and finish the race, but her leg was very sore. I came in first in the men's 55–59 age group. We had completed our tune-up for the half-distance race that was one month away.

Maggie's leg hurt as we prepared for the next race. She went to physical therapy and continued to train, and we thought it was a nagging injury she just needed to work through. When you're competing in triathlon, something usually hurts. It is just part of the sport. The offseason is the time to recover.

The start of the race was delayed until 8:30 a.m. when the first swimmers hit the water, amid two-foot whitecaps. Maggie had a strong swim and bike, but she was in major pain during the run. She finished in five hours and thirty-five minutes, which was good enough for second place in the 20–24 women's age group and thirty-fourth woman overall. Her run time was twenty minutes slower than what she was capable of, and we decided it was time to go in for an MRI.

The MRI confirmed that Maggie had a stress fracture in her leg caused by the fall in the first Madison triathlon. The fact that she completed a half-distance triathlon on a broken leg was a testament to Maggie's determination and pain tolerance, but the message was clear that she needed to shut it down for the season.

Maggie was in tears and devastated that her season was over, and she wouldn't be able to work out for an unknown period of time. Wendy reminded her that things happen for a reason and that she would recover quickly. We canceled the remaining races on her calendar, and Maggie had to find some new activities to fill her time as she recovered.

A week later, I gave her a call. "Hey, Maggie, do you want to go to a grad party with Mom and me? It's a nice day, and there will be food!"

"Sure, I'll go." She didn't even hesitate. "I don't have anything else going on."

The party was at a friend's place in St. Louis Park, a twenty-minute drive from our house. It was a nice summer day, and we greeted the graduate and his parents, went through the food line—loading up on Chipotle—and sat down.

A few minutes later, a young man sat next to me. He introduced himself as Paul, and I noticed he was wearing a Specialized bike hat.

Specialized is the brand of bike that Maggie, Wendy, and I ride, and we got into a conversation about cycling. Paul had done some bike touring and had worked at a bike shop. Maggie and Wendy joined in the conversation. I didn't sense anything in the air between Paul and Maggie. But as it turned out, the women had their radar up!

Lesley Oran, a friend of Paul's family, sauntered over to where we were sitting.

Loudly enough for all at the table to hear, she asked Paul, "How's your job going at the *Bernard Group*?"

Lesley was making the point that this guy was not only employed but had a great job—something the father of a young lady might want to know.

"Really well." Seizing the opportunity, Paul lifted a small smile. "We've been swamped lately."

Lesley continued, "I heard you were just promoted. Congratulations!"

On the drive home, Wendy asked Maggie what she thought about Paul. It soon became clear that he had made a good impression.

The timing wasn't lost on us. Maggie wouldn't have been at the party if we hadn't canceled all her races. Had God orchestrated an injury to allow a chance encounter at a graduation party?

As Maggie and Paul began officially dating, we were able to spend a lot of time with him and found him to be fun and easygoing yet very driven and motivated like Maggie. He had grown up in the church but drifted away from the Lord after high school, as many people do. Fortunately, he'd been led back to church and a renewed faith.

We discovered Paul's many talents and interests, including photography, cycling, hiking, and camping, and loved that he had the energy to keep up with Maggie! You could see the transformation in Maggie as her confidence in the relationship grew. She had met the guy she wanted to marry and their commitment to each other developed quickly.

One Saturday in April, ten months after meeting, Paul asked Maggie to go to the North Shore of Lake Superior. They stopped for lunch in Duluth, then hiked around Gooseberry Falls. They came to an open area looking out over the lake.

Paul said, "I'm going to set up my camera on the tripod and play around with some photos."

Unbeknownst to Maggie, he hit the "record" button.

Returning to her side, he seemed a little nervous. "Maggie. . ." He cleared his throat. "I love you, and I want to spend the rest of my life with you."

As she held her breath, he dropped to one knee.

"Will you marry me?"

Maggie could only stammer, "Y-yes!"

The tears started to flow from both of them. They spent the afternoon at Split Rock, and then called family and friends on the ride home to share the wonderful news.

God had been preparing Maggie's right guy for just the right time.

CHAPTER SEVENTY-ONE

W endy and I were absolutely thrilled for Maggie and Paul. They decided to hold their wedding in our back yard, and we had five months to prepare. Needless to say, we were very busy!

The End and the Beginning
by Tad Weiss, September 23, 2019

It has been two years and a day since our last post, and I'm pretty sure this will be the last one. Disney and the Hallmark Channel are the masters of fairy-tale endings, but our God is pretty good at them too!

Fifteen months ago, Maggie met Paul Swanson at a high school graduation party for Jake Beitel, the son of our friends Clayt and Dawn. They were very intentional in their dating, and things progressed quickly. Paul proposed to Maggie in April, and they set a wedding date of September 21.

We had hundreds of people praying for a nice fall day so we could hold the wedding outside by the lake. With advancements in technology, you now can get fifteen-day weather forecasts on your smartphone. My advice is, if you're planning an outdoor wedding, don't look at a fifteen-day forecast!

Our forecast looked perfect two weeks out, then slowly worsened as the big day approached. The day before, the prediction was for showers and thunderstorms, mainly in the afternoon.

I asked God how He could let this happen! We know He controls the wind and the waves. I was perplexed, confused, tired, wired, and a little angry, but we would make this work and it would be great, inside or out.

Our message at church the previous Sunday had been on John 6—Jesus feeds the five thousand with two fish and five loaves of barley.

When Jesus sees that you are overwhelmed, He tests you. That may seem harsh, but He has His reasons. Jesus already knew He was going to perform the miracle, but He tested the disciples, Philip and

Andrew, as well as the little boy who had the fish and bread. He tested them so they could learn, so they could see that He alone can meet every need, and so they could see the sweetness of His love!

The morning of the wedding, the forecast sharpened further with showers and thunderstorms between 4:00 and 5:00 p.m. The time of the wedding—you guessed it—was 4:00 p.m.

We really wanted to have the ceremony in open air, by the lake, and decided to continue to monitor the weather. We had 275 people coming, and a four o'clock thunderstorm would be a disaster if we weren't under the tent.

We were busy throughout the morning making final preparations. At two o'clock, it was decision time; we had to set up the chairs for the guests, either under the tent or outside by the lake. Wendy and I agreed that under the tent was the safer option.

I took one last peek at the radar, but there was no way to know the right answer. I felt overwhelmed, tested, frozen in indecision.

I said to Paul, "Looks like a good chance of rain right at four o'clock."

"I don't know." Looking up at the so-far rain-free sky, Paul said, "I really want to have the wedding outside."

"I'm a risk taker," Mike, one of the groomsmen, said decisively. "Let's go for it!"

So, we set the chairs up outside. There was no more planning or praying; God knew what we wanted, and it was in His hands.

It was nearly four o'clock. and the guests were being seated. The sky was filled with fluffy clouds, but not a drop of rain. The grandparents, then Paul's parents and Wendy were escorted in.

Next the bridesmaids and groomsmen. And it was time to walk Maggie down the aisle.

Paul saw Maggie in her wedding gown for the first time, and the look on his face was beyond description. The sun broke through the clouds, the rain failed to appear, and the wind of the Holy Spirit kept us cool.

The ceremony was beautiful, and the bride and groom were absolutely stunning! We had so many people tell us that they had never seen a happier couple. God showered them with so much love and they couldn't keep it inside.

After the ceremony, the families and wedding party ran off for photos while the guests enjoyed the reception. Dinner was followed by speeches and toasts, dessert, and the dance. The dance floor was filled for over two hours straight, overflowing into the tent and outside into the yard. Maggie and Paul's friends are so much fun, and we had the time of our life. God was honored, and we celebrated all that He has done for Maggie, for Paul, and for us!

So how did I do on my "test?" You would think that after having a front-row seat to see the miracle God performed in protecting, saving, and healing Maggie, that my faith would be stronger. I should have known He would control the rain, the wind, and the waves for us at four o'clock on Saturday.

It is so clear in hindsight, after all He has done for Maggie and for us, that this was an easy one for Him. But I worried and doubted, refreshed my phone countless times, and resigned to take the safe approach. I was acting like Philip, doubting that Jesus could do it. Paul and Mike were like the little boy. They trusted, and I went along. And we saw the glory of God and His love for us in the most beautiful of ceremonies. So, I wouldn't give myself an "F," maybe a "C–." The good news for me is that I saw the power and sweetness of Jesus again, and maybe next time, I'll do a little better.

Wendy and Peter remember talking months after Maggie's accident about her healing. She was making great progress, but it was going to be a long road. Wendy told Peter that she believed Maggie's healing would be complete when she found a man that loved her completely, just as she is. Wendy was right, and Maggie found that man in Paul. More accurately, God held this guy back for Maggie, until the time was right. He knew the future, we just had to live it out.

We can't thank you all enough for your prayers for Maggie, for us and our family over the past five years. Our only regret about the wedding is that we couldn't invite every one of you. You have been so instrumental in our lives, and we love you all and thank you for caring for us so deeply.

So, this is The End, but just of this CaringBridge site. Maggie and Paul started a New Beginning on Saturday, as Mr. and Mrs. Paul and Maggie Swanson. It is a new beginning for us too, and we look forward to seeing what adventures God has in mind for us next.

All praise, honor and glory to God and His Son Jesus, our Lord and Savior!

"And we know that in all things God works for the good of those who love him, who have been called according to his purpose" (Romans 8:28).

Pam Benbow, October 7, 2019

What a way to end that journey and start a new one! You need to write a book.

EPILOGUE

Twenty-five meters. That is the distance Maggie traveled from the point of impact into God's loving hand. He caught her, saved her, carried her, and healed her. It was a very long distance for Maggie to travel from being hit by a bus, and a very large miracle He performed in saving her life.

I also picture twenty-five meters as the distance between God and me before the accident. I believed in Him but wanted to keep my distance and run my life on my terms. That was a very short distance for me to cover but required me to give up the illusion of control with which I lived my life. Running to my Savior didn't take long, and it was the best decision I've ever made.

Long or short, near or far, it doesn't matter. God is waiting for you, too, with open arms.

We believe that God prepared Maggie from a young age for the assignment that only He knew was coming. Her faith and tenacity were developed at a young age. Ecclesiastes 9:10, a verse she was asked to memorize in kindergarten, described how Maggie approached life: "Whatever your hand finds to do, do it with all your might."

The ability to trust in God when facing an uncertain future isn't easy for anyone, and it wasn't for Maggie. But her faith remained solid as she trusted that God would redeem the accident for her. Her tenacity was on display during her rehabilitation, and it continues to be demonstrated in her triathlon training and racing.

Maggie's physical makeup and aerobic capacity helped her in singing, swimming, and playing the flute throughout her childhood and in her triathlon career later on. That same lung capacity pumped oxygen to her brain and body when she was hanging on to life by a thread and allowed her to completely recover from the accident. As Wendy and I look back on Maggie's childhood, we can clearly see how God prepared her to survive the accident and recover and to point others to Christ through her journey.

God allowed a stripping away of parts of Maggie's life, only to restore them later. Loss and change are difficult to face, but we all trusted that God had a bigger plan in mind.

Over the last eight years, Wendy and I have been asked hundreds, if not thousands, of times how Maggie was doing in her recovery and whether she had regained the abilities she had before the accident. We always try to give a thoughtful answer.

Mentally, Maggie's cognitive abilities are back to where she was prior to the accident. She is four years into her career as a Certified Financial Planner®, having passed the CFP® exam, and she's learning a fourth language. Her age and fitness level helped her to recover, and we are so thankful there are no lasting repercussions from her traumatic brain injury.

Physically, her fitness exceeds her level prior to the accident. She continues to compete in triathlon, a sport she might not have found if not for the accident.

In September 2021, Maggie competed in her first full-distance triathlon, IRONMAN Wisconsin. We believed that a young woman who had been on her deathbed seven years prior could complete one of the most grueling endurance events in sport, and she did! She finished in tenth place out of 503 women with a time of eleven hours and six minutes. All things are possible with God.

God willing, Maggie and I will race together in the 2022 IRONMAN Wisconsin race and raise money for the IRONMAN Foundation and other charities that support people in need.

Emotionally, Maggie's recovery in this area ended up being the biggest challenge. Her family and friends helped her get through the long months and years until she met Paul. With his support, combined with family and friends, she's doing exceptionally well.

Maggie and Paul bought a fixer-upper near us, and they welcomed another Dakota sport retriever, Hobie, in November of 2021. They have a great community of friends and attend a vibrant church. Maggie knows that Paul, her family, and her friends love her just the way she is.

Spiritually, Maggie had strong faith before the accident, and although she asked God a lot of questions, her faith never wavered.

If she could turn back time and prevent the accident from happening, would she do it? No. She knows that God can take a terrible accident and use it for good, and she has seen it play out in her own life. This is a powerful lesson, and one she will be able to fall back on in the future. She's excited to see how God wants to use her life to help tell His story.

What about me? If I could go back to June 5, 2014, and stop the accident from happening, would I? As difficult as it was to see my daughter suffer, I would say, "Not a chance." I've had a front-row seat to watch God do His thing. Life is better in the front row as a committed follower of Christ, trusting God, especially in the most difficult of circumstances.

So is *this* the end? Yes and no. It's the end of the book and the end of Maggie's recovery from the accident. But the process of sanctification, or growing in likeness to Jesus, continues for all of us until God calls us home.

Until then, we'll give thanks to God and run the race set before us.

THE END

ENDNOTES

Chapter 2

1 CaringBridge was started in Minnesota in 1997, www.caringbridge.org.

2 The Evangelical Alliance Mission (TEAM), https://team.org/.

Chapter 8

3 SEND International is an interdenominational Christian mission agency, https://send.org/.

4 Angel MedFlight, medical transport, https://www.angelmedflight.com/.

Chapter 13

5 Feed My Starving Children, https://www.fmsc.org/.

Chapter 15

6 Bebo Norman, "I Will Lift My Eyes," *Between the Dreaming and the Coming True* (Essential Records, 2006).

7 Third Day, "Born in Bethlehem," *Christmas Offerings* (Essential Records, 2006).

8 Third Day, "Show Me Your Glory," *Come Together* (Essential Records, 2001).

9 Third Day, "Cry Out to Jesus," *Wherever You Are* (Essential Records, 2005).

10 Third Day, "I Believe," *Wire* (Essential Records, 2004).

Chapter 21

11 Michael W. Smith, "Healing Rain," *Healing Rain* (Reunion, 2004).

Chapter 23

12 Michael Franti, "Life Is Better with You," written by Michael Franti and Jay Bowman, *All People* (Capitol, 2013).

Chapter 27

13 John Eckhardt, *Prayers that Bring Healing* (Charisma House, 2010).

14 Brandon Heath, "Give Me Your Eyes," *What If We* (Reunion, 2008).

Chapter 32

15 Philip Yancey, *The Question That Never Goes Away*, (Zondervan 2013).

Chapter 44

16 Randy Alcorn, *Heaven* (Tyndale House Publishers, 2011), 578.

Chapter 44

17 Casting Crowns, "Praise You in This Storm," *Lifesong* (Reunion Records, 2005).

Chapter 53

18 Sally Lloyd-Jones, *Thoughts to Make Your Heart Sing* (Zonderkids, 2014).

19 Video of Maggie's first run, w.ww.youtube.com/watch?v=99QDA38t0j4.

Chapter 54

20 Casting Crowns. "Until the Whole World Hears," *Until the Whole World Hears* (Reunion Records, 2009).

Chapter 61

21 Richard Foster, *Celebration of Discipline* (HarperCollins Publishers, 1978).

Chapter 62

22 TreeHouse, https://treehousehope.org/.

Chapter 64

23 IRONMAN, https://www.ironman.com/.

Chapter 66

24 Chris Tomlin, "How Great Is Our God," *Arriving* (Sixsteprecords, September 2004).

ORDER INFORMATION

To order additional copies of this book, please visit
www.redemption-press.com.
Also available at Christian bookstores and Barnes and Noble.

CPSIA information can be obtained
at www.ICGtesting.com
Printed in the USA
JSHW012033310722
28703JS00003B/11